Library of New Testament Studies

653

Formerly the Journal for the Study of the New Testament Supplement series

Editor
Chris Keith

Editorial Board
Dale C. Allison, Lynn H. Cohick, R. Alan Culpepper,
Craig A. Evans, Jennifer Eyl, Robert Fowler, Simon J. Gathercole,
Juan Hernández Jr., John S. Kloppenborg, Michael Labahn, Matthew V. Novenson,
Love L. Sechrest, Robert Wall, Catrin H. Williams, Brittany E. Wilson

Jesus and the Empire of God

Royal Language and Imperial Ideology in the Gospel of Mark

Margaret Froelich

LONDON • NEW YORK • OXFORD • NEW DELHI • SYDNEY

T&T CLARK
Bloomsbury Publishing Plc
50 Bedford Square, London, WC1B 3DP, UK
1385 Broadway, New York, NY 10018, USA
29 Earlsfort Terrace, Dublin 2, Ireland

BLOOMSBURY, T&T CLARK and the T&T Clark logo are trademarks of
Bloomsbury Publishing Plc

First published in Great Britain 2022
This paperback edition first published in 2023

Copyright © Margaret Froelich, 2022

Margaret Froelich has asserted her right under the Copyright, Designs and
Patents Act, 1988, to be identified as Author of this work.

For legal purposes the Acknowledgments on p. x constitute an extension
of this copyright page.

Cover design: Charlotte James

All rights reserved. No part of this publication may be reproduced or transmitted in
any form or by any means, electronic or mechanical, including photocopying,
recording, or any information storage or retrieval system, without prior permission
in writing from the publishers.

Bloomsbury Publishing Plc does not have any control over, or responsibility for, any
third-party websites referred to or in this book. All internet addresses given in this
book were correct at the time of going to press. The author and publisher regret any
inconvenience caused if addresses have changed or sites have ceased to exist, but
can accept no responsibility for any such changes.

A catalogue record for this book is available from the British Library.

Library of Congress Cataloging-in-Publication Data
Names: Froelich, Margaret, author.
Title: Jesus and the empire of God : royal language and imperial ideology
in the Gospel of Mark / by Margaret Froelich.
Description: London ; New York : T&T Clark, 2022. |
Series: The library of New Testament studies, 2513-8790 ; 653 |
Includes bibliographical references and index. |
Summary: "Margaret Froelich argues that the Gospel of Mark portrays the
Kingdom of God as a conquering empire and Jesus as its victorious
general and client king"– Provided by publisher.
Identifiers: LCCN 2021025395 (print) | LCCN 2021025396 (ebook) |
ISBN 9780567700841 (hb) | ISBN 9780567700858 (epdf) |
ISBN 9780567700872 (epub)
Subjects: LCSH: Bible. Mark–Criticism, interpretation, etc. |
Jesus Christ–Kingdom–Biblical teaching. | Jesus Christ–Royal office–Biblical teaching.
Classification: LCC BS2585.52 .F76 2022 (print) |
LCC BS2585.52 (ebook) | DDC 226.3/06–dc23
LC record available at https://lccn.loc.gov/2021025395
LC ebook record available at https://lccn.loc.gov/2021025396

ISBN: HB: 978-0-5677-0084-1
PB: 978-0-5677-0088-9
ePDF: 978-0-5677-0085-8
ePUB: 978-0-5677-0087-2

Series: Library of New Testament Studies, volume 653
ISSN 2513-8790

Typeset by Newgen KnowledgeWorks Pvt. Ltd., Chennai, India

To find out more about our authors and books visit www.bloomsbury.com
and sign up for our newsletters.

Contents

Abbreviations of Modern Works	vii
Acknowledgments	x
Introduction	1
1 Empire Criticism	**7**
Methodology	7
Theoretical Approaches	9
Sociohistorical Approaches	21
Applications within This Study	23
2 Kingdom and Imperium	**29**
Roman Self-Understanding	29
Judean Monarchic Ideology	31
Mark's Kingdom of God	32
Conclusion	38
3 Rulership	**41**
Ideal Roman Kings	41
Messiahs	44
Titles for Jesus and Other Royal Language in Mark	45
Hierarchy in God's Kingdom	54
Conclusion	56
4 Military and Conquest	**61**
Rome's Place in the Mediterranean History of War	61
Warfare and Expansionism in Hellenistic Israel	64
Generals and Military Leadership	65
Peace and War in Rome	66
Battlefield Gods	68
Markan Militarism	70
Conclusion	79

5 Salvation	83
Salvation in Hellenistic and Roman Culture	83
Freedom	84
Judaic Soteriology	85
Salvation in Mark	85
Conclusion	89
6 Jesus as the Son of God	91
Divinity and Divinization in the Ancient World	92
The Divinity of Jesus	96
Jesus and Cosmic Power	99
Conclusion	102
7 The Values of Empire	105
Greco-Roman Ideals and Values	106
Judean Values	111
Mark	112
Does Mark Overturn Majority Values?	118
Conclusion	123
Empire and the Death of the Hero	124
Appendix A: Judea before the War	127
Rulership, War, and Expansion	127
Economics	129
Factions and Interests	132
How the War Started	139
Appendix B: Comparisons with Matthew and Luke	143
Bibliography	151
Subject Index	165
Index of Ancient Authors	167

Abbreviations of Modern Works

AB	The Anchor Bible
ABD	Freedman, David Noel, ed. *The Anchor Bible Dictionary*. 6 vols. New York: Doubleday, 1992
ABRL	The Anchor Bible Reference Library
AJEC	Ancient Judaism and Early Christianity
AJP	*The American Journal of Philology*
BBB	Bonner biblische Beiträge
BCAW	Blackwell Companions to the Ancient World
BDAG	Danker, Frederick William, ed. *A Greek-English Lexicon of the New Testament and Other Early Christian Literature*. 3rd ed. Chicago: University of Chicago Press, 2000
BETL	Bibliotheca Ephemeridum Theologicarum Lovaniensium
BibInt	Biblical Interpretation Series
BMW	The Bible in the Modern World
BPC	The Bible and Postcolonialism
BRLJ	Brill Reference Library of Judaism
BTB	*Biblical Theology Bulletin*
BTS	Biblical Tools and Studies
BZNW	Beihefte zur Zeitschrift für die neutestamentliche Wissenschaft und die Kunde der älteren Kirche
Cathedra	*Cathedra: For the History of Eretz Israel and Its Yeshuv*
CBQ	*Catholic Biblical Quarterly*
CBR	*Currents in Biblical Research*
ClAnt	*Classical Antiquity*
ClB	*Classical Bulletin*
ClQ	*Classical Quarterly*
CRINT	Compendia rerum iudaicarum ad Novum Testamentum
CSNTCO	Claremont Studies in New Testament and Christian Origins
EDNT	Balz, Horst, and Gerhard Schneider. *Exegetical Dictionary of the New Testament*. 3 vols. Grand Rapids, MI: Eerdmans, 1990
ERAW	Edinburgh Readings on the Ancient World
FGrH	Jacoby, Felix. *Die Fragmente der griechischen Historiker*. 3 vols. Berlin: Weidmann, 1923–57.
FOTL	The Forms of Old Testament Literature
FRLANT	Forschungen zur Religion und Literatur des alten und neuen Testaments
GBS	Guides to Biblical Scholarship
GPBS	Global Perspectives on Biblical Scholarship
HCS	Hellenistic Culture and Society

Historia	*Historia: Zeitschrift für alte Geschichte*
HNT	Handbuch zum neuen Testament
HSCP	*Harvard Studies in Classical Philology*
HTR	*Harvard Theological Review*
HTS	*HTS Teologiese Studies/Theological Studies*
Int	*Interpretation*
JBL	*Journal of Biblical Literature*
JECH	*Journal of Early Christian History*
JHSJ	*ournal of the History of Sexuality*
JRJ	*ournal of Religion*
JRASup	Journal of Roman Archaeology Supplementary Series
JSHJ	*Journal for the Study of the Historical Jesus*
JSJ	*Journal for the Study of Judaism*
JSJSup	Supplements to the Journal for the Study of Judaism
JSNT	*Journal for the Study of the New Testament*
JSNTSup	Journal for the Study of the New Testament Supplement Series
JSOTSup	Journal for the Study of the Old Testament Supplement Series
JTS	*Journal of Theological Studies*
KLJS	Kogod Library of Judaic Studies
LBS T&T	Clark Library of Biblical Studies
LNTS	Library of New Testament Studies
LSJ	Liddell, Henry George, Robert Scott, Henry Stuart Jones, and Roderick McKenzie. *A Greek-English Lexicon*. Rev. and augm. Throughout. Oxford; New York: Clarendon Press; Oxford University Press, 1996
LSTS	Library of Second Temple Studies
NA28	Nestle, Eberhard, Erwin Nestle, Barbara Aland, Kurt Aland, and Institut für Neutestamentliche Textforschung, eds. *Novum Testamentum Graece*. 28., rev. Aufl., 2. korr. Druck. Stuttgart: Deutsche Bibelges, 2013
NCI	The New Critical Idiom
NIDOTTE	Silva, Moisés, ed. *New International Dictionary of New Testament Theology and Exegesis*. 2nd ed. 5 vols. Grand Rapids, MI: Zondervan, 2014
NIGTC	The New International Greek Testament Commentary
NovTSupp	Supplements to *Novum Testamentum*
NTOA	Novum Testamentum et Orbis Antiquus
NTT	New Testament Theology
OECS	Oxford Early Christian Studies
OGIS	Dittenberger, Wilhelm. *Orientis graeci inscriptiones selectae: Supplementum sylloges inscriptionum graecarum*. 2 vols. Leipzig: S. Hirzel, 1903. http://hdl.handle.net/2027/gri.ark:/13960/t75t7gx7g
OPIAC	Occasional Papers of the Institute for Antiquity and Christianity
ORCL	Oxford Readings in Classical Studies
OTK	Ökumenischer Taschenbuchkommentar zum Neuen Testament
OTL	The Old Testament Library
OTM	Oxford Theological Monographs
SAC	Studies in Antiquity and Christianity

SBEC	Studies in the Bible and Early Christianity
SBG	Studies in Biblical Greek
SBL	Society of Biblical Literature
SBLDS	Society of Biblical Literature Dissertation Series
SBLECL	Society of Biblical Literature Early Christianity and Its Literature
SBR	Studies of the Bible and Its Reception
Smyth	Smyth, Herbert Weir, and Gordon M. Messing. *Greek Grammar*. 13th ed. Cambridge, MA: Harvard University Press, 1984
SNT	SMS Society for New Testament Studies Monograph Series
SNTW	Studies of the New Testament and Its World
StBibLit	Studies in Biblical Literature
TDNT	Kittel, Gerhard, ed. *Theological Dictionary of the New Testament*. Translated by Geoffrey W. Bromiley. 10 vols. Grand Rapids, MI: Eerdmans, 1964
TSAJ	Texte und Studien zum antiken Judentum
WBC	Word Biblical Commentary
WUNT	Wissenschaftliche Untersuchungen zum neuen Testament

Acknowledgments

I have so many people to be grateful for.

None of this would have happened without the support of Greg Riley, Dennis MacDonald, and Tom Phillips. Their knowledge, insight, and willingness to let me experiment have made me into the academic I am now.

Many of my friends and colleagues deserve to be listed here. I can name a few. My mother, Gina Froelich, taught me to love the *Chicago Manual of Style*; her editing and questions helped make my second draft readable. Jeanne Coats let me make things with my hands when my head needed a break. Kirianna Florez kept my schedule honest with weekly writing sessions. Christopher Zeichmann's dissertation paved my way into much of the recent scholarship on the Judean War and Mark's treatment of the temple. Michael Kochenash's work on Augustan propaganda in Luke–Acts provided a needed model and point of reference for mine on Mark. Christopher Crawford knows at least as much about the research process as I do and proved it when he fell down a rabbit hole with me and spent four hours hunting down a single, relatively minor citation. Susana Funsten has consistently supported my work and the development of my career with encouragement, lunches, and draft notes.

The support, advice, and work of Chris Keith and Sarah Blake at Bloomsbury have been invaluable for this inaugural publishing effort. I couldn't have done any of it without the libraries of the Claremont School of Theology and Willamette University, and the Digital Theological Library. Willamette's extra week off for the winter holidays was a godsend to the revision process.

Finally and most importantly, thanks to Jordan for everything. Revising—and nearly doubling the length of—a book during a pandemic has been an experience that cannot be summed up by simple words, and I did it with his support, love, and ability to talk down my deadline anxiety with math.

Introduction

Input determines output. Methodology determines the shape of the results. That is the guiding principle of this book, which is, at its core, an experiment in input. The field of New Testament studies is full of inputs that we its practitioners often take for granted. The existence of a "New Testament" is one of them—Paul certainly was not aware of it. Categories like "Christian," "Jewish," "Bible," "religion," and "supernatural" pervade the way we think and write about these 2000-year-old texts and the people who wrote and worked with them, and we do not often think about the ways in which these categories determine our conclusions from the outset. Working outside of such categories is difficult because they are so endemic to Western culture and, relatedly, because even those of us who want to work outside of them have not yet developed sufficient or sufficiently recognized language to do so well.

In this book I, to the best of my ability, put aside especially the categories of "Christianity" and "religion" to read the text we call the Gospel of Mark as a product and piece of first-century (Hellenized) Judean culture within the Roman empire. In doing so I have gained new insights into this text and the ways it is the same as and different from other texts of the period, and into the values and cultural assumptions the author (whom, for statistical reasons, I will assume was male) meant to challenge, and which ones he meant to uphold or even did not consciously recognize. I am not alone in this kind of endeavor, as my bibliography will show, but a number of my conclusions go farther than previous work, or in different directions.

For scholars interested in the historical contexts of the New Testament and the birth of what we call Christianity, the social, political, administrative, military, economic, and religious factors of the Roman empire have long been fruitful starting points. While Roman characters (or characters representing Rome), such as the centurion at the cross or the governors portrayed in Acts, offer some of the most obvious entry points into this field of inquiry, for the past several decades an increasing body of work has been devoted to looking more deeply at how life under *imperium* informed the most basic fabric of the Jesus tradition. These studies engage with a range of evidence outside of the biblical text, particularly epigraphy, archaeology, and Greek and Latin literature.[1]

A great number of these studies, though by no means all of them, focus on Luke and Acts, separately or as a duology. Of the Evangelists, that author is the one most obviously concerned with issues of Roman administration—such as correct names and titles for Roman governors and client rulers—and the narrative of Acts ends in the *urbs* itself. The Roman empire and its culture are also important touchstones for the study of the book of Revelation, especially for its connection to *Nero redivivus* and its apparent mythologization and eschatologization of persecution against Christ believers.[2] In recent years the Gospel of Mark has likewise been gaining its share of attention from the empire critics, as many of the secondary sources referenced throughout this study will attest.

Empire criticism is especially relevant for Mark because of the Gospel's most likely date. With a very few exceptions,[3] scholars in the twentieth and twenty-first centuries have tended to date Mark in the fifteen or so years surrounding the destruction of Jerusalem by Roman forces in 70 CE. Consensus, therefore, teeters on the fulcrum of the Judean War. A number of commentators judge the date of the Gospel with little more specificity than before or after 70, usually on the basis of passages such as the preface to ch. 13, the temple saying (15:57–58), the tearing of the temple veil (15:38), and the like. If the scholar judges the saying to be sufficiently accurate in its depiction of the events of the siege or destruction, the Gospel was written after the war. If not, or if the scholar finds the passage believable as Jesus's or Mark's foretelling, the Gospel was written before.[4] As it stands, the majority accepts the temple saying to be a *vaticinium ex eventu* and thus places the Gospel in or after 70. Since the turn of the twenty-first century this majority has become nearly solid, notwithstanding a few significant outliers,[5] such that some recent works have forgone argument altogether, considering the matter more or less closed.[6] This study follows the majority of scholarship in situating Mark after 70, looking back on the recent war and destruction. I infer from 14:28 and 16:7 that Galilee is a likely center of Mark's community, or at least the place where he would like the center to be.[7]

Mark and the Judean War: The Focus of the Study

Maia Kotrosits has offered an intriguing alternative to the more common ways of thinking about the text and its author and community. What if, she posits, "Christian identity"—for whatever that might mean in a particular time and place—was not necessarily the driving motivation for many of what we now call the "early Christian" texts?[8] Instead of centering the texts on straightforward and even binary confessional categories, she observes the ambivalence the authors show toward Roman authority, Israelite tradition, and even other Christ-believers. The primary organizing principles in her analysis are diaspora and empire, and she argues that the authors, rather than attempting to create a singular Christian identity suitable for *post facto* recognition, are processing the pain of dispossession and oppression as well as the realities of collusion versus resistance.[9]

Kotrosits examines the second-century texts in her book as records of pain, grief, and trauma. She attributes these feelings to empire and diaspora broadly, without much specific analysis of the actions or environments of the Roman empire. Mark, however, has a specific and reasonably well-attested source of trauma: between the years of 66 and 73 CE, Roman legions led by Cestius Gallus, Vespasian, Titus, and finally Lucius Flavius Silva violently put down a rebellion in Judea. They laid siege to Jerusalem, burned and toppled the temple, and, in a haunting exploit, built a ramp out of dirt up the side of the 1,300-foot plateau fortress of Masada rather than simply starve out the remaining rebels.[10] Whatever Mark and his community thought of Rome or the revolutionaries before the start of the war, by the time of composition it is obvious that the Roman boot cannot be shifted by human means. Rather than creating or disseminating a purely confessional or ecclesiological position, the author finds himself needing to reassess his and his community's very place in the cosmos and their outlook toward the conquerors. The purpose of this study is to work on a small piece of this reassessment, specifically the question of rulership and authority.

I have begun with the premise that the Gospel of Mark was written in the aftermath of the destruction of Jerusalem and its temple. Thus, I set out to find how applying this lens to the entire text, not simply the passages that make explicit reference to the temple or Roman control, might affect interpretation of it. In my research on this topic I have come to one overarching conclusion, with several subpoints. Primarily, *Mark does not imagine an alternative structure for the Kingdom of God*. The Gospel operates under a set of assumptions that are endemic to its cultural location. That is, Mark does not propose radically new meanings for concepts such as "king," "kingdom," or even "god." Rather, it works within expected connotations of these terms and others in order to reimagine their significance for a population that has faced military, economic, and social violence. The observations that have led me to this conclusion are that

- God's kingdom is stratified. It exists under divine authority and is ruled by God and God's agent, Jesus. It has ranks of status determined by understanding of and adherence to Jesus's teachings.
- God's kingdom is military and is at war with its enemies. Jesus is portrayed as a conqueror over demonic forces (who often surrender outright) and, in some Son of Man passages, as a general at the head of angelic armies. The Jerusalem leadership is portrayed as rebelling against God. Individual people must choose sides.
- Just as the word "kingdom" is used with its expected meanings, Jesus is portrayed as a ruler in the expected roles. Using Roman imperial language, and taking up some of the concerns of Augustan propaganda, Mark casts Jesus as fulfilling the Roman ideals of rulership. This includes an understanding of Jesus's divinity partially on the models of Hellenistic and Roman ruler cults.

These conclusions are distilled from a variety of interconnected textual and cultural evidence. I have divided my discussion into broad topics. After establishing my approach and my place within the discussion in Chapter 1, I turn to ideas of imperium and sovereignty writ large in Chapter 2, before addressing kingship specifically in Chapter 3. Chapter 4 addresses specifically military issues, including generalship. Chapter 5 begins to take the discussion out of the solidly military-political with a discussion of salvation, both pre- and post-eschatological. Chapter 6 addresses civic religion and Jesus's place in the Hellenistic concept of god-kings, and Chapter 7 caps the work with a reflection on Markan values. Appendix A examines some of the background contexts that led to the Judean War, as a way of creating a foothold for understanding Mark's project. Appendix B charts Mark's use of significant vocabulary compared to Matthew and Luke.

Throughout this book, I observe and describe the interweaving portrayals of authority and power in the Gospel of Mark and will demonstrate that for its earliest audiences Mark is not cryptic in its critique and appropriation of imperial authority, despite ambivalence in its treatment. Instead it intentionally and directly positions Jesus and the Kingdom of God as conceptual competitors with the emperor and Rome. By "conceptual," I mean that, counter to the claims of some liberationist and empire-critical theorists, Mark is not advocating a practicable alternative community on a proto-anarchist model. On the contrary, if we decide to read Mark primarily as a postwar document rather than a confessional one, it is possible to understand it as an attempt to reestablish a sense of divine justice and control in the face of the catastrophic failure of armed rebellion. The overthrow has already been attempted and has failed; Mark's Jesus is an answer to what the author sees as the inevitability of Roman rule for the present time, but simultaneously a stubborn insistence that the dignity of those who have suffered will be vindicated when the ultimate cosmic order is revealed.

Notes

1. A small selection of work from the past twenty years: Christopher Bryan, *Render to Caesar: Jesus, the Early Church, and the Roman Superpower* (Oxford: Oxford University Press, 2005); Warren Carter, *The Roman Empire and the New Testament: An Essential Guide*, Abingdon Essential Guides (Nashville, TN: Abingdon Press, 2006); Richard A. Horsley, ed., *Hidden Transcripts and the Arts of Resistance: Applying the Work of James C. Scott to Jesus and Paul*, Semeia 48 (Atlanta, GA: SBL, 2004); Michael Kochenash, "Empire without End: Juxtaposing the Kingdom of God with Rome in Luke-Acts" (Dissertation, Claremont School of Theology, 2017); Scot McKnight and Joseph B. Modica, *Jesus Is Lord, Caesar Is Not: Evaluating Empire in New Testament Studies* (Downers Grove, IL: InterVarsity Press, 2013); Amanda C. Miller, *Rumors of Resistance: Status Reversals and Hidden Transcripts in the Gospel of Luke*, Emerging Scholars (Minneapolis, MN: Fortress Press, 2014); Eben Scheffler, "Luke's View on Poverty in Its Ancient (Roman) Economic Context: A Challenge for Today," *Scriptura* 106 (2011): 115–35.
2. E.g., Christopher A. Frilingos, *Spectacles of Empire: Monsters, Martyrs, and the Book of Revelation*, Divinations (Philadelphia: University of Pennsylvania Press, 2004); J. Nelson Kraybill, *Imperial Cult and Commerce in John's Apocalypse*, JSNTSup 132 (Sheffield: Sheffield Academic Press, 1996); Thomas Witulski, "Der römische Kaiser Hadrian und die neutestamentliche Johannesapokalypse," in *Die Johannesapokalypse: Kontexte - Konzepte - Wirkungen*, ed. Jörg Frey, James A. Kelhoffer, and Franz Tóth, WUNT 287 (Tübingen: Mohr Siebeck, 2012), 79–116; Shane J. Wood, *The Alter-Imperial Paradigm: Empire Studies and the Book of Revelation*, BibInt 140 (Leiden: Brill, 2016).
3. Notably James G. Crossley, *The Date of Mark's Gospel: Insight from the Law in Earliest Christianity*, JSNTSup 266 (London: T&T Clark, 2004); Adolf Harnack, *The Date of the Acts and of the Synoptic Gospels*, trans. J. R. Wilkinson, vol. 4, Crown Theological Library 33 (London: Williams & Norgate, 1911); and N. H. Taylor, "Palestinian

Christianity and the Caligula Crisis. Part II. The Markan Eschatological Discourse," *JSNT* 18, no. 62 (October 1996): 13–40.
4. "The freshness of its colouring, the simplicity of its teaching, the absence of any indication that Jerusalem had already fallen when it was written, seem to point to a date earlier than the summer of A. D. 70," Henry Barclay Swete, *The Gospel According to St. Mark: The Greek Text with Introduction, Notes, and Indices*, 3rd ed. (London: Macmillan, 1913), xl. For pre-70 on the basis that the temple saying is inaccurate, Martin Hengel, *Studies in the Gospel of Mark*, trans. John Bowden (London: SCM Press, 1985), 14–28; E. P. Sanders and Margaret Davies, *Studying the Synoptic Gospels* (London: SCM Press; Philadelphia, PA: Trinity Press International, 1989), 18. For post-70 on the basis that the temple saying is accurate, Walter Schmithals, *Das Evangelium nach Markus*, 2 vols., OTK (Gütersloh: Gütersloher Verlagshaus Mohn, 1979), 2:558; William Telford, *The Theology of the Gospel of Mark*, NTT (Cambridge: Cambridge University Press, 1999), 13; Gerd Theissen, *The Gospels in Context: Social and Political History in the Synoptic Tradition* (Minneapolis, MN: Fortress Press, 1991), 259; Joel Marcus, "The Jewish War and the *Sitz im Leben* of Mark," *JBL* 111 (1992): 441–62. For post-70 on the basis of chapter 13 as *vaticinium ex eventu*, Burton L. Mack, *A Myth of Innocence: Mark and Christian Origins* (Philadelphia, PA: Fortress Press, 1991), 315. For post-70 focused on the image of the torn temple veil, e.g., Johannes Schreiber, *Theologie des Vertrauens* (Hamburg: Furche, 1967), 34–41, 66–82; Donald Juel, *Messiah and Temple: The Trial of Jesus in the Gospel of Mark*, SBLDS 31 (Missoula, MT: Scholars Press, 1977), 206; Craig A. Evans, *Mark 8:27–16:20*, WBC 34B (Nashville, TN: Thomas Nelson, 2001), 509. For a post-70 interpretation of the parable of the tenants (Mark 12:1–9), William E. Arnal, "The Parable of the Tenants and the Class Consciousness of the Peasantry," in *Text and Artifact in the Religions of Mediterranean Antiquity: Essays in Honor of Peter Richardson*, ed. Stephen G. Wilson and Michel Desjardins (Waterloo, ON: Wilfrid Laurier University Press, 2000), 135–57.
5. E.g., Adela Yarbro Collins, *Mark: A Commentary*, ed. Harold W. Attridge, Hermeneia (Minneapolis, MN: Fortress Press, 2007), 13–14; Joel Marcus, *Mark 1–8: A New Translation with Introduction and Commentary*, The Anchor Bible 27 (New York: Doubleday, 1999), 37–9. This is a slight shift from Marcus's earlier position (1992), which acknowledged the possibility that an acute observer pre-70 would accurately guess the outcome of the war, but states a stronger preference for the retrospective option. Marcus, "The Jewish War."
6. In particular, Gabriella Gelardini's commentary of nearly one thousand pages, which by its argument assumes a date post-70, devotes two sentences to date and provenance: "For no few interpreters there is much to suggest the Gospel was written during the war or shortly after. And even if it may no longer be a plausible hypothesis, nevertheless some accept that it was written in Rome for a Roman audience." Gabriella Gelardini, *Christus Militans: Studien zur politisch-militärischen Semantik im Markusevangelium vor dem Hintergrund des ersten judisch-romischen Krieges*, NovTSupp 165 (Boston, MA: Brill, 2016), 22 (my translation).
7. For a complete argument for Mark's Galilean provenance, see Christopher B. Zeichmann, "Capernaum: A 'Hub' for the Historical Jesus or the Markan Evangelist?," *JSHJ* 15, no. 1 (2017): 147–65. Aspects of Mark that are often put forward as evidence of Roman provenance, particularly the frequent Latinisms, have other possible explanations (see note 16 of Zeichmann's article). More importantly however, a strict Rome/Galilee dichotomy is artificial. There are countless imaginable scenarios that

would have a person familiar with or even brought up in Roman culture spending his adulthood in Galilee, or vice versa, after the war.
8. Maia Kotrosits, *Rethinking Early Christian Identity: Affect, Violence, and Belonging* (Minneapolis, MN: Fortress Press, 2015), 1–20, https://doi.org/10.2307/j.ctt9m0tqr.
9. Kotrosits, *Rethinking*, 117–46.
10. Jos. *War* 7.8–9. Josephus's reliability concerning the siege and conquest of Masada have been criticized, although the ramp is indisputable.

1

Empire Criticism

The analysis of Mark in this study has its basis in the historical and political contexts of its composition. Historical criticism prioritizes the historical, cultural, social, and economic matrices of New Testament texts in order to understand their places in and contributions to early Jesus reverence and Christianity.[1] Thus, examples and uses of historical criticism are wide-ranging and often involve the application of subdisciplines or other hermeneutical models. In large part, this study makes use of rhetorical, historical, intertextual, and narrative exegetical methods. This chapter outlines major contributions to some of those approaches to show the foundations on which I build and to highlight some of the gaps in the research that this book fills.

Methodology

Primarily, this book takes a narrative approach to the Gospel in combination with historical and comparative literary approaches. Consideration of Mark as a narrative will help demonstrate how narrative elements such as character, plot, flow, and perspective convey or limit discourse in Mark. Narrative theory also helps differentiate Mark's world from the historical realities of the first century—for example, the distinction between "the crowd" as a character in Mark and the real, historical populace of prewar Galilee and Judea—which will allow me to draw conclusions about the author's possible goals. Through descriptions of historical developments and circumstances in the Hellenistic and early Roman periods, I situate both the Judean War and Mark within the trajectory of Roman expansion. My use of texts such as the *Res gestae divi Augusti*, 1 Maccabees, or the *Aeneid* demonstrates currents in culture and thought to which Mark's author would reasonably have had exposure. The combination of these approaches removes some of the "uniqueness" of Mark and of the first-century Jesus movement, but at the same time highlights what was unique about them.

The current chapter surveys several different approaches to Markan studies that have influenced my own research. Imperial-critical and postcolonial approaches have been especially helpful in discerning the types of questions to ask and in framing the answers to them. Although the content of this book is historical and exegetical with little reference to theory, the methodological underpinnings I outline in the next few sections make up an important foundation to the entire study.

Throughout this book the reader will find in-depth studies of significant words and phrases from the Gospel of Mark. These terms are examined in three ways in their historical contexts: with brief summaries of their uses and meanings in pre-New Testament literature; in their narrative contexts within Mark; and in the ways that Matthew and Luke show consistency with or difference from the Markan text. Analysis of Mark's particular use of this language both in the narrative flow of the Gospel and in the cultural and historical contexts of the early to mid-70s—for example, the fact that the word ἐξουσία (authority) only appears in relation to Jesus (see Chapter 3 of this study)—allows claims regarding Mark's characterization of Jesus within the story and for his audience. Comparison of Mark to the other Synoptics brings uniquely Markan strategies and concerns to the fore.

Mark's Community

I refer to Mark's community repeatedly throughout this study, and so it will be helpful to outline some of the assumptions that go into my discussion. First, I find it more than likely that Mark's intended audience consists primarily of people who are already Jesus followers, and perhaps have been for some time. There is much scholarly discussion of Mark's purpose and audience, but my justification for this opinion rests largely on three themes in the Gospel. First, there are various details that clearly expect the audience to have previous knowledge. The reference to Rufus and Alexander in 15:21 and "let the reader understand" in 13:14 indicate address to insiders. Likewise, the division between insider and outsider in ch. 4, where the parable saying (4:11) can just as easily be read as a statement to the audience as to the disciples. Second, the ambiguous treatment of the Twelve suggests some degree of factionalism, or at least disapproval of certain leaders, groups, or ways of interpreting or acting. Such disputes are by definition internal, though they may be aired to outsiders when there is competition for new membership or other benefit. Finally, the Gospel's focus on suffering as integral to discipleship is a call for renewed or strengthened commitment, not a means of attracting popularity or acceptance. In contrast to Acts, which portrays the martyrdoms of Stephen and others as evidence of the strength and truth of their faith, Mark insists that suffering is *necessary* and even inevitable but not, in itself, glorious. The Boanerges will suffer, but their suffering will not lead to their glorification (10:35–40). Chapter 13 not only advocates flight from danger but also admits that persecution must be endured. Compared to the glorification and joy of martyrs in Acts and later Christianity, this heavy doom can be a bracing message for insiders, but it is not an evangelization strategy.[2]

Otherwise, I use "community" and "audience" somewhat loosely—with the evidence available I am loathe to attempt a fuller description. In fact, I am hesitant to assign said community a unified relationship to the temple, Rome, or the war. Mark, as an author, has identified a problem—the failure of Judean rebellion and Messianic, maybe even parousic, hopes—and has set out to solve it. The extent to which other Jesus followers in the region shared his concerns or went along with his solution is, unfortunately, unrecoverable to us. This study addresses Synoptic reception of Mark where relevant, but the authors of Matthew and Luke are each writing for different sociopolitical situations and with different agendas in mind. They represent intentional rejections of Mark's approach in some ways and intentional adoptions in others and, overall, simply the shifting needs of the growing and diverse Jesus movement at different periods in time.

Theoretical Approaches

Narrative Criticism

Since William Wrede's contribution[3] there has been steady interest in the Gospel of Mark as a fully formed, intentional literary product. Specifically, narrative and rhetorical criticisms ask what meaning an interpreter can discover from the text of Mark itself, as it has reached us. Putting aside questions of form, redaction, and source history, narrative critics instead consider the perspective of the implied author and audience[4] and the text's strategies toward internal meaning. Three major studies of narrative Christology will demonstrate the method's strengths and weaknesses.

Robert Tannehill

Tannehill's 1979 article assesses the Gospel's portrayal of Jesus through development of his "commission" or "task." He states that a "unified narrative sequence" consists of the (direct or implied) imparting of such a commission; movement toward and obstacles impeding its fulfillment; and its final completion or abandonment.[5] Tannehill traces Jesus's commission from the baptism to the crucifixion, although it is not a simple trajectory. As he moves toward the fulfillment of his commission, "Jesus assumes certain roles in relation to other persons in the narrative," for example, the disciples, the Jewish leadership, those who approach Jesus for healing, and the demons. How these relationships play out over the text's various subplots adds nuance to the commission and Christology. As the narrative proceeds it reveals that Jesus's function is not the same vis-à-vis all of the characters. For example, his role as savior does not extend to the demons.[6] The text receives further complication as characters other than Jesus receive and develop their own commissions. In particular, Tannehill understands Mark to contain three major commissions: Jesus's, which produces the central plot line of the Gospel; that of the disciples, which is to participate in Jesus's own commission as "subordinate … but sharing";[7] and that of the Pharisees and other authorities to destroy Jesus.[8] Other characters, such as supplicants in need of healing, have their own commissions confined to individual pericopes. Mark demonstrates and develops its Christology in the places where Jesus's thread crosses the many others.

Paul Danove

More recently, Danove takes a detailed look at the ways in which the Gospel of Mark creates internal meaning by characterization, context, and the rhetorical use of individual units of language.[9] He analyzes the Gospel from two points of departure: an investigation of "the ways in which the narrative cultivates specific meanings for words" and "a … study of how the unfolding of the narrator establishes the possibility for interpretive responses."[10] The Gospel's—and any narrative's—rhetorical strategies, Danove argues, build on, confirm, or deconstruct the audience's preconceived understandings of words, phrases, situations, and characters in order to construct meaning for the narrative as a whole.[11] In Mark this includes developing the relationships between God and Jesus and also Jesus and other characters (e.g., the disciples, opponents, or suppliants),[12] as well as developing the audience's understanding of titles such as "Son of Man" and "Christ."[13] He concludes, in agreement with Theodore Weeden,[14] that the purpose of Mark's Gospel is to problematize the audience's preexisting belief in Jesus as a θεῖος ἄνηρ and their favorable identification with the disciples.[15]

Elizabeth Struthers Malbon

Malbon's work has long focused on narrative characterization and the complex relationships between text, author, audience, and characters. Her book *Mark's Jesus* turns that attention to the main character of the Gospel. Rather than focusing on character development through plot (Tannehill) or repetitions in language and rhetoric (Danove), Malbon asserts that "characters are known by what they say and what they do and by what others (the narrator and other characters) say and do to, about, or in relation to them."[16] She divides her analysis into five parts, detailing the various ways in which Jesus, the narrator, and the other characters in Mark express their own beliefs about Jesus, and how Jesus responds to and compares with the expectations of the narrator, other characters, and audience. She concludes that Mark consists of complex layers of "creative tension" between the statements and actions of Jesus and those of the other characters and even the narrator. Importantly, she finds that while Mark's narrator is attempting to tell the story of a powerful divine being, Mark's Jesus repeatedly thwarts that plan, resisting or resignifying titles and expectations that would glorify him, such as Messiah and Son of God, and preferring a humble self-conception, epitomized in the title Son of Man.[17]

Summary and Critique

When applied correctly, narrative criticism fills in a number of the gaps that other methods leave. It follows in the spirit of Wrede, in that it forces the interpreter to carefully consider the *story* a text tells and its purpose, rather than mining it for evidence of source traditions. This approach accounts for the author's control of his material: even when relying on sources, authors choose the stories they tell and the strategies they use to tell them. Conversely, it also allows the interpreter to consider a text's impact on its readers, acknowledging that meaning is a product of interaction between audience and text: a reader who is unaware of an earlier source or model will not take any meaning from it. It avoids the like-equals-like prescriptivism of structuralist and history-of-religions approaches. Thus, studies like those of Tannehill, Danove, and Malbon are able to contribute important insights to our understanding of Mark.

In practice, a major weakness of the narrative approach is that on its own it often abstracts the text from its historical anchoring, proposing and prioritizing readings that can apply to any text of any provenance. This universalizing results in conclusions with little intrinsic content. Thus, Tannehill concludes that Mark's Jesus is an "eschatological salvation bringer,"[18] and Ole Davidson identifies Jesus's "three fundamental roles, the *wonder-worker*, the *proclaimer* and the *savior*."[19] These assessments are accurate enough (and fairly self-evident from the text of Mark) but abstract. The work of determining contextual meaning falls to other interpreters. All three of these quoted categories are extremely dependent on context—an Ephesian in the first century would read the word "savior" fundamentally differently than a Southern Baptist in the modern United States. Despite her focus on the "implied reader," Malbon spends little time contextualizing that reader in a particular time or place, specification of which would seriously affect the reading of the text. Any reader of any background can make some kind of coherent meaning of any text, but such conclusions often tell us more about that reader than about the text or its author. The benefit and weakness of narrative criticism, therefore, is its broad applicability to an understanding of the Gospel in any context, from the historical investigation to the modern ecumenical Bible study.

Political Criticism

The specific historical foundations lacking from many studies of Gospel narrative fall into many categories. Importantly, a number of assumptions go unquestioned: the definitions of some words and ideas are treated as self-apparent (e.g., Tannehill's and Davidsen's conclusions about Jesus highlighted above); there is often exclusive reference to the Hebrew Bible to explain concepts that appear in the texts and *milieux* of Second Temple and Hellenistic or Roman cultures, chronologically and culturally more relevant to Jesus literature; and post-credal Christian theological categories and vocabulary are often read back into the earliest Jesus-centered texts and communities.

This scope results from and is sustained by a twofold error. First, modern Westerners tend to understand religion as a distinct, even optional phenomenon that can and should be experienced separately from other aspects of culture; second and more concretely, even as scholars we often read early Christians and their texts as isolated from their surrounding contexts, particularly non-Jewish/Judean contexts. We understand the texts of the New Testament, as religious documents, to refer to religious—that is, metaphysical—realities, which overlap with more material concerns only in the immediate and individual lives of adherents, rendering them universally applicable in ways that, similarly to the downsides of narrative criticism, mask real historical contexts, concerns, and limitations. This religion-versus-life dichotomy is apparent in the secondary literature on apocalyptic texts and communities: scholars often debate whether texts such as Daniel and Revelation should be read as more "political" or more "religious," even though theorists have long understood the anachronism of these categories for ancient thought worlds.

Increased interaction with the field of classics, and especially the proliferation in biblical studies of social, historical, anthropological, and political methodologies, has destabilized these dichotomies. There are three major types of political analysis relevant to this study: liberation criticism, postcolonial criticism, and empire-critical analysis. Despite my Oxford commas, these are not necessarily discrete avenues of study as they apply to Gospel interpretation; they approach the text from a single general starting place—that "empire," colonialism, or other politics of domination were part of the basic realities of New Testament texts, their authors, and their earliest audiences. All three undertake to interpret the texts as dynamic responses to both the everyday and transcendent concerns of their authors and audiences. Applied to exegesis, these approaches result in thicker descriptions of New Testament texts, as well as the lives of their communities. This involves recognizing and analyzing power dynamics that have often been ignored or taken for granted in earlier scholarship, especially in an effort to determine what perspectives are dominant (in the text itself and in its interpretation) and how the text can be seen to create, reify, or challenge power structures. In practice, these criticisms all tend to assume a hierarchy of domination that has the Roman empire at the top. Thus they often overlap both in questions asked and conclusions reached, although there are some basic differences of approach.

James C. Scott and Infrapolitics

As a political scientist and anthropologist, Scott does not fall neatly into any one of the subdisciplines that I describe below. However, his work is relevant for all of them. In particular, his book *Domination and the Arts of Resistance*,[20] a study of resistance in highly stratified societies (primarily American antebellum slavery, the Indian caste system, and early-modern European peasant or serf societies) can help clarify Mark's position in the chaotic world of postwar Galilee and addresses some of the gaps in the other political methodologies.[21]

The novelty and significance of Scott's book is that he puts to paper and systematizes a common and familiar dynamic. In the evidence he analyzes, Scott observes what he calls "public transcripts" and "hidden transcripts," which exist in any unequal relationship. He states, "The process of domination generates [both] a hegemonic public conduct and a backstage discourse consisting of what cannot be spoken in the face of power."[22] The public transcript is, to put it somewhat poetically, the story that a society tells about itself to itself and outsiders. Rules of etiquette, leadership titles, and mythic or rationalizing justifications for the status quo are all examples. The public transcript includes behaviors and attitudes, and often reasons for both. It constrains both dominants and subordinates (though obviously the latter to a greater degree) in their speech and actions while outsiders or members of the other group are present. The public transcript also includes beliefs that the dominant class holds or purports to hold about the subordinate class, which can often be leveraged by subordinates in subtle acts of resistance.

The hidden transcript, on the other hand, is the story that a segment of a society tells only to itself about the full society. This is the social rebel making pig noises at (or out of hearing of) police officers, the significance of the Moses narrative to enslaved African Americans, or ribald songs questioning the king's lineage. Although Scott takes great pains throughout the book not to privilege the "truth" of the hidden over the public transcript, or vice versa, as far as what each says about a society, it is clear that the hidden transcript by its nature challenges the public one. The relationship between the two is complicated by the fact that there are various stratifications within any society, each of which has its own set of public and hidden transcripts. It is further complicated because the nature of the hidden transcript is such that it often leaves sparse evidence or none at all. Outsiders are most often treated to the public view of things through direct experience or surviving records. Since outward adherence to the public transcript is usually the safest mode of behavior for subordinated people, Scott warns that "we are in danger of making a serious mistake ... whenever we infer anything at all about the beliefs or attitudes of anyone solely on the basis that he or she has engaged in an apparently deferential act."[23]

Scott emphasizes that the hidden transcripts of subordinated groups are forms of resistance. Everyday resistance in the forms of gossip, grumbling, pilfering, folk culture, religion, poaching, and so on "could hardly be mounted without a lively backstage transcript of values, understandings, and popular outrage to sustain it."[24] Those values, understandings, and outrage are resistance, both because they provide infrastructure for more material forms of resistance and because they implicitly challenge the veracity and influence of the public transcript.

One crucial feature of Scott's argument for application to the Gospel of Mark is the assumption that *resistance* is not necessarily the same as *revolt*. Throughout the book Scott emphasizes that the hidden transcript is hidden because of the risks inherent in exposing it. "The first open statement of a hidden transcript, a declaration that breaches the etiquette of power relations, ... carries the force of a symbolic declaration of war."[25] In the vast majority of cases, resistance against elites does not seek the overthrow of the entire system, but rather to reestablish some experience of dignity and control among subalterns.[26] In an interview, Scott makes reference to a small Malaysian community that resisted a new tax not by attempting to skirt it but by paying it with a substandard variety of rice.[27] The "tax rice," used only for that purpose, still required labor and cropland to produce, so the material gains of this resistance would have been minimal. Its value, then, would have been in the knowledge that the community had pulled one over on the authorities—the private assertion of dignity and control. Whereas Tat-Siong Benny Liew interprets Mark's apocalyptic bent as "passive" and claims that the Gospel "defers" action against oppression (see the section dedicated to Liew below), Scott allows us to see even the fantasy of revolt or divine comeuppance as an effective kind of resistance in its own right.

Here it is necessary to address a frequent misreading of Scott in biblical studies. The phrase "hidden transcript" is often understood literally, in the sense of a written text that makes heavy use of allegory or is otherwise encrypted.[28] This approach treats the biblical text as a cypher with a key, a puzzle that can be solved by substituting the correct references in a one-to-one pattern. While Scott certainly addresses this kind of resistance,[29] he is clear that it is only part of the phenomenon: "I argue that a partly sanitized, ambiguous, and coded *version of the hidden transcript* is always present in the public discourse of subordinate groups."[30] The hidden transcript itself, spoken and lived among subalterns when they are unobserved by outsiders, is not "sanitized, ambiguous, and coded" in that way, and it is more than stories and words. The complete hidden transcript is the structural underpinning of the dignity of a subordinated group, and it includes rituals, behaviors, and unarticulated beliefs as much as spoken and written material.

This is an important distinction for Mark, because it is my contention that the Gospel is *not* a public version of the hidden transcript, disguised from the outsider's view, although we might experience it that way in the modern world. For the author, and for the earliest audiences, Mark is explicit in its claims and positions. The alternative phrasing that Scott uses occasionally, "private transcript," is perhaps more accurate. First, I have already stated that Mark is a text for insiders.

The second observation is the Gospel's unapologetic use of Roman imperial language and titles. A phrase like το εὐαγγελίον τοῦ χριστοῦ (to paraphrase Mark 1:1) reads to modern Westerners as a religious statement that might allow for a range of interpretation, but in the Roman empire, in the aftermath of the destruction of Jerusalem, a claim to be the Messiah would have been understood primarily in political and even military terms (as Peter proves for us in ch. 8; see also Acts 1:6; Jos. *Ant.* 17.10.7; *War* 2.13.5). Similarly, ὁ υἱὸς τοῦ θεοῦ, a major title of Augustus here adapted for Jesus, is a direct and explicit challenge to the cosmic legitimacy of the Roman emperors.[31]

Thus, to the extent that Mark's appropriation of imperial titles and vocabulary is *not* surreptitious and would be immediately recognizable to a contemporary audience, there are various possibilities for where the Gospel might exist on the spectrum of hidden and public transcripts. Further, consideration of Scott's work should lead to an examination of what we think we know about Roman responses to the early Jesus movement, and vice versa, and the ways in which followers of the movement did or did not publicly assert themselves.

Liberation Criticism

Liberation criticism is rooted in the liberationist theologies of Central and South America, which quickly spread to Black American, continental African, Asian, and feminist and womanist theologies. Generally, and to do the field no justice, liberationist approaches to the Bible focus on ways in which biblical texts can empower oppressed communities or otherwise serve as examples for their liberation. The origins of these theologies mean that "liberation" is usually expressed in socio- or econo-political terms.

A major liberationist reading of the Gospel of Mark is Ched Myers's commentary, *Binding the Strong Man*. Myers criticizes what he calls "theological hermeneutics":

> This tradition has exposited the Gospels in a way analogous to mining for precious metals: the "gold" of timeless and universal theological principle or churchly dogma is carefully extracted from the "ore" of historical or social peculiarities, which are sluiced away. Wrested away from history and practice, the kerygma thus becomes the domain of abstract thought or "spiritual" reflection. ... Such a suppression of the fully human, concretely socio-historical character of the Gospel is nothing less than a perpetuation of the docetic heresy.[32]

In contrast, Myers asserts that "Mark's Gospel originally was written to help imperial subjects learn the hard truth about their world and themselves. ... His is a story by, about, and for those committed to God's work of justice, compassion, and liberation in the world."[33] For Myers, Mark "is a narrative for and about the common people," and as such is something of an anomaly of surviving ancient literature, which primarily demonstrates the perspectives and concerns of the privileged classes. As evidence of Mark's proletarian bent, Myers points to the prominence of crowds, John the Baptist's "subversive promise of a new order," recurring themes of "hunger and hopelessness," and even the crowd's turn against Jesus in ch. 15 as "one who, as far as they were concerned, failed to deliver on his promises."[34]

Ultimately, Myers's Mark is apocalyptic, but Myers rejects twentieth-century interpretations of the apocalyptic as escapist, pessimistic, and passive.[35] Instead, he reads apocalyptic texts like Daniel, Revelation, and Mark as "political manifestoes of nonviolent movements of resistance to tyranny."[36] One basis for this reading is his dating of Mark before the fall of the temple. He defends this supposition with what he considers unfulfilled or erroneous elements of otherwise *ex eventu* prophecy. Most prominently, he refers to 13:1–2—the incorrect prediction of the temple's fall "stone by stone" as opposed to burning, as other accounts of the war describe,[37] and the disciples' question preceding it—as evidence that the temple still stood at the time of writing; and the demonic Legion, nonetheless driven into the sea, as evidence that "the historical power represented by Roman legions ... was ... intact."[38] Likewise, Myers's Mark rejects movements such as the Pharisees and Essenes largely on the bases of their attitudes toward hierarchy and elitism and the place of the poor in their worldviews; and demonstrates a complex but nonaligned attitude toward the Judean rebels, supporting and even mimicking their socioeconomic goals (e.g., the destruction of the public archives to erase debt) but ultimately disapproving of their defense of the temple as a "return to the politics of domination."[39] Mark thus intends to model a resistance centered on "radical discipleship" and "nonaligned radicalism,"[40] and bolster a community founded on egalitarian, nonhierarchical structures that both elevate those traditionally marginalized (e.g., the poor, women) and restrict the powers and privileges of leadership.[41]

Within this framework, Mark's Jesus emerges as a prophet, priest, and "rebel king" of a populist movement.[42] Intertwining plot strands develop the character of Jesus as creating a messianic, discipleship-based community; proclaiming liberation and healing to the oppressed; and "challenging the authorities to choose justice and compassion over domination."[43] In this context, Mark and Mark's Jesus both demonstrate ambivalence toward political titles such as Messiah, retaining it as "the cornerstone of the early church's confession," but preferring ὁ υἱὸς τοῦ ἀνθρώπου (which Myers translates as "Human One") as an anti-dominational, nonhierarchical, apocalyptic designation more in line with Mark's ideology.[44]

Some aspects of Myers's work illustrate the limitations of liberation criticism for New Testament study. The language of liberation as Myers uses it is closely tied with twentieth-century liberation theology (which he directly cites in his afterword). Indeed, Myers's image of Mark's community in some ways resembles a Latin American or eastern European resistance group, or a peaceful resistance movement as idealized by post facto portrayals of Mahatma Gandhi and Martin Luther King, Jr.[45]

Central to this image is the imagination of Mark as "a coded discourse of resistance that could elude Roman censors and military intelligence."[46] However, Myers gives no reference to any structures or practices that might have amounted to official censorship or relevant "military intelligence" in the Roman empire. Such a reading of Mark paints the text as a revolutionary tract and the Roman authorities on the lookout for that type of dissent. While it is beyond question that ancient communities or movements in resistance to power structures could use the written word for various purposes, the idea that indirect references to opponents in apocalyptic texts serve only the utilitarian purposes of plausible deniability—stitches in a Frenchwoman's knitting—betrays a distinctly and even simplistically modern understanding of text and resistance. The literacy rate in the ancient Mediterranean was quite low,[47] and even assuming primarily oral circulation of Mark, what information there is of the first- and second-century Jesus communities does not support an image of the kind of underground political resistance that has flourished since the early twentieth century, or even that buttressed the Judean revolts against Rome, and that Myers seems to have in mind.[48] Finally, as I discussed above in my outline of Scott's work, Mark's text is not so covert as Myers imagines.

Postcolonial Criticism

As a general approach, postcolonialism "has been concerned with the elaboration of theoretical structures that contest the previous dominant western ways of seeing things."[49] This approach has been developing since the 1980s as a way to give a voice to subaltern (i.e., subjugated or otherwise considered of lower status) peoples in the analyses of their own situations. In particular, many of its champions understand postcolonialism as a way to understand the ongoing effects of European colonialism even after the end of direct colonial rulership.[50] Although New Testament texts (and especially Mark, in the perspective of this study) cannot strictly be called "*post*colonial" in that sense, this kind of analysis is well situated to help interpret those texts. Postcolonialism understands the producers and early audiences of New Testament texts as colonized subjects and the texts themselves as negotiating, accepting/collaborating with, or resisting Roman power, and can help the interpreter see the complexity inherent in colonialist, subaltern, and anticolonialist enterprises.[51]

Tat-siong Benny Liew

In an important postcolonialist interpretation of Mark, Liew begins by staking his claim in postmodernist territory, rejecting "the modern [that is, ideologically Modern] notion or ideal of universal truths or standards that are applicable at all times, at all places, and for all people."[52] To put it simply, context matters—both of the text and of the reader. Liew understands postmodernism to be fundamentally interested in "political and ethical questions" in order to "bring about change and transformation."[53] For biblical interpretation, this means recognizing the role that the Bible has played in oppressive structures as well as its potential for liberation, and how it is the interpreter's location and goals that make the difference.

Similarly to Myers, Liew regards Mark as "a piece of colonial literature written under Roman colonization."[54] Also in line with Myers, he reads Mark as apocalyptic and (therefore) political literature, though his interpretation of the apocalyptic differs from Myers's. He notes a tendency in Markan scholarship to "segregate the sociopolitical and apocalyptic dimensions of Mark,"[55] in which the former devalues the parousia as a mechanism for coping with the loss of the war or sublimates it to the crucifixion and instead emphasizes the gradual flowering of the kingdom (e.g., Myers); and the latter spiritualizes the conflicts faced by Mark's community as Jewish/Christian ideological struggles or dots on the map of salvation history.[56] In contrast, Liew argues that apocalypticism is itself a product of colonialism, citing not only the chain of colonizing forces in the history of Israel but also, by way of example, the narrative outline of the book of Daniel, "presenting history in a succession of kingdoms."[57]

Liew departs from Myers in some important ways. Where Myers reads the Gospel of Mark as the manifesto of a movement, a blueprint for radical living, Liew finds it to be rather less action oriented. He defines the apocalyptic in general as "simply the belief that God will soon intervene in history to erase all evil and demonic powers, and usher in a new age of perfect divine sovereignty"[58] and regards apocalyptic texts as "ultimately not factual information but matters of fantasy and desire."[59] Mark, then, resists domination not through a call to revolutionary action of whatever kind but by "promising the utter destruction of both Jewish and Roman authorities *upon Jesus' resurrected return*."[60] In fact, for Liew, "Mark's politics of parousia … by the way it views evil and suffering as unalterable conditions short of God's direct intervention, is basically a politic of postponement and passivity."[61]

Further, in contrast to Myers and some other political readings of Mark, Liew acknowledges that the Gospel is not so much a repudiation of hierarchy as a refocalization of it. At no point does Mark question hierarchy or centralized authority as such. The text simply asserts that the "current" powers are illegitimate and even Satanic, that humans occupy only two strata of the hierarchy—those who follow and those who do not—and that true authority belongs to God and his appointed agent Jesus.[62] As such an agent, however, Jesus is repeatedly stymied in his mission both by opposition and the intractability of his disciples.

Liew reads Mark as if it were a novel, self-contained and reflecting but not meant to particularly inform the lives of its early audience. This leads him, throughout his book and particularly in chapter 5, to read Jesus's mission, as Mark portrays it, as a failure. He understands the appeals to necessity (δεῖ) in the passion predictions and other discussions of the crucifixion to indicate Jesus's resignation to this failure, and even interprets the parable of the wicked tenants as indicating God's surprise that the opposition is so stiff.[63] This fatalistic reading disregards the purpose of the Gospel as a tool of and for post-crucifixion Jesus communities, and makes precisely the same mistake that the disciples and crowd do in chs. 14–16: they see the crucifixion as the failure of Jesus's plan, rather than an integral part of it. For Liew, the Gospel of Mark is a fully enclosed world where the last page, dour as it is, marks the end of the story, which cannot be the case.

Simon Samuel

Simon Samuel reaches somewhat different conclusions. He identifies colonial power as operating on both external (Roman) and internal (Jerusalem) levels[64]—an observation implicit in both Myers's and Liew's discussions of Mark's treatment of the Jerusalem cult. Further, he notes that, according to many postcolonial theorists, "in a colonial/post-colonial context there is no overly rigid binary opposition between the colonizer and the colonized for both are often caught up in a complex reciprocal relationship of desire and derision."[65] For Samuel, a postcolonial discourse is "a complex, ambivalent and incongruous discourse that accommodates and disrupts the colonialist perceptions and perspectives of domination."[66] The implications for reading Mark are promising for thick analysis. The conclusions of Myers and Liew "boil down"—for Myers, to a vision of revolutionary, radical, pacifist resistance; and for Liew, to a cynical record of submission to authoritarian power. Samuel, however, reads Mark as an ambivalent text that occupies a precarious space between colonized and colonizer, demonstrating resistance and acquiescence, mimicry and otherness.

To demonstrate the applicability of postcolonial method to the Gospel of Mark, Samuel looks to other texts of the late Hellenistic/early Roman period. In particular, he focuses on Chariton's novel *Chaereas and Callirhoe* as an example of the ambivalence and in-betweenness felt by many colonized subjects. He notes that the novel genre developed primarily in the eastern Mediterranean, and thus novelists were Greeks under Roman authority (or even perhaps native Asiatics under Greek and then Roman authority). Further, Hellenization and Roman philhellenism produced "hybrid cultures" as well as opportunities for Greeks to claim certain kinds of superiority over the colonizing Romans.[67]

Samuel also briefly investigates Jewish writings of the Hellenistic and early Roman periods, especially 1 Maccabees, Josephus, and the Qumran texts. He finds a variety of responses to Roman power, ranging from allegiance against Antiochus Epiphanes IV in 1 Maccabees, to apocalyptic demonization in the Dead Sea Scrolls, to apologeticist collusion in Josephus. A repeated and crucial theme in his analyses of Jewish literature and of Chariton is *ambiguity*. There is no monolithic Greek or Jewish response to Rome or imperial rule, and even individual texts demonstrate both a desire for freedom from outside rule as well as an acceptance of imperial mastery as beneficial, necessary, or simply impossible to resist. Notably, Samuel points out that the Sibylline Oracles portray Rome as *both* a weapon of God "to punish Israel for going astray from him" (3.268ff) *and* a "barbarian" rule that God will bring low (3.350–355).[68] To further bring home Samuel's point, observe that in this case both citations come from the same oracle.

Thus finding that roughly contemporary writings lend themselves to postcolonial analysis, Samuel is confident to read Mark similarly. He criticizes the analyses of Myers, Liew, and others as "essentialist," particularly when they describe the Gospel in terms of pure resistance or a return to pure "Israelite" culture and values.[69] For Samuel, Mark's Jesus is a "conundrum" that reflects the Markan community's hybrid, interstitial position. As a minority both under Roman domination and among the primarily Judean culture of Galilee and Judea, the Markan community as imagined by Samuel is not in a position either to fully resist or fully accommodate imperializing power. One strategy that the text uses to negotiate this precarious position is the universalization of some Jewish apocalyptic ideas: crucially, Mark transforms Daniel's ὁ υἱὸς τοῦ ἀνθρώπου from a figure representing the salvation of "Israel's elect" to one that brings together "a transcultural community … from the ends of the earth to the ends of the heavens."[70] An outsider to both Rome and Israel, Samuel's Mark refuses to take sides, and instead attempts to delimit a new territory that welcomes the elect regardless of their origins.

Thus, Samuel's methodology helps to develop an understanding of Mark that is postcolonial in its awareness and critique of power structures throughout the text, attentive of narrative and historical contexts, and open to the ambiguities and multiple valences of a text addressed to a cultural minority attempting to differentiate itself from its parent communities and simultaneously survive in a world where novelty is suspect and social conformity is a primary measure of loyalty and belonging.

Empire Criticism

Drawing from liberationist, postcolonialist, and more traditional sociopolitical and economic approaches, empire-critical studies are primarily specific to the study of Second Temple Judaism and especially the New Testament, and produce historical and literary interpretations that assume and look for evidence of responses to Roman occupation and violence. My study falls comfortably within that definition, as do many of its sources. The next few pages summarize two of the major architects of empire criticism.

Richard A. Horsley

Horsley has been an influential voice in empire-critical studies for over two decades. His early monograph, *Jesus and the Spiral of Violence*, sets the tone for much of his later work.[71] He investigates the Gospel tradition for evidence concerning the historical Jesus's approach to violence, and counter to previous work that favors a nonviolent Jesus in contrast to the violent (and ahistorical, Horsley contends) Zealot movement, he concludes that Jesus cannot be shown to have particularly advocated or repudiated violence as such. Instead, he argues that Jesus worked within and engaged with a violent system in order to oppose violent oppression. He "announced a good deal of imminent divine violence," but, on the other hand, "there is no indication that he advocated acts of violence" from his followers.[72] His description of Jesus is somewhat comparable to Myers's, if not quite as idealistic: for Horsley, the historical Jesus's mission "focused on village communities [and] an alternative social order of cooperation and social justice free of oppression."[73]

In his treatment of Mark, Horsley criticizes the bulk of modern biblical scholarship as primarily theological, depending on categories and assumptions more at home in modern Christian communities than in first-century Galilee.[74] Instead, he advocates reading Mark as a "people's history," in which Jesus's conflicts with the Pharisees can be understood not as debates over such modern ideas as morality and religion but over local and popular (i.e., Galilean) versus elite (Jerusalem) control over culture, politics, and economics.[75]

Like Myers, Horsley tends toward dualistic thinking. He relies on a sharp differentiation between Hellenistic and Israelite cultures that has been losing consensus in scholarship for some time.[76] His construction of Galilee as "popular" and Jerusalem as "elite" ignores Herodian rulership and Galilean cities such as Sepphoris and Tiberius. Further, in this book he gives no date or provenance for Mark, and in some ways treats Mark more as a record of Jesus's experience than an interpretation of the author's own. In his interpretation of the Gospel as anti-Roman, he assumes the historical situation of the 20s and 30s CE, or at least makes no sustained reference to Roman military action, preferring less specific allusions to "Roman rule" and the like. Thus unpinning the Gospel itself from history, Horsley reads it as just a story—a story about real political situations and with a basis in history, but with no apparent reference to the author's own time and situation. Overall, "Mark's Jesus" in *Hearing the Whole Story* is not different from the historical Jesus of Horsley's other work, and both are concerned with creating an egalitarian, village-based society rather than with theology.[77]

Despite all of this, Horsley's understanding of the disciples in Mark assumes a later, if unspecified, date for the Gospel. He reads them as representing (for Jesus) the renewal of Israel and its twelve tribes,[78] and (for Mark) the failure and error of the Jerusalem Christian leadership. Counter to Paul's representation of Peter and the other "pillars," and to the later Gospels' rehabilitation especially of Peter, in Mark "the disciples have no authority based on their having witnessed the resurrection." Additionally, they consistently misunderstand Jesus especially in relation to issues of leadership, service, and power, a trend that Horsley interprets as a foil "for Jesus' insistence that his movement be egalitarian, with no heads who enjoy veneration, power, and privilege."[79]

Warren Carter

Carter's only monograph specifically focused on Mark is a work of feminist criticism, not explicitly empire criticism.[80] However, that book is rooted in his earlier empire-critical work, and as a major voice in empire-critical studies he deserves an overview here. At first glance, Carter's approach is similar to Horsley's, in that he attempts to interpret the Gospels primarily through the lens of Roman imperial domination, and the common thread of his empire-critical work is an interest in the details of social, political, and economic structures that create or enable oppressive violence. His bibliography favors Matthew,[81] which he dates and contextualizes roughly to 80s Antioch.[82] He reads Matthew in terms largely familiar to the reader versed in empire and postcolonial criticism:

> The Gospel presents a *social* challenge in offering a different vision and experience of human interaction and community. Instead of a hierarchical, exploitative, exclusionary community based on "their great ones being tyrants over them" (20:25–26), it creates and inclusive, merciful, egalitarian community based on practical, merciful, loving service to others. ... The Gospel also presents a

theological challenge. It contests the imperial theology or worldview that claims the world belongs to Jupiter and to Rome. ... It refuses to accept Rome's claims to sovereignty, Rome's theological sanctions, and Rome's vision of social interaction that benefits a few and causes hardship to most.[83]

Similarly, Matthew's Jesus "challenges imperial claims that the emperor embodies divine sovereignty and presence, and that the emperor, as the agent of the gods, ensures societal well-being."[84] This reading of Matthew's Jesus is similar to my argument in Chapter 4 of this study, an examination of Mark's engagement with imperial theology.

In his work on Matthew, Carter reaches similar conclusions as Myers and Horsley regarding Jesus's nonviolence and egalitarianism, but a fuller account of his approach to these matters is available through his interpretation of the Gospel of John. In this work, he criticizes idealist, "monolithic" approaches to the Roman empire in John, which "reject any accommodation between the empire and John's Gospel." Carter reminds us of the importance of imitation and "a mix of distance and participation, compliance and defiance" in subaltern strategies of resistance and survival.[85] In John, which Carter situates in late-first-century Ephesus,[86] this plays out partly in the imitation and resignification of apotheosis. John's Gospel both imitates this idea and renders it null: it demonstrates the glory of Jesus by including him in this tradition, and ironically divests the tradition of its special glory by promising ascension to *all* who follow Jesus (e.g., John 14:1–30).[87] Where Myers and Horsley read the Jesus tradition as a wholesale rejection of imperial values and structures, Carter sees a more complex, subtle process of negotiation, appropriation, and resignification closer to the postcolonial critics.

Sociohistorical Approaches

Mark and the Judean War

Werner Kelber

Mine is not the first study of Mark to address it as a response to the war. Kelber's 1973 monograph understands the Gospel to be a kind of Christian Deuteronomistic history, explaining and justifying the disaster of 70 CE through a reimagining of Jesus.[88] For Kelber, Mark responds to the destruction of the temple and of the "Jerusalem church" by portraying its pillars as fearful, misunderstanding, and ultimately cowardly.[89] I do not dispute Kelber's conclusions, but I do approach the text from a somewhat different angle. My use of scare quotes earlier in this paragraph more or less sums up the major differences between Kelber's approach and mine. The strict dichotomy between Christian and Jew is alive and well in Kelber's book, although he allows for a category of "Jewish Christians,"[90] whereas I have serious reservations about the helpfulness for historical research not only of the dichotomy but even of the English terms themselves (as well as terms such as "church"), as far as what they potentially connote for the modern reader. I avoid using them in this study where possible, particularly in reference to the first century. Further, Kelber assigns Mark's primary motivation as ecclesiastical and religious. The evangelist *"reinterprets* the life and death of Jesus for his own time and people."⁹¹ While Jesus is without a doubt the protagonist of the story, my reading presumes that Mark's purpose is rather to reinterpret the cosmology and worldview of the community in light of the Roman destruction, using Jesus as a lens rather than the focus. This is perhaps a subtle difference, and certainly a matter of scholarly choice.

Mark and the Roman Military

Gabriela Gelardini

Likewise, Gelardini examines the Gospel of Mark as a postwar product and therefore interwoven both literarily and contextually with military language and assumptions. She criticizes previous imperial-critical work on Mark as too vague, as not taking into account the profound importance of the military in maintaining Roman rule in general as well as specifically in the Levantine/Judean context. Further, she recognizes that characterization of Mark primarily as an anti-imperial *Gegensevangelium* artificially limits interpretation. Observing the ubiquity of war in the ancient world, and noting its particular prominence as part of regime changes, she asks to what extent Jesus's inauguration of the Kingdom of God might follow the same rules.⁹² Her subsequent analysis reveals a Gospel that both opposes Roman rule and simultaneously constructs a new divine reign. By way of conclusion, Gelardini interprets the end of Mark through the lenses of the Flavian triumph, held in Rome after the defeat of Judea, and the rituals of the Jerusalem temple that were ignored or desecrated by both sides during the war.⁹³ In this reading, Jesus emerges at once as the cleansing Yom Kippur sacrifice, the defeated leader who is executed as part of the Roman triumph, and, after his resurrection, the general *redivivus* amassing his troops in Galilee for conquest.⁹⁴

Christopher Zeichmann

In a monograph and an article, Zeichmann demonstrates that (1) the military was an integrated and ambiguous or even, in some ways, positive aspect of life in first-century Israel; (2) attitudes toward the military must be understood in regional and temporal terms (e.g., the experience of the military in the Decapolis during the war would have been fundamentally different from that experience in Judea); and (3) there was no monolithic "Roman military," and as much as possible, soldiers in Mark should be interpreted as agents of their local command structures, rather than of "the empire" writ large.⁹⁵ Crucially, in his dissertation Zeichmann observes that the Gospel's attitude toward soldiers reflects a larger societal trend that distinguished and stereotyped soldiers by rank. Regular enlisted men appear faceless, either as morally neutral tools of their commanders (e.g., soldiers carry out the arrest and execution of John the Baptist in ch. 6, but Herod appears as the main grammatical subject of 6:16 and 17, and thus acquires the blame) or as sadistic bullies (i.e., the soldiers of the Jerusalem garrison in ch. 15, torturing Jesus despite Pilate's relative ambiguity toward the matter). Meanwhile, more highly ranked soldiers have more agency (such as the centurion at the cross) or make up a sector of the local elite class (the χιλίαρχοι in 6:21).⁹⁶

In terms of the present discussion, Zeichmann's conclusions show that the question of "Roman authority" in Mark is more immediately a matter of local rulership, in contrast, for example, to Luke-Acts' globalizing rhetoric and appropriation of imperial propagandizing strategies.⁹⁷ However, Zeichmann's earlier work somewhat overstates Mark's disinterest in the empire at large. He claims that "the nonexistence of a consistent depiction of the military suggests that the author did not operate with 'empire' or 'Roman army' as salient categories when composing the Gospel,"⁹⁸ a perplexing conclusion given his convincing argument throughout the dissertation that a historical understanding of the Roman military precludes a "consistent depiction" in the first place. A few pages later, he argues (against postcolonial and imperial-critical scholars such as Horsley) that a characterization of Mark as anti-Roman is largely indefensible, because the Gospel does not espouse the "naïve" and decidedly modern nonhierarchical ideals that these scholars assign to it; instead he rightly contends that the Gospel is a clear product of its context and is concerned with the illegitimacy of earthly authorities versus the Kingdom of God, not with the concept of hierarchy per se.⁹⁹ As a critique of Horsley this is quite valid, but here and in the above quote Zeichmann on the one hand conflates the Roman military, whatever its form(s), with the empire itself, counter to his own analysis; and on the other assumes that an anti-Roman position must necessarily also be an ideologically anti-imperial one, and that is patently not the case.

Applications within This Study

The chapters that follow make use of these and other methods and lenses in combination. More traditional exegetical methods, such as narrative analysis of characters and their relationships to each other, or the rhetorical investigation of specific vocabulary, are here rooted in (and therefore return results appropriate to) political and power-aware inquiry. This combination of methods produces a reading of Mark that does not separate "religious" from "political," or apocalypticism from concrete resistance, and, further, does not romanticize the nature and goals of Mark's resistance to Roman domination.

Notes

1. See Craig L. Blomberg and Jennifer Foutz Markley, *A Handbook of New Testament Exegesis* (Grand Rapids, MI: Baker Academic, 2010), 63–92; Edgar Krentz, *The Historical-Critical Method*, GBS (Philadelphia, PA: Fortress Press, 1975); Gerhard Maier, *Biblische Hermeneutik*, Monographien und Studienbücher (Wuppertal: R. Brockhaus, 1990), 226–47.
2. Collins (*Mark*, 96–102) represents the scholarly debate about Mark's audience as primarily about whether Mark wrote to a specific community or to "all Christians." I am not staking ground in that debate at this time, except perhaps to point out that both ends of that spectrum assume that Mark is fundamentally "scripture" and was written as such. I believe that there are more possibilities for interpreting the Gospels.

3. William Wrede, *Das Messiasgeheimnis in den Evangelien* (Göttingen: Vandenhoeck & Ruprecht, 1901).
4. Elizabeth StruthersMalbon, *Mark's Jesus: Characterization as Narrative Christology* (Waco, TX: Baylor University Press, 2009), 7. Cf. the critique of reader-response criticism and the implied reader in particular in Thomas E. Phillips, *Reading Issues of Wealth and Poverty in Luke-Acts*, SBEC 48 (Lewiston, NY: Edwin Mellen Press, 2001), 45–79.
5. Robert C. Tannehill, "The Gospel of Mark as Narrative Christology," *Semeia* 16 (1979): 60–1.
6. Tannehill, "Narrative Christology," 63.
7. Tannehill, "Narrative Christology," 65.
8. Tannehill, "Narrative Christology," 66.
9. Paul L. Danove, *The Rhetoric of Characterization of God, Jesus, and Jesus' Disciples in the Gospel of Mark*, JSNTSup 290 (New York: T&T Clark, 2005).
10. Danove, *Rhetoric*, 2.
11. Danove, *Rhetoric*, 11–18.
12. Danove, *Rhetoric*, 84.
13. Danove, *Rhetoric*, 83, 85–6.
14. Theodore J. Weeden, *Mark: Traditions in Conflict* (Philadelphia, PA: Fortress Press, 1971).
15. Danove, *Rhetoric*, 157–8, 162.
16. Malbon, *Mark's Jesus*, 14.
17. Malbon, *Mark's Jesus*, 132–40.
18. Tannehill, "Narrative Christology," 63.
19. Ole Davidsen, *The Narrative Jesus: A Semiotic Reading of Mark's Gospel* (Aarhus, Denmark: Aarhus University Press, 1993), 334, italics original.
20. James C. Scott, *Domination and the Arts of Resistance: Hidden Transcripts* (New Haven, CT: Yale University Press, 1990).
21. My research has uncovered only a few published works that explicitly make use of Scott's book for Gospel studies, although there is somewhat more engagement in Pauline studies. Two representative examples are Horsley, *Hidden Transcripts*; and Sung U. Lim, "A Double-Voiced Reading of Romans 13:1–7 in Light of the Imperial Cult: Original Research," *HTS* 71 (2015): 1–10, http://www.hts.org.za/index.php/HTS/article/view/2475. Of the major authors outlined later in this chapter, Scott earns a brief citation in Simon Samuel, *A Postcolonial Reading of Mark's Story of Jesus*, LNTS 340 (London: T&T Clark, 2007), 123n56, but is not cited in either Tat-siong Benny Liew, *Politics of Parousia: Reading Mark Inter(Con)Textually*, BibInt 42 (Leiden: Brill, 1999) or Ched Myers, *Binding the Strong Man: A Political Reading of Mark's Story of Jesus* (Maryknoll, NY: Orbis Books, 1988). The latter, having been published before *Domination and the Arts of Resistance*, could have had access to Scott's earlier work on peasant societies, but it seems that Scott was not on the radar of New Testament studies before the late 90s. Warren Carter cites another of Scott's works, *Weapons of the Weak: Everyday Forms of Peasant Resistance* (New Haven, CT: Yale University Press, 1985), in Warren Carter, *Matthew and Empire: Initial Explorations* (Harrisburg, PA: Trinity Press International, 2001), 18–19. On the other hand, Scott's terminology of the "hidden transcript" has taken on something of a life of its own in biblical studies (see pages 13 and 14).
22. Scott, *Domination*, xii.

23. Scott, *Domination*, 23. See also pages 87–9 on the public transcript as historical record and the necessity of secrecy in the hidden transcript.
24. Scott, *Domination*, 190.
25. Scott, *Domination*, 8.
26. Scott, *Domination*, 188; Warren Carter, "James C. Scott and New Testament Studies: A Response to Allen Callahan, William Herzog, and Richard Horsley," in Horsley, *Hidden Transcripts*, 89–90.
27. Benjamin Ferron, Claire Oger, and James C. Scott, "'When the Revolution Becomes the State It Becomes My Enemy Again': An Interview with James C. Scott," The Conversation, accessed February 7, 2019, https://web.archive.org/web/20191217101657/http://theconversation.com/when-the-revolution-becomes-the-state-it-becomes-my-enemy-again-an-interview-with-james-c-scott-98488.
28. E.g., Gelardini, *Christus Militans*, 25–26; Hyun Chul Paul Kim, "Two Mothers and Two Sons: Reading 1 Kings 3:16–28 as a Parody on Solomon's Coup (1 Kings 1–2)," in *Partners with God: Theological and Critical Readings of the Bible in Honor of Marvin A. Sweeney*, ed. Shelley L. Birdsong and Serge Frolov, CSHBS 2 (Claremont, CA: Claremont Press, 2017), 83–99.
29. For example, see the discussion of Brer Rabbit in the folk stories of American enslaved people: Scott, *Domination*, 19, 163–6.
30. Scott, *Domination*, 19, emphasis mine.
31. This is not a unanimous position. Edwin Broadhead, in his study of New Testament titles for Jesus, briefly discusses "Son of God" as a title for Hellenistic rulers but does not mention the Roman emperors at all, instead focusing on Davidic and other Hebrew Bible precedents. (*Naming Jesus: Titular Christology in the Gospel of Mark*, JSNTSup 175 [Sheffield: Sheffield Academic, 1999], 116–23.)
32. Myers, *Strong Man*, 9, emphasis original.
33. Myers, *Strong Man*, 11.
34. Myers, *Strong Man*, 39.
35. Myers, *Strong Man*, 415–16.
36. Myers, *Strong Man*, 417.
37. Jos. *War* 6.4.5. However, contrary to Myers's argument, *War* 7.1.3 describes Titus's order to have the temple and the rest of the city pulled down.
38. Myers, *Strong Man*, 417–18. I take issue with Myers's assumption that the technical end of the war equates to the limit of military influence on local culture. Rarely has an imperializing power ended a local rebellion and then simply left. More specifically, *legio X Fretensis*, after sacking Jerusalem, brought about the fall of Masada in 73 and remained a fixture in the region, eventually ending the Bar Kochba revolt. The legion was garrisoned there until at least the fourth century. References to the military and its influence in Mark by no means limit the Gospel to a date pre-70. For the history of the Tenth, see Werner Eck, *Rom und Judaea: Fünf Vorträge zur römischen Herrschaft in Judäa* (Tubingen: Mohr Siebeck, 2007), 50–1.
39. Myers, *Strong Man*, 428–31.
40. Myers, *Strong Man*, 334.
41. Myers, *Strong Man*, 434–8.
42. Myers, *Strong Man*, 444–6.
43. Myers, *Strong Man*, 120–1.
44. Myers, *Strong Man*, 122–3.
45. See especially Myers, *Strong Man*, 431–44.
46. Myers, *Strong Man*, 419.

47. See the discussion in Greg Woolf, "Literacy or Literacies in Rome?," in *Ancient Literacies: The Culture of Reading in Greece and Rome*, ed. William A. Johnson and Holt N. Parker (Oxford: Oxford University Press, 2009), 46–68; and my discussion on scribes in Appendix A.
48. There are two surviving records of intentional Roman investigation into early Christianity from the Roman perspective. In the early second century, Pliny the Younger (Letter 10.96) interrogated and tortured Christians, and required sacrifice to the emperor. More than fifty years later, Celsus wrote a treatise against Christian doctrine. Neither scrutinize Christian texts for evidence of treason; Pliny does not mention texts at all. Both suggest that Christian meetings are illegal under laws forbidding associations (Orig. *Cels.* 1) and question the morality and integrity of Christians (e.g., Orig. *Cels.* 9, where Celsus appears to accuse them of charlatanism). While there is certainly evidence that royal titles for Jesus could be used against Christians at trial, it does not seem that Romans treated New Testament or any other Jesus-centered texts as possible evidence of armed rebellion, or that Roman officials focused in any particular way on written texts when bringing Christians to trial or execution.
49. Robert Young, *Postcolonialism, A Very Short Introduction* (Oxford: Oxford University Press, 2003), 4.
50. Leela Gandhi, *Postcolonial Theory: A Critical Introduction* (New York: Columbia University Press, 1998), 7.
51. A brief note on vocabulary: Throughout this project I use the terms "colonialism," "colonization," and "imperialism" as they are understood in contemporary postcolonial theory. In that context these terms refer to functional and ideological categories, rather than actual strategies of migration, inhabitation, or conquest. They refer to dominance in cultural and social arenas as much as political and economic ones and have inherent connotations of stratification, exploitation of subaltern classes, and devaluation of the Other. They do not directly overlap with the vocabulary of concrete settlement and rulership. Thus, Roman colonization, in the sense of cultural, social, economic, and/or political domination, may or may not be accompanied by Roman *colonies*, cities founded outside of the city of Rome for the express purpose of settling Roman people. Likewise, a power may practice imperialism in its relationship to other powers without exerting the direct administrative control usually required to classify it as an empire in modern terms.
52. Liew, *Politics*, 3.
53. Liew, *Politics*, 4–5.
54. Liew, *Politics*, 22.
55. Liew, *Politics*, 47.
56. Liew, *Politics*, 48–54.
57. Liew, *Politics*, 57–8.
58. Liew, *Politics*, 46.
59. Liew, *Politics*, 60.
60. Liew, *Politics*, 149, emphasis mine.
61. Liew, *Politics*, 130.
62. Liew, *Politics*, 93–108.
63. Liew, *Politics*, 113.
64. Samuel, *Postcolonial Reading*, 2.

65. Samuel, *Postcolonial Reading*, 11. Here Samuel particularly cites Homi Bhabha, *The Location of Culture* (London: Routledge, 1994) and Gayatri Chakravorty Spivak, *In Other Worlds: Essays in Cultural Politics* (New York: Routledge, 1988).
66. Samuel, *Postcolonial Reading*, 3.
67. Samuel, *Postcolonial Reading*, 37–9.
68. Samuel, *Postcolonial Reading*, 64–5.
69. Samuel, *Postcolonial Reading*, 82–6.
70. Samuel, *Postcolonial Reading*, 153–4.
71. Richard A. Horsley, *Jesus and the Spiral of Violence: Popular Jewish Resistance in Roman Palestine* (Minneapolis, MN: Fortress Press, 1993).
72. Horsley, *Spiral of Violence*, 318–19.
73. Richard A. Horsley, *Jesus and Empire: The Kingdom of God and the New World Disorder* (Minneapolis, MN: Fortress Press, 2003), 14.
74. Richard A. Horsley, *Hearing the Whole Story: The Politics of Plot in Mark's Gospel* (Louisville, KY: Westminster John Knox Press, 2001), 27–8.
75. Horsley, *Hearing the Whole Story*, 149–76, esp. 156–76.
76. E.g., Horsley, *Hearing the Whole Story*, 87: "Far from having assimilated into the general Hellenistic culture under the Roman imperial order, Mark and its audience identified strongly with Israelite cultural tradition and set themselves in opposition to the Roman imperial order." This statement falsely equates Hellenistic culture with Roman imperialism, and treats both as monoliths. See Tat-siong Benny Liew, Review of *Hearing the Whole Story: The Politics of Plot in Mark's Gospel* by Richard A. Horsley, *CBQ* 64 (2002): 576–7.
77. T. Engberg-Pedersen, Review of *Hearing the Whole Story: The Politics of Plot in Mark's Gospel,*" *JTS* 54 (2003): 233–4, https://doi.org/10.1093/jts/54.1.230.
78. Horsley, *Hearing the Whole Story*, 87.
79. Horsley, *Hearing the Whole Story*, 95–6.
80. Warren Carter, *Mark*, ed. Sarah Tanzer, Wisdom Commentary 42 (Collegeville, MN: Liturgical Press, 2019).
81. See especially Carter, *Matthew and Empire*; Warren Carter, "Sanctioned Violence in the New Testament," *Int* 71 (July 2017): 284–97, https://doi.org/10.1177/0020964317698764.
82. Carter, *Matthew and Empire*, 44–53.
83. Carter, *Matthew and Empire*, 53, emphasis original.
84. Carter, *Matthew and Empire*, 57.
85. Warren Carter, *John and Empire: Initial Explorations* (New York: T&T Clark, 2008), 13.
86. Carter, *John and Empire*, 343.
87. Carter, *John and Empire*, 326–7.
88. Werner H. Kelber, *Mark's Story of Jesus* (Philadelphia, PA: Fortress Press, 1979).
89. Kelber, *Mark's Story*, 91–6.
90. Kelber, *Mark's Story*, 14.
91. Kelber, *Mark's Story*, 88, emphasis original.
92. Gelardini, *Christus Militans*, 23–6.
93. Gelardini, *Christus Militans*, 884–94, esp. 892–4.
94. Gelardini does not comment on the provocative parallel that her use of "*redivivus*" creates between Jesus and the mythical Nero, gathering armies in the East.

95. Christopher Zeichmann, *The Roman Army and the New Testament* (Lanham, MD: Fortress Academic, 2018), 1–48; "Military Forces in Judaea 6–130 CE: The *Status Quaestionis* and Relevance for New Testament Studies," *CBR* 17, no. 1 (2018): 86–120.
96. Christopher Zeichman [sic], "Military-Civilian Interactions in Early Roman Palestine and the Gospel of Mark" (Toronto, University of St. Michael's College, 2017), 180–2.
97. See n. 1 in the introduction to this study.
98. Zeichman, "Military-Civilian Interactions," 174.
99. Zeichman, "Military-Civilian Interactions," 186–7.

2

Kingdom and Imperium

The Gospel of Mark is about the Kingdom of God. Jesus's central teachings in the Gospel, especially the parables of ch. 4, focus on the nature of the kingdom, and the individual episodes that make up Mark's narrative build and refine a structure of possible relationships individuals can have to the kingdom. This chapter will show that the Kingdom of God in Mark functions like an earthly political kingdom, both in the nature of its activities and in the ideology it uses to promote itself. The first half of the chapter will discuss ancient conceptions of state sovereignty, especially the self-conception of Rome. Turning then to the Gospel of Mark, the chapter will analyze its understanding of the hierarchical structure of God's kingdom, its portrayal of the kingdom's expansion and administration, and the appeals to tradition and justice that undergird the implicit claim that the Kingdom of God is more legitimate than any other.

The major conclusion of this chapter is that, counter to some interpretations of Mark, the Gospel's Kingdom of God is not a reimagining of the idea of kingdom. For Roman and Judean authors, a legitimate kingdom is divinely ordained, fulfills (and updates) tradition, and is consistent with the proper order of the cosmos. Mark's understanding is no different, and he portrays ἡ βασιλεία τοῦ θεοῦ with these same elements and strategies.

Roman Self-Understanding

In the collective Roman mind, Rome was not an accident. Particularly in the Augustan age and beyond, literature, art, and rhetoric lauded the divine mandate of Rome. In Virgil's *Aeneid*, the premier and broadly known etiology of the empire, the legendary past looks forward to the Augustan present, prophesying not in broad and cryptic language but in the recitation of specific names, genealogies, and events, to show that the reign of Augustus was salvation to the *patria*, the will of the gods, and the inevitable work of fate.

Prophecy is a major feature of the *Aeneid*'s narrative, particularly prophecy about Augustan-era Rome. In the first book, Venus reminds Jupiter of a promise he made before the opening of the poem, that "the Romans were to arise; from them, even from Teucer's restored line, should come rulers, to hold the sea and all the land beneath their sway" (Virg. *Aen.* 1.234–37 [Fairclough, LCL]). Confirming the goddess's memory of his promise, Jupiter then adds to it: "For these [Romans] I set neither bounds nor periods of empire; dominion [*imperium*] without end have I bestowed" (1.278–79). He even announces Augustus: "From this noble line shall be born the Trojan Caesar, who shall limit his empire [*imperium*] with ocean, his glory [*fama*] with the stars" (1.286–87). Likewise, in book 3 Apollo promises lordship over the world to Aeneas's descendants (3.97).[1]

Besides prophetic speeches, two scenes represent Roman history as being on a single determinative track, willed by the gods and even built into the operations of the cosmos. In book 6, a throng of souls (*animae*) comprises many of the famous men of Roman history, awaiting their turns to drink of Lethe and return to the physical world (6.703–885). A peculiar feature of this narrative is in Anchises's description of the people: unlike everyone else Aeneas meets on his journey in the underworld, these men are known as who they will be after their new birth into the future Rome—as Aeneas's heirs—rather than as who they were before they died, even though they have not yet drunk of the memory-killing waters. Rome's fated greatness is such that it reaches into the underworld and rewrites its own prehistory. Anchises's recitation of their names and deeds frames Roman history as a single and unstraying historical arc. Book 8 similarly casts Virgil's past and present as Aeneas's inevitable future in its description of the shield that Venus gives to her son (8.626–728).

Outside of the *Aeneid*, Rome's divine mandate is often expressed in the divinization of Rome itself. Military expansion into the Greek east was accompanied by the goddess Roma (Ῥώμη), whose cults became common throughout Greece and Asia. Cults of the Hearth of the Romans, the People of the Romans, and even of the Roman senate are attested in various locations.[2] Price refers to such phenomena as "cults of Roman power."[3] This casting of Rome virtually as its own tutelary deity, and that especially of the far-flung regions under its *imperium* from the second century BCE onward, further anchors the characterization of Rome as both divinely favored and an essential part of the workings of the cosmos.

All of this is part of a larger schema in art, literature, and thought that emphasizes Rome's status as the rightful world power. Strabo, writing in the early first century CE, matter-of-factly expresses Roman world domination and takes for granted that the mark of a good general is expansion: "The greatest generals are those who can rule land and sea, and bring together nation and city into one administration [ἐξουσίαν] and government [διοίκησιν πολιτικήν]" (Strab. 1.1.16). The importance of conquest in Roman culture is apparent in its celebration. The triumph was the highest honor to which a Roman could aspire, such that the emperors were known to limit the celebration of triumphs (sometimes replacing them with "triumphal honors" such as decoration and speeches rather than the parade) as a method of limiting the glory attainable by individuals.[4]

However, late republican and imperial authors are mindful to characterize Roman expansion and military action as just, necessary, and ultimately defensive. In his oration in support of Pompey, Cicero reminds the senate that the glory of Rome "involves the safety of your allies and friends, in whose defence your forefathers undertook many great and serious wars" (Cic. *Leg. man.* 2.6 [Hodge, LCL]). Augustus is insistent that his military actions were liberative and defensive: he "liberated the *res publica*" (*RGDA* 1.1), achieved peace "throughout the whole *imperium* of the Roman people" (13), defeated pirates (25.1), and "made peaceful" many border regions (26). The language of liberation and pacification in border regions, alongside language that criminalizes resistance (e.g., "bandit"), both of which persist largely unquestioned into modern treatments of Roman military history, styles Rome as a necessary and primarily beneficial, civilizing influence on a chaotic world.

The common thread here is order: Rome, and particularly imperial Rome after Augustan propaganda, is the intended and only possible result of fate and divine will. It is part of the cosmic order and also reflects it (e.g., Cic. *Rep.* 1.36, where Scipio compares monarchy to the reign of Jupiter; and *Aen.* 1.76–80, in which Aeolus functions as a client ruler under Juno's patronage). Through expansion, Rome brings the inhabited world so completely under its—and therefore the gods'—ordering influence that highly idealistic texts like the *Aeneid* can define Romanness in terms of disparate peoples brought together into the divine plan.[5]

Judean Monarchic Ideology

The realities of post-exilic rule in Judea are difficult to parse. Under Persian and Hellenistic empires, Yehud/Judaia/Judea was administrated by foreign governors (i.e., their authority was external, even in cases where the individual governors were native), but there are limited sources for internal power structures—the roles and authority of aristocracy and especially the high priesthood. David M. Goodblatt has shown both that there emerged a priestly monarchy in the early Second Temple period and that, concurrently, there developed an ideology supporting it based in historical Judean cultic and monarchic traditions.[6]

More recently, David C. Flatto has complicated the discussion of internal Judean authority (real and ideological) in his study of biblical jurisprudence in the Second Temple and Rabbinic periods.[7] As the title of the book suggests, Flatto identifies a persistent, though not always unanimous, ideology of nonmonarchic juridical power in Judean and later Jewish writings. This does not negate the importance of the kingship (or of the discussion of it) even in Rabbinic thought.[8] Rather, Flatto notes that in contrast to ancient near eastern texts like the Code of Hammurabi, which situate the king as the source and ultimate decider of law, Hebrew tradition understands Torah to come directly from God, mediated through Moses at Sinai. The king, in Hebrew etiology, came much later.

Therefore, while the kingship remained an important aspect of tradition and ideology as a symbol of national cohesion and identity, a king was not the linchpin or sole preserver of cosmic order. That role belonged to God through Torah. In that way, Hebrew ideology bears similarities to Roman and Western Greek thought, which both understand kings—when kings are present—to be administrators of law but not sources of it, cosmically speaking.

Messianic thought and the role of the king in Hebrew tradition are more fully discussed in Chapter 3. More salient to this chapter is the fact that monarchy remained an important focus of discussion and ideology for Judeans throughout the Second Temple and Roman periods. Judean resistance to imperial rulership was a constant through the Hellenistic and Roman periods, sometimes expressed primarily through the ideological importance of the kingship, rather than through material revolt. Even when self-rule was relegated to the distant future or to eschatological fantasy, it remained a persistent focus of Judean and Jewish literature in ways that have no comparison among many other subalterns to Roman rule.

Mark's Kingdom of God

A fundamental principle of this study is the idea that no part of the Gospel of Mark was formed in a vacuum. Therefore, aspects of the texts that have taken on specific theological meanings in Christianity must be examined to determine whether those meanings ring true in the text's historical *milieu*, without the accretion of two thousand years of tradition and theology. Thus we turn to the phrase "Kingdom of God." To begin to understand what Mark means by this, it is best to begin with the phrase itself and its use in the Gospel. With that established, I can turn to the whole picture of the Kingdom of God in the Gospel and compare it to ideas of sovereignty in Roman and Judean ideology.

Use of Βασιλεία in Mark

The βασιλ- group of words is common and wide ranging. βασιλεύς appears repeatedly in Homer, as does the verb βασιλεύω, and βασιλεία as "kingdom" or "sovereignty" appears at least as early as Aeschylus (*Pers.* 589). As a constellation these words refer to rulers and the things and actions of rulership: the basic translation of the masculine noun is "king," although it often appears as a more general "lord," "master," or "leader," somewhat synonymous with κύριος. It also denotes divine rulers and is quite frequently a literary or cultic title of Zeus. It does not indicate any particular kind of king—for example, hereditary versus elected; polis versus regional or imperial— except that it can in some contexts connote a legitimate ruler in contrast to τύραννος, a usurper.[9] In the New Testament the word group likewise refers to both mundane and divine dominion, and βασιλεία in particular appears frequently with reference to the "kingdom" or "reign" of God—in the Gospels almost exclusively in the technical term ἡ βασιλεία τοῦ θεοῦ (or οὐρανοῦ in Matthew).

In the LXX βασιλ- words often translate words of the root מלך.[10] K. L. Schmidt describes its more metaphysical and ethical uses in some Hellenistic Jewish sources, associated especially with wisdom or virtue and including the phrase βασιλεία τοῦ θεοῦ in Wis 6. In Philo, Schmidt observes a tendency to delineate kingship from priesthood, giving the latter precedence, as well as a lack of an eschatological concept of βασιλεία.[11]

In New Testament usage, except in a few cases (e.g., the parable of the pounds in Luke 19:12–27), βασιλεία in reference to an earthly power is set in contrast to that of God; see, for example, the "kingdoms of the world" in Matt 4:8//Luke 4:5, as well as uses of ἐξουσία and δύναμις in similar contexts (see Chapter 3 of this study). As the temptation pericope implies, earthly kingdoms fall under the dominion of Satan, whose own βασιλεία is at odds with that of God (e.g., Mark 3:23–24//Matt 12:26//Luke 11:18).[12] An issue for understanding ἡ βασιλεία τοῦ θεοῦ, however, is the fact that βασιλεία can refer either to a physical kingdom—that is, a ruled people or expanse of land—or, more abstractly, to "kingship" or "sovereignty" as concepts. Thus, while the standard translation (and the one used most frequently in this study) is "Kingdom of God," interpreters have chosen a variety of ways to render the phrase, and in any case the reader should be aware that both connotations are possible, even simultaneously.

The word βασιλεία appears twenty times in Mark, fourteen in the phrase ἡ βασιλεία τοῦ θεοῦ, with a fifteenth eschatological use (13:8). The other five refer to earthly kingdoms or the Satanic one. Both of these references to earthly kingdoms appear in the context of Jesus's apocalyptic prophecy. Verse 13:8—"nation [ἔθνος] will rise against nation, and kingdom against kingdom"—reflects imagery and language from earlier Jewish prophetic and apocalyptic works.[13] In this case, as in Isa 19, the prophecy alludes to wars that will weaken or punish the enemies of the elect in preparation for the accession of a divinely ordained βασιλεία.[14]

Verse 9, in contrast, envisages a more stereotypically "New Testament" prophecy.[15] The emphasis on individual suffering (as opposed to the tribulations of Israel writ large) that makes its way through the canonical New Testament and beyond has little analogue in the Hebrew Bible.[16] Without making too much of the Gospel author's specific knowledge, we should also keep in mind Christian traditions about the deaths of figures such as Paul and James; certainly the response to the request of James and John in ch. 10 points to traditions about the sufferings and deaths of Jesus's inner circle.

In both of these verses, "kingdoms" and "kings" are generalized images that evoke more specific references in the audience's minds, but do not require them. Historical or cultural particularities of administration or authority are not crucial to the meaning here. Even a modern English speaker, for whom both terms represent politically archaic—bordering on obsolete—concepts, understands the implications: all-consuming war on the one hand and judicial persecution on the other. Thus, they are also not specifically eschatological in themselves, but do contribute to the eschatological imagery of the passage, and thus help cast Mark's eschatology as based in the political and military realities of its context.

Mark's Kingdom of God Propaganda

Like Virgil and the author of 1 Maccabees, Mark understands the kingdom in his narrative to be divinely ordained, an integral part of the cosmic order, and just in its actions. R. T. France clearly summarizes Mark's use of Hebrew prophecy in ch. 1: "Mark begins his book with a prologue designed to appeal to Jewish expectations of the fulfillment of the hopes of Israel."[17] The composite prophecy in 1:2–3 serves the same function as the entire *Aeneid*: to originate contemporary events in the distant past, revealing the predetermined and divinely established arc of history, even as Jesus (like Augustus) updates and reinterprets tradition (2:21–22). The appearance of Moses and Elijah in ch. 9, the linking of Jesus to David in chs. 10 and more ambivalently in ch. 12, the passion predictions and appeals to necessity (δεῖ), and the disputes over Torah interpretation also contribute to this sense of Jesus as the culmination of a fixed historical trajectory rooted in Israel's divine chosenness.

In Mark Jesus shows himself, and therefore the kingdom he represents, to be an important part of the workings of the cosmos through his manipulation of nature. His control over weather (4:35-41), ability to walk on water (6:45-52), and manipulation of physical resources (6:30-44; 8:1-10) demonstrate a fundamental integration into and control over cosmic laws beyond what normal human beings experience. Likewise, the daytime darkness and the tearing of the temple veil (15:33, 38), like the omens that presage and accompany the deaths of emperors (Suet. *Aug.* 97; *Tib.* 72, *Cal.* 52, etc.), show divine and cosmic investment in the life and fate of Jesus.

The fundamental justice of the Kingdom of God is expressed in Jesus's ethical teachings. Repentance (e.g., 1:4, 15) and forgiveness (e.g., 2:5-12; 6:12; 11:25) are the basic mechanisms for approaching and being admitted into the Kingdom of God. Within, the Kingdom is stratified based not on influence, wealth, legal status, or socioeconomic class but on one's adherence to Jesus's teachings. Although the word δίκαιος, habitually translated "righteous" in texts considered primarily Christian or Jewish and "just" most everywhere else, only appears twice in the narrative (2:17; 6:20), pericopes such as the widow's mite (12:41-44) and the temple act (11:15-19), and disputes such as that over the alabaster jar (14:3-9) demonstrate a complex engagement in issues of right action and how to identify "proper" members of the Kingdom of God. The repeated contrast between ostentatious wealth and service (10:17-27; 12:38-44) shows a value system quite different from that in play among local elites, according to Mark's rhetoric.[18]

The Kingdom of God has both a present and future connotation in Mark, which is quite intelligible in light of the various possible meanings inherent in βασιλεία that require separate vocabulary in English and German. In other words, the phrase ἡ βασιλεία τοῦ θεοῦ naturally refers both to a present *reign* or *sovereignty* and a future *kingdom*.[19]

An issue in the interpretation of Mark's kingdom is the translation of ἤγγικεν in 1:15. The NRSV reads, "has drawn near." C. H. Dodd argues that it should be "has arrived."[20] Whether one understands the kingdom to be "near" or "arrived" can make the difference between a primarily realized or primarily future eschatology in Mark, although Collins bridges the issue nicely: "'The time is fulfilled and the Kingdom of God has drawn near,' implies that the prophesies of scripture are in the process of being fulfilled."[21]

"Process" is perhaps the best way to understand Mark's kingdom. The text repeatedly refers to movement into the βασιλεία and its own movement toward potential subjects. Besides ἤγγικεν in 1:15, we find the verbs ἔρχομαι (9:1) and εἰσέρχομαι (9:47; 10:15, 23-25)—the βασιλεία comes, but it must also be entered. Likewise, one may receive it (δέχομαι; 10:15), await it (προσδέχομαι; 15:43), or be close to it (οὐ μακρὰν ἀπό; 12:34). In 10:15 ("Truly I say to you, whoever does not receive the Kingdom of God as child will not enter it"), "receiving"—that is, approaching and responding to—the βασιλεία in the correct manner is a prerequisite to entering it at all. In Mark, the βασιλεία approaches but does not overtake, at least in the present. If we understand the present βασιλεία more in terms of "sovereignty" than territorial "kingdom," then God provides the opportunity to come under his lordship, but submission must be volunteered. This comes out especially in the parables of ch. 4, which envision ἡ βασιλεία τοῦ θεοῦ through the metaphor of growth, and those things that encourage or inhibit it. This vocabulary of motion and response reflects international relations in the sense that it requires an "inside" and an "outside": at least one other place for a person to be located before the new βασιλεία approaches and from which to respond. It further mirrors Mediterranean *Realpolitik* in its conditionality and the implicit threat lurking beneath οὐ μὴ εἰσέλθῃ εἰς αὐτήν in 10:15b.

This does not end the discussion, however. The βασιλεία coming in verse 9:1[22] is not the growing and nourishing lordship of God in the world, as portrayed in the parables of ch. 4, but the imminent eschatological conquest; Chapter 4 of this book discusses military aspects of Mark in more detail and the possibility of martial imagery in ἐληλυθυῖαν ἐν δυνάμει. Although the word βασιλεία does not appear in ch. 13, vv. 24–27 reflect 9:1 and expand upon it. The consequences for those who remain outside the βασιλεία are explicit in 9:42–48: hell, burning fire, and the worm that never dies. The threat of 10:15b, the defeat that awaits the one who does not enter, comes to light here in ch. 9.

In that sense, ἡ βασιλεία τοῦ θεοῦ operates much like the Roman empire and other expansionist states and their rulers. Postcolonial and empire-critical interpretations of the Gospels emphasize Roman expansion by military means, but the military aspect of expansion worked in tight concert with economic and political methods. Rome's superior military might and willingness to use it was the basis for such alliances and ensured that their terms favored Rome itself. The threat and use of military action, the support and sometimes installment of favorable local leaders, and economic strongarming tactics were all ways that Rome maintained control over far-flung lands. Nonetheless, there is a similar basic pattern in Roman expansion as in that of Mark's Kingdom of God: there are incentives to belonging, at least for elite decision-makers, and so the approach of sovereign to subject is reciprocal up to a point. However, those who resist the approach of the sovereign will eventually be subdued.

ἡ βασιλεία τοῦ θεοῦ in Matthew and Luke

There are significantly more references to ἡ βασιλεία τοῦ θεοῦ in Matthew and Luke, and especially Matthew (including references to ἡ βασιλεία τοῦ οὐρανοῦ) than there are in Mark. This is primarily a function of the greatly expanded material in both later Gospels compared to Mark, especially the parables in Matthew (see the large section of Matt 13 citations in Appendix B). However, there are still a number of passages that have parallels in Mark where one or both of the later Gospels has added βασιλεία.

The nature of the kingdom shifts slightly between Mark and the later Gospels. Many of Matthew's additions are explicitly eschatological, including the parable of the tares and its interpretation (Matt 13:24–30, 36–43); the parable of the net (Matt 13:47–50); the dispute over who is the greatest;[23] and the promise of thrones (Matt 19:28). Luke's additions are fewer, and those that point to eschatology emphasize the delay of the end in a way that Matthew does not (e.g., the parable of the pounds, Luke

19:12–27). Overall, and going beyond simple occurrences of the vocabulary, neither of the later Synoptics presents a theology of the kingdom that is drastically different from Mark's: all include the basic elements of both realized and future eschatology, and all express the future at least partly in apocalyptic imagery. However, each emphasizes its eschatology in a different way. Matthew's focus on punishment and reward, and Luke's on delay, highlight both the immediacy and the relative lack of reward/punishment of Mark's eschatology. While Mark does not lack consequences for being outside of the kingdom, the Gospel does not emphasize them as dramatically as Matthew; and compared to Luke (especially considering Acts 1:7), Mark 13 seems to promise a more immediate end.

Satan's Kingdom in Mark

A fourth kingdom in the Gospel of Mark, beside those of God, Herod, and Rome, is that of Satan. Satan himself, like God, operates largely in the background—he has agents active in the story and he is the subject of disputes, but his only direct action in the text is a brief mention in ch. 1 regarding the temptation (1:13). Compare this to Matt 4:1–11 and Luke 4:1–12, which both greatly extend the scene to describe the nature of the temptation and give the devil speaking lines. Luke also adds the influence of Satan to Judas's betrayal (Luke 22:3). Otherwise, Satan, like God, is only present in Mark through his agents.

The controversy of 3:20–30 makes clear that the demons and "unclean spirits" throughout Mark operate under the dominion of Satan (especially 3:22: "by the ruler [ἐν τῷ ἄρχοντι] of demons he casts out demons").[24] The long and short of this confrontation is that in the world of Mark's Gospel, Jesus's authority to conduct exorcisms can only come from one of two sources, God or Satan, and one's understanding of Jesus's activities depends heavily on which option one believes is most likely. On a basic level, this leaves the reader with the impression of a highly dualistic world. Nonetheless, this dualism has its limits—the text does not understand Satan to be *equal* to God. The demons' fear of Jesus (e.g., 5:7) and the ease with which he dispatches them show clearly that Jesus's authority is greater than the demons', from which it follows that God's power is greater than Satan's. Some scholars have gone so far as to say that Satan himself is ultimately under God's control, not only in the sense of cosmic superiority and eschatological defeat but also as another active agent of the divine.

This position is represented by Elizabeth Shively.[25] In her character study of Satan, she finds that "Mark presents a consistent portrait of Satan as one who acts under the sovereign will of God both to test Jesus (1.12) and to drive him to the cross (δεῖ, 8.31)."[26] Shively's understanding of Mark's narrative assumes that the testing in 1:13 continues throughout and drives the action of the entire Gospel until the crucifixion, when the cry of dereliction signals Jesus's ultimate passing of the test, not in its despair but in its apparently determined faithfulness: in her quote of the passage Shively italicizes the possessive pronoun, "*my* God."[27] However, in addition to its focus on a rather minor detail of 15:34, this position fails to account for the syntax of 1:13. Here is the passage in Greek, with the verbs emphasized: καὶ **ἦν** ἐν τῇ ἐρήμῳ τεσσεράκοντα ἡμέρας **πειραζόμενος** ὑπὸ τοῦ σατανᾶ. Generally, we should expect the present participle to indicate time coincident with the main verb, or an action that is the intended purpose of the main verb, which in this case (ἦν) expresses a simple or narrative past ("he *was* in the wilderness *being tested* [or *to be tested*] by Satan").[28] The same construction appears in the very next verse ("he *went* to Galilee *preaching* [or *to preach*] the gospel of God") and in v. 39 ("he *went* throughout Galilee *preaching* [or *to preach*] in their synagogues"). In all of these cases the action indicated by the participle is happening as a part or intent of the action of the main verb. Since by this syntax the action of *being tested* in 1:13 is connected to the state of *being in the wilderness*, when Jesus leaves the wilderness for Galilee we should understand that this particular testing has also come to an end.

On these grounds, Shively's assertion that Satan is another agent of God, though desirable from the standpoint of strict monotheism, finds little purchase.[29] Rather, Mark repeatedly pits Satan against God, as in 3:20–30, and imagines both as diametrically opposed sources of power. Further, the devil and demonic activity are notably absent following ch. 13 and play no apparent role in the arrest or passion. The appeals to necessity in the passion predictions do not indicate the activity of Satan, but the will of God and/or the immutable workings of the cosmos, which will come to fruition through human hands. They are comparable to the appeals to prophecy and divine will throughout the *Aeneid*, and, in their content, recall the fated (and thus unavoidable) deaths of Homeric heroes.

Even if Satan is not a persistent thorn in Jesus's side specifically, he certainly exercises his dominion in the lives of the Galilean people. For every exorcism the Gospel narrates, an untold number happen off-screen; the authority Jesus is able to delegate to his disciples includes exorcism, as does the power working through the other exorcist in ch. 9. Dramatic episodes like the Gerasene demoniac (5:1–20) and the boy with seizures (9:14–29) highlight what is apparently a constant problem in the region.

Postcolonialists and other interpreters focused on the political aspects of Mark tend to read the demonic realm as representing dominating powers. Liew notes parallels between the vocabulary of Jesus's temple act (11:15–19) and that of the Beelzebul controversy (3:20–30) and argues that this language casts the Jerusalem establishment as similarly demonic.[30] Myers suggests that since the first exorcism takes place in a synagogue (1:21–28), we should understand the demonic throughout the Gospel to be representative of "the dominant Jewish social order."[31] Perhaps most famously, many scholars have read 5:1–20 as a brazen statement of anti-Roman sentiment, due to the Latinism and military reference of the demons' name ("Legion") and, for some, the apparent reference to the symbols of *legio X Fretensis*.[32]

Again, the Beelzebul controversy is relevant. Mark 3:20–30 depicts Satan as the ruler (ἄρχον) of a rival, but weaker, kingdom. The image of "a kingdom divided against itself" recalls the fractured local politics of Judea and Galilee in the centuries and decades leading up to the war. Besides loyalists to Rome such as the Herodian dynasty, even the "rebels" did not make common cause. Josephus attests to multiple parties of various levels of resistance to Rome and to each other.[33] The historian gives firsthand descriptions of disputes such as that between himself and the city of Taricheae on the western shore of the lake (*War* 2.21.1–5). To allegorize this passage through the lens of the war, the demonic is not Myers's monolithic "dominant Jewish social order," but the balkanized Judean/Galilean socio-econo-political landscape as a whole. That explains why demons appear both in the synagogue and with apparent reference to the Tenth Legion. The situation on the ground cannot easily be divided into Roman versus Jewish, or even rebel versus sympathizer. It is complex and multilayered. For the Gospel of Mark, one apparent division is elite versus nonelite, but even that is merely a surface reading that glosses over considerable nuance. For example, although Jesus condemns the rich at various points in the Gospel, Jairus, as a leader of the synagogue, is elite at least at the village level, and the anointing woman has access to an expensive item like the alabaster jar. Ultimately, the Kingdom of God consists of those who follow Jesus, and the kingdom of Satan of those who do not. Both groups may include rich and poor, Jew and Gentile, Galilean and Jerusalemite.

Even putting aside any specific allusion to the events of the war, Mark 3:24 depicts an "international" situation. To what will a divided kingdom fall? To another kingdom. While it is true that Rome did not employ any notably unique brutalities or ideologies in its expansion through Asia Minor, Syria, and the Levant, it was able to expand to such a vast region by virtue of its superior strength—that of both its armies and its allegiances. Interpreting Mark 3:20–30 through this history, it is possible to see Satan here as representative of a weaker kingdom being defeated and annexed by a stronger one.

Conclusion

The βασιλεία τοῦ θεοῦ is a kingdom: both *Reich* and *Herrschaft*, nation and sovereignty. In the mid-70s, in the immediate aftermath of the Judean War, and in the early days of the crystallization of "Christianity" as a distinct tradition, it is possible and fruitful to read this language not as containing spiritualized political metaphors but as political in its own right. Mark's Kingdom of God, like the *imperium* of Rome, expands, approaches, and offers its allyship. Also like Rome, it defeats those who challenge it and punishes those who reject it. It justifies itself using the same strategies as Roman propaganda and rhetoric—appeals to prophecy and tradition, claims of superior justice, and claims of cosmic significance. This chapter began by challenging portrayals of Rome as uniquely and exclusively brutal, not to minimize the damage of imperializing conquest, but to suggest the possibility that such conquest would have been understood in its historical *milieu* as normal in its ideology and practice. Therefore, assuming these expectations, there is no reason to read the language of βασιλεία in Mark as fundamentally different from its connotations in the author's immediate context. Mark sets up God's kingdom as a rival to other local and imperial rulerships, claiming that those who submit to God's rule will be better off under it, just as Roman and Judean literature claim about their own ideologies. The next chapter will look more closely at Jesus as the king of this kingdom, God's agent and conquering general.

Notes

1. For a closer discussion of the role of prophecy in the *Aeneid*, see A. D. Botha, "Aspects of Prophecy in Virgil's *Aeneid*," *Akroterion* 37, no. 1 (1992): 6–14; James J. O'Hara, *Death and the Optimistic Prophecy in Vergil's Aeneid* (Princeton, NJ: Princeton University Press, 1990).
2. S. R. F. Price, *Rituals and Power: The Roman Imperial Cult in Asia Minor* (Cambridge: Cambridge University Press, 1984), 41–2. For a comprehensive study of the cults of Roma and their inscriptional evidence, see Ronald Mellor, ΘΕΑ ῬΩΜΗ: *The Worship of the Goddess Roma in the Greek World*, Hypomnemata 42 (Göttingen: Vandenhoeck & Ruprecht, 1975). Andrew Erskine discusses the cult of the senate in "Greekness and Uniqueness: The Cult of the Senate in the Greek East," *Phoenix* 51, no. 1 (1997): 25–37.
3. E.g., Price, *Rituals and Power*, 40.
4. Karl Galinsky, *Augustan Culture: An Interpretive Introduction* (Princeton, NJ: Princeton University Press, 1996), 385.
5. J. D. Reed, "Vergil's Roman," in *A Companion to Vergil's Aeneid and Its Tradition*, ed. Joseph Farrell and Michael C. J. Putnam, BCAW (Chichester: Wiley-Blackwell, 2010), 73–6.
6. David M. Goodblatt, *The Monarchic Principle: Studies in Jewish Self-Government in Antiquity*, TSAJ 38 (Tübingen: J.C.B. Mohr [P. Siebeck], 1994).
7. David C. Flatto, *The Crown and the Courts: Separation of Powers in the Early Jewish Imagination* (Cambridge, MA: Harvard University Press, 2020).
8. Besides Goodblatt, see Gerald J. Blidstein, "The Monarchic Imperative in Rabbinic Perspective," *AJS Review* 7/8 (1982): 15–39; Yair Lorberbaum, *Disempowered King: Monarchy in Classical Jewish Literature*, KLJS 9 (New York: Continuum, 2010), https://doi.org/10.5040/9781472548481.
9. Hermann Kleinknecht, "βασιλεύς," TDNT 1:564.
10. For a description of the various mundane and divine concepts of kingship in the Hebrew Bible, see Gerhard von Rad, "βασιλεύς," TDNT 1:565–71.
11. Karl Ludwig Schmidt, "βασιλεύς," TDNT 1:574–75.
12. Schmidt, "βασιλεύς, κτλ," TDNT 1:580.
13. E.g., Isa 19:2. For similar language that does not use βασιλεία, cf. 2 Chr 15:6; 1 En. 99:4.
14. Marvin A. Sweeney, *Isaiah 1–39: With an Introduction to Prophetic Literature*, FOTL 16 (Grand Rapids, MI: Eerdmans, 1996), 264–6; Otto Kaiser, *Isaiah 13–39: A Commentary*, trans. R. A. Wilson, OTL (Philadelphia, PA: Westminster Press, 1974), 97–112. Note, however, the lack of eschatology in the Isaiah passage: the divinely mandated order is a temporal one. God, though in ultimate control of history and worldly powers, will not reign directly.
15. "They will hand you over to councils and you will be beaten in synagogues, and you will be stood up before governors and kings for my sake because of your witness."
16. Lester L. Grabbe, *Judaic Religion in the Second Temple Period: Belief and Practice from the Exile to Yavneh* (London: Routledge, 2000), 271–3. NA28 makes note only of New Testament texts in the marginalia for vv. 9–13, including the Synoptic parallels at Matt 24:9 (which is not a complete parallel, and omits the mention of kings) and Luke 21:12 and 2 John 8.
17. R. T. France, *Divine Government: God's Kingship in the Gospel of Mark* (London: SPCK, 1990), 21.

18. It is similar, however, to the general mistrust of ostentation that we see in Livy 1.pr.10–12 and Suetonius's critiques of Nero and other less favored emperors, and that Augustus implicitly wards off in his catalogs of payments, donations, and patronages (e.g., *RGDA* 15, 17, and appendix).
19. A succinct description of this dual function may be found in France, *Divine Government*, 14–15.
20. C. H. Dodd, *Parables of the Kingdom*, rev. ed. (New York: Charles Scribner's Sons, 1961), 37–8. Cf. Marcus, *Mark 1–8*, 172–3, arguing against Dodd that while both valences are possible, the most common occurrence in the NT and other Greek literature is "has come near."
21. Collins, *Mark*, 154.
22. "Truly I say to you that some are standing here who will not taste death until they see the Kingdom of God coming ἐν δυνάμει."
23. Matt 18:1 names it a dispute over the greatest in the kingdom; cf. Mark 9:34, where it seems simply to be a question of the greatest among the Twelve.
24. For a brief excursus on the name Beelzebul and its connection to Satan, see Collins, *Mark*, 229–31.
25. Elizabeth Shively, "Characterizing the Non-Human: Satan in the Gospel of Mark," in *Character Studies and the Gospel of Mark*, ed. Christopher W. Skinner and Matthew Ryan Hauge, Library of New Testament Studies (London: Bloomsbury T&T Clark, 2014), 127–51, https://doi.org/10.5040/9780567669766.
26. Shively, "Characterizing," 150.
27. Shively, "Characterizing," 150.
28. Smyth §1872a. See also Constantine R. Campbell, *Verbal Aspect and Non-Indicative Verbs: Further Soundings in the Greek of the New Testament*, SBG 15 (New York: Peter Lang, 2008), 22; Buist M. Fanning, *Verbal Aspect in New Testament Greek*, OTM (Oxford: Oxford University Press, 1990), 407.
29. This is true, at least, of the argument that Satan is God's agent *with the purpose of testing Jesus*. It is not out of the question that an early reader might understand Satan to be a servant of God generally; this idea, contrary to the Enochian and medieval Satan-as-rebellious-angel, finds precedence in the endcaps of Job. However, this is not a particular focus of the text of Mark, and some military aspects of the Gospel (see Chapter 4 of this book) would seem to preclude it.
30. Liew, *Politics of Parousia*, 74.
31. Myers, *Strong Man*, 143.
32. Among many others: Horsley, *Hearing the Whole Story*, 141–8; Bryan, *Render to Caesar*, 48–50; John Dominic Crossan, *The Historical Jesus: The Life of a Mediterranean Jewish Peasant* (San Francisco, CA: HarperSanFrancisco, 1991), 314–18. See Zeichman, *Military-Civilian Interactions*, 138n391 for a longer (but still incomplete) list.
33. E.g., *War* 2.20.3, in which a party of those who had pursued the Roman governor of Syria out of Jerusalem returned to the city and turned their violence upon some there who supported Roman rule; and especially *War* 4.3.6–14, detailing the tremendous chaos that Josephus claims gripped Jerusalem before the siege.

3

Rulership

Mark's portrayal of Jesus as a ruler is multivalenced and resists straight allegorizing. In the passion narrative Jesus is a titled and crowned king (βασιλεύς); in ch. 10 an eschatological sovereign; in ch. 13 a successful general. He is at once ruler and client ruler, *imperator* and agent, bearer of authority and conduit of someone else's power. This chapter will look closely at the ways that Mark situates Jesus within the context of rulership available to postwar Galilee, by examining language that explicitly denotes rulership or leadership—specifically royal titles and the words βασιλεύς and ἐξουσία—and by comparing Jesus to other rulers in the text and to the ideals of kingship modeled through Roman and Jewish cultures.

Ideal Roman Kings

In books 1 and 2 of his *Republic*, Cicero builds images of the ideal state and ideal ruler. The character Scipio asserts that the best kind of state is governed by a combination of three systems—monarchy, aristocracy, and democracy—that serve as checks and balances for each other to avoid descent into tyranny or anarchy. In Scipio's model, both the ideal king and the ideal state prioritize justice and order.

When pressed, Scipio admits that in the absence of this balanced system, he finds the best of the three forms of government to be monarchy, stating, "the name of king seems like that of a father to us, since the king provides for the citizens as if they were his own children, and is … eager to protect them" (1.35). He reasons that the cosmos itself is a monarchy, whether one adheres to the polytheist system ruled by Jupiter or the philosophical system ruled by the Platonic Mind (1.36). Further, the human psyche follows the same pattern: the baser instincts and emotions are, ideally, ruled by rationality as a single function (1.37). Thus Scipio argues that kingship is the most natural model, and simultaneously that kings have in the cosmos and their own anthropology examples that set the standard for good kingship.

It is a high standard, and for Scipio the weakness of monarchy is that although it is the best "simple" form of government (2.23), it is a hair's breadth away from the worst form, tyranny (1.42): "And this form of government is the most liable of all to change, because one man's vices can overthrow it and turn it easily toward utter destruction" (2.23). Cicero, through Scipio, consistently contrasts good kings and tyrants as "just" and "unjust," respectively. Just kings, exemplified in the text especially by Romulus (2.3–12), Numa (2.13–20), and Servius Tullius (2.21–22), are ones who expand the state and who establish and respect aristocratic powers, the rights of citizens, and the priesthoods. That is, for Scipio, ideal kings demonstrate military might, promote Scipio's own ideal form of mixed government, and show appropriate piety toward the gods.

Notably, Scipio's model of kingship does not require strict heredity. Romulus may be excused from this example, as the son of Mars and Rhea Silvia, and in any event the first king and thus no one's successor. Numa, however, was a Sabine, and was deliberately appointed instead of seeking a Roman candidate (2.13); and Servius was born and raised a slave and took power over the heads of his predecessor's natural children (2.21).[1] At least ideally, then, Scipio separates *genius* and the qualities necessary for kingship from ethnicity, lineage, and social status.[2]

Augustus and his partisans take up Cicero's model to justify the focus of power into one man, keenly aware of the political crisis of Julius Caesar's dictatorship and the delicate ideological situation it created for his successor. The *Res gestae divi Augusti*, a long inscription found in Rome (in Latin) and Ancyra (in Greek) that gives an apparently autobiographical summary of Augustus's reign, repeatedly emphasizes the emperor's claimed reliance on the apparati of the republic for his position and power. Although the inscription begins with a declaration of his independent (*privato consilio et privata impensa*) and heroic liberation of the *res publica*, it quickly pivots to honors and duties freely awarded by the senate and the people (*RGDA* 1). Throughout the piece, Augustus denotes his participation in and support and even revival of traditional Roman modes of administration and public piety. In earlier chapters he frequently calls attention to high honors and offices that he declined despite the wishes of the SPQR. Chapter 5 is standard:

> Even though the post of dictator was conferred upon me both when I was absent and when I was present by both people and senate in the consulship of Marcus Marcellus and Lucius Arruntius, I did not accept it. I did not decline to manage the corn supply during a very severe grain shortage, and I administered it in such a way that within a few days I freed the entire community from pressing fear and danger through my expenditure and supervision. When the consulship too was conferred upon me at that time for a year and in perpetuity, I did not accept it.[3]

Augustus's careful avoidance of overt claims to power is part of a larger project, on the part of the emperor and his propagandists, to portray Augustus as highly conscious of his duty to the restoration of the state rather than the establishment of a new one. In 27 BCE the senate awarded him with the *clipius virtutis*, a shield with an inscription honoring him and listing his virtues: *virtus, clementia, iusticia*, and *pietas*. Although these are not the so-called cardinal virtues (*prudentia, fortitudo, temperentia*, and *iusticia*),[4] neither are they incompatible. Karl Galinsky reads the four virtues of the *clipius* as, in the context of Octavius/Augustus, particularly in reference to war and conquest.[5] Taken together after Actium, the list of virtues portrays a ruler who is strong but not overbearing and who exercises his power for the good of the state.

Further, the *clipius*, like later examples of Augustan literature, emphasizes reference to the past as a solid foundation on which to build the future. As the heir and successor of Julius Caesar, claiming legitimacy in part through Caesar's divinity, Augustus must at the same time be seen as healing the wounds in the republic that allowed for Caesar's dictatorship in the first place. Livy's introduction is stereotypical in its idolization of the past, but is also emblematic of the rhetoric surrounding the end of the republic and the beginning of the principate:

> For the rest, either love of the task I have set myself deceives me, or no state was ever greater, none more righteous or richer in good examples, none ever was where avarice and luxury came into the social order so late, or where humble means and thrift were so highly esteemed and so long held in honour. For true it is that the less men's wealth was, the less was their greed. Of late, riches have brought in avarice, and excessive pleasures the longing to carry wantonness and licence to the point of ruin for oneself and of universal destruction.[6]

Augustus, who wished to be seen as far from avaricious, showered money on the people and the legions, restored dozens of crumbling shrines and neglected priesthoods, and, to hear him and his propagandists tell it, reinstated the rule of law as the functioning principle of Rome (e.g., *RGDA* 8; 11; Suet. *Aug.* 33–34). In fact, Augustus, or his after-image, was so committed to restoring the virtues of the past that Suetonius has him concerned even with clothing styles (Suet. *Aug.* 40.5).

The image of the ideal ruler as embodied in Augustus comes into further relief in comparison to his successors. In Suetonius, descriptions of satisfactory and even admirable administrative careers are undercut by litanies of vices and personal failings. Tiberius, who enacted reforms in line with frugality, morality, and hygiene (Suet. *Tib.* 33–35), was on the other hand tight-fisted (48), inimical toward his family (50–53), and neglectful of the gods (69), not to mention drunk and sexually deviant (42–43). At the beginning of his reign, Nero "declared that he would rule according to the principles of Augustus, and he let slip no opportunity for acts of generosity and mercy, or even for displaying his affability" (Suet. *Nero* 10.1 [Rolfe, LCL]). Nonetheless, his egoism (25, 30–31), greed (32), violence (33–34), and cowardice (47–49) make up the legacy that most interests Suetonius.

Through these representative examples the shape of the ideal ruler in the early Roman empire begins to emerge. Beyond effective administrative achievements, he must demonstrate commitment to a Rome that extends from the legendary past into the eternal future (through, e.g., restorative or new building projects). He must show disregard for his own wealth through magnanimity such as food tickets, building projects, or cash payments to the public and soldiers. He must rule with the cooperation of the traditional apparati of state, and, as a jurist, must uphold the rule of law while simultaneously cultivating a reputation for mercy. And he must display appropriate attention to his duty as a member of Roman society, including piety toward the gods.

Messiahs

From a perspective more native to Mark, messianic ideology portrays a more autocratic king, though not a tyrannical one. The legislative body of the Roman system is replaced by Torah. Just as Livy and Virgil appeal to the legendary past of Rome to legitimize the principate, early Jewish messianism, in its most common form, looks back to David, especially through the Psalms, to express postexilic and Hellenistic hopes for restored self-rule. In the Hebrew Bible, the noun משיח is exclusively a royal title (e.g., 1 Sam 24:7; Hab 3:13; Ps 84:10), although verbal and adjectival forms can apply to others.[7] Shemaryahu Talmon identifies the Dead Sea Scrolls as a major source, though not the earliest one, for the eschatological casting of the Messiah that dominates Second Temple and later stages of the idea.[8]

In broad strokes, the image of the Messiah is comparable to the kind of prophetic and nostalgic legitimization of Augustus in the *Aeneid* and Livy discussed earlier in this book. Removed from millenarian concerns, the Messiah is characterized as a king of the Davidic lineage who will restore Israel to greatness and independent rule. While our Roman sources usually contrast Augustus and his reign with an image of Roman government and culture sliding for centuries into degeneracy, in Jewish sources the Messiah takes on both a Deuteronomistic role—restorer of Torah—and a salvific one—defeater of foreign rulers. In both cases the hoped-for king is *restorative* of the way things "should" be and once, legendarily, were. That is, as Talmon succinctly observes, "the conception of the 'Age to Come' is intrinsically conceived as the memory of the past projected into the future."[9]

Emphasis on the Davidic lineage of the Messiah is explicit in Jer 23:5–6, where the Lord promises to "raise up for David a righteous branch" (NRSV). Likewise, Isa 11:1 promises a "shoot from the stump of Jesse." The rest of Isa 11 details the expectations for this figure. He will reign over an era of cosmic peace extending even into the animal realm (vv. 6–9); be a champion for the poor and marginalized (vv. 3–5); gather the people of God from diaspora (vv. 12–13); and defeat the enemies of Israel (vv. 14–16). Similar themes appear in the *Damascus Document*, found both at Qumran and in fragments at Cairo. The text looks forward to the reign of "the Anointed of Aaron and Israel,"[10] which will be marked by the end of wickedness (CD 12.22–23; 13.20–22) and thus the restoration of righteousness. 1 Maccabees portrays Mattathias and his sons as such salvific figures in their opposition to Antiochus IV and their restoration of Judaic practice.

In the Judean War and its buildup, messianism was a common rallying point for rebel leaders of varying significance.[11] During the first century, at least eight men besides Jesus emerged as leaders of popular movements that, according to our sources, drew on biblical and post-biblical traditions about salvific kings in their resistance to Herodian and Roman rule: Athronges (Jos. *Ant.* 17.10.7), Simon of Perea (*Ant.* 17.10.6; *War* 2.4.2), Judas ben Hezekiah (*Ant.* 2.10.5; *War* 2.4.1), Judas of Galilee (*War* 2.8.1), the Egyptian (*Ant.* 20.8.6; *War* 2.13.4-5; Acts 21:38), Theudas (*Ant.* 20.5.1; Acts 5:36–38), Simon bar Giora (throughout *War*), and Manahem (*War* 2.17.8-9). For the most part, these figures are messianic on the historic, rather than eschatological model. That is, their primary function was to lead the people in driving out foreign or illegitimate rulers.

It is notable that in the Hellenistic sources, the connection between the Messiah (or untitled salvific ruler) and the Davidic line becomes somewhat weakened. The *Damascus Document*'s anointed figure is not explicitly Davidic, and the Hasmoneans, as Levites, explicitly were not. Except for Simon bar Giora, the rebel leaders in Josephus are not explicitly Davidic (Josephus describes Athronges as a shepherd, but does not connect this to David). In these sources, any Davidic lineage might be taken as further legitimizing, but not necessary so long as the figure fulfills at least one of the primary expectations of ideal kingship: restoring Judaic practices, routing "wickedness," and establishing independent rule over Judea or the whole land of Israel.

Titles for Jesus and Other Royal Language in Mark

The Gospel of Mark casts Jesus in many different roles. By examining the titles used for him in the text, we can come to a clearer understanding of those roles in the context of first-century culture and history.

ὁ βασιλεὺς τῶν Ἰουδαίων

The world βασιλεύς appears twelve times in Mark, eleven of them in reference either to Herod or to Jesus as ὁ βασιλεὺς τῶν Ἰουδαίων/Ἰσραήλ. The appearance of this title in the passion narrative points to a treason charge against Jesus, which leads to his crucifixion. R. T. France suggests that the phraseology is foreign: Jews would refer to the King of Israel or the Messiah, as the priests do at 15:32.[12] Jesus's enigmatic reply to Pilate's interrogation in v. 2 (σὺ λέγεις) has been variously interpreted as a qualified positive,[13] a sarcastic negative ("So *you* say"),[14] or intentionally evasive.[15] Pilate's question cannot, of course, be sincere—he is well aware of the official administration of the region. In the author's more immediate context, Josephus tells us that some revolutionary leaders called themselves βασιλεύς.[16] Here, then, it is best understood that Pilate is presenting the charges brought by the priests (see the parallel questioning and Jesus's unqualified response in Mark 14:61–62) in anticipation of a plea.[17]

Herod Antipas

In the strictest sense it is, of course, historically inaccurate both to refer to Mark's Herod without disambiguation and to refer to him as a βασιλεύς.[18] Antipas held the title τετραάρχης, and unsuccessfully sought that of βασιλεύς from the emperor.[19] However, "the strictest sense" by definition leaves no room for popular or literary usage,[20] and in studies like the present one it gets us nowhere to nitpick the author on his own *milieu*.

As tetrarch, Antipas[21] controlled the noncontiguous regions of Galilee and Perea (the eastern Jordan valley south of the lake) as a client of Rome. He controlled his own army, and famously sponsored building projects in Sepphoris and the construction of Tiberius as his capital. In Mark, this Herod's "kingship" largely manifests as the ability to imprison and execute for the sake of his personal reputation, without reference to legal statute or procedure. He also has—or claims to have—functional ownership over everything within his borders (vv. 22–23). The motif of a king or other powerful man giving exorbitant gifts to or in exchange for a woman is ubiquitous, found both in Homer and the Hebrew Bible, and in cases like this one the hyperbolic offer showcases the dire consequences of the deceptively simple boon actually requested.[22]

From the text's perspective, Herod oversteps his rights in marrying Herodias, and gets in over his head in the process. This is significant, because as the second densest cluster of βασιλ- words in the Gospel, the flashback demands attention both in contrast to ἡ βασιλεία τοῦ θεοῦ and ὁ βασιλεὺς τῶν Ἰουδαίων (a title that was officially held by Antipas's father and by later Herodian scions).

Most often, interpreters compare the Herod scene and the passion narrative for the two deaths, where John and Jesus are analogues to each other, respectively opposite Herod and Pilate; or with reference to contemporary resurrection traditions.[23] However, it is also possible to compare them in a different way. The two scenes contain nearly equal occurrences of βασιλεύς, a word that otherwise only appears in a very general reference in ch. 13. Both scenes depict their central characters as kings, playing them off of each other. From that angle, form-critical classifications of the Herod scene as a "court anecdote" have more merit than those that identify it as a martyrology or a legend strictly about John the Baptist.[24]

As noted above, the title ὁ βασιλεὺς τῶν Ἰουδαίων (or, perhaps, ὁ τῶν Ἰουδαίων βασιλεύς) was historically granted to Herod the Great, but not to Herod Antipas, despite his petition. Other members of the dynasty, particularly Agrippa I and Agrippa II, gained the title βασιλεὺς from Roman emperors. Mark refers to his Herod as βασιλεύς, but withholds the full title. Instead he applies it to Jesus, but only through the mouths of people who do not believe it—it is a mockery, not a confessional title, within the narrative. Whereas every occurrence of the full title in ch. 15 drips with irony, the application to Herod of the simple βασιλεύς is, literally if not historically, matter-of-fact. Finally, in ch. 6 Herod demonstrates his kingship through a luxurious party and the imprisonment and execution of John the Baptist; but Jesus's kingship in ch. 15 is inseparable from his suffering and death. In other words, Jesus's kingship, in contrast to Herod's, is not explicitly imagined in terms of κράτος—that is, might or sovereignty[25]—except eschatologically. Further, while Herod wields κράτος in the sense that his orders are obeyed, he has little actual control over the situation and operates out of a combination of fear and ambition. Jesus, on the other hand, comes to accept his present lack of control and understands his circumstances in the passion narrative as part of God's κράτος and will, not to be resisted.[26]

βασιλεύς in the Synoptic Tradition

Both later Synoptics have overlooked or rejected Mark's rhetorical strategy. Matthew removes βασιλεύς from several verses of his account of Herod's banquet, although he retains the narrative itself; and Luke severely shortens the narrative and chooses to refer to Herod by his correct title, tetrarch (Mark 6:14–27; cf. Matt 14:1–10//Luke 9:7). Both later Gospels retain some of the accusations against Jesus as "king of Israel" or "king of the Jews," but not all of them. Their additions, especially in Matthew but also in Luke, water down Mark's focused use of the term, and in the process highlight how focused it really is. Significantly, both later Evangelists add references to Jesus as king that are meant to be taken seriously. For example, to the triumphal entry Matthew adds the quotation of Zech 9, "Behold, your king comes to you" (Matt 21:5), and in the same scene Luke changes "blessed is he who comes in the name of the Lord" (Mark 11:9//Matt 21:9) to "blessed is the king who comes in the name of the Lord." Matthew's teaching on the sheep and the goats (Matt 25:31–46) refers to the eschatological Son of Man several times as "the king." Contrast these passages with Mark, who never refers to Jesus with the word βασιλεύς outside of the passion narrative and never places it in the mouth of someone speaking in earnest. Like βασιλεία, this term has a particular rhetorical use in Mark, not just as a title but as a part of Mark's Christological innovations in light of the historical moment.

ὁ υἱὸς Δαυίδ

Allusions to Jesus as king earlier than ch. 15 demonstrate the same ambiguity toward the undoubtedly political title Son of David as Jesus voices in Pilate's presence—perhaps a "yes, but," and perhaps a "no." Like ὁ βασιλεὺς τῶν Ἰουδαίων, ὁ υἱὸς Δαυίδ never comes directly from the narrator—it is a title that other characters give to Jesus (10:48, and an allusion at 11:11). Jesus indirectly accepts the title Messiah at 8:29–30, and he will claim it outright at 14:61–62; in between, at 12:35–37, he calls into question the identification of the Messiah with David's son. But earlier, in 10:46–52, he seems to accept the Davidic title from Bartimaeus. Broadhead observes that in both scenes the title is treated ambiguously: "The healing [of Bartimaeus] is associated with Jesus himself, with no direct connection to the title (10.49, 51–52). Conversely, the scene in 12.35–37 is abstracted from the person of Jesus."[27]

Earlier scholarship has debated the historicity of Bartimaeus's declaration of Jesus as Son of David and the redaction history of the passage, on the evidence of the double address to Jesus ("Son of David" in vv. 47–48 and "teacher" in v. 51) and the apparently inconsistent behavior of the crowd, who silences Bartimaeus and then encourages him to approach Jesus.[28] Whether or not Mark redacted an earlier account, however, the fact remains that he chose the compositional form of the story, so from the point of view of narrative it is important to consider what that language might evoke.

Reading the pericope as part of a document that is aware of and interactive with its immediate political landscape, the Davidic title and the crowd's reaction to it take on a different kind of sense. It is almost certain that Mark is aware of an earlier tradition regarding Jesus as the descendant of David. Paul, of course, continually refers to Jesus with the title Χριστός, and it is difficult—though not impossible, as I have discussed—to separate the title from the Davidic lineage.[29] However, up until this point Jesus has actively rejected the expectations of the Davidic Messiah, if not the title itself (8:29–30).

Reading 10:47–48 together with 11:11, with the Judean War in the background, a motive for the crowd's behavior emerges. Bartimaeus's declaration of Jesus as the Son of David is without context for the crowd, who has not been present for the passion predictions, and therefore comes across as a declaration of rebellion. Their attempt to silence him is not a rejection of the title per se but a momentary panic at the outbreak of this portion of the hidden transcript into the open. Bartimaeus has not necessarily said anything wrong, but something *dangerous*. By that reading, their encouragement to him in v. 49 does not constitute a reversal of their attitude, but rather an attempt to re-hide the transcript. The crowd's own investment in the return of Davidic rulership and acceptance of Jesus as that ruler—in a period when the issues of local leadership and the suitedness of individual local leaders are at a fever pitch—is apparent in the cry at 11:11, at Jesus's triumphal entry into the city. Myers explains their abandonment of Jesus at the trial and crucifixion as an expression of their disappointment when he does not fulfill their hopes.[30] Jesus's discussion of David in 12:35–37 seems designed to head off this disappointment, but ultimately even the Twelve are unable to adjust to this new notion of messiahship.

ἐξουσία

This term first appears in text in the seventh century[31] or, more securely, the sixth.[32] It maintains a consistent basic meaning through the Hellenistic and Roman periods, which is that of *authority, permission,* or *license*.[33] The translation "power" too easily confuses it with δύναμις for the purposes of this exegesis, but Foerster and Silva both emphasize that ἐξουσία refers to power in the sense of possibility—both by lack of prevention (without obstacle) and by explicit grant or commission from a higher force—rather than, as Foerster puts it, "intrinsic ability."[34] The translation "right" is sometimes appropriate. It is common in legal, political, and military contexts, and in some cases refers to an office or appointment; Dionysius of Halicarnassus uses the plural in the same sense as the English phrase "the authorities."[35] It can also take on a negative meaning: Foerster notes that it can be synonymous with ὕβρις in the sense of "taking liberties" and thus "arrogance" or abuse of authority.

It is a critical concept in LXX Dan 7, where it translates the Aramaic שלטן (dominion) and exemplifies the conflict between God and the worldly powers. Silva refers also to the apocalyptic tradition at Qumran, where "emphasis is placed on the contrast between the dominion of Belial and that of the Prince of Light."[36] The plural, ἐξουσίαι, appears in some New Testament texts alongside or synonymous with ἄρχαι, in reference to the metaphysical powers of the heavens or the world (e.g., Col 1:16).

It appears ten times in Mark, all before ch. 14. All of these occurrences bear some connection to Jesus: in seven cases Jesus is explicitly the one bearing authority (1:22, 27; 2:10; and 11:28 [twice], 29, and 33). Twice the disciples receive authority from Jesus (3:15 and 6:7), and once the implicit subject is Jesus, in a parable in which a landowner gives ἐξουσία to his slaves to do their work while he is away (13:34).

Anne Dawson's reading of the ἐξουσία texts in Mark privileges the meaning "freedom." Although ἐλευθερία does not appear in Mark, Dawson argues that the Gospel nonetheless "witnesses to the concept of freedom," and she does so by connecting Mark closely to the *Res gestae divi Augusti*. In that text, "although the word *libertas* (liberty) occurs at the beginning of the text, it is the language or 'vocabulary' of the office of the *triumvir potestas*, rendered in the Greek as δημαρχικὴ ἐξουσία …, that conveys the sense of the meaning of freedom that the *Res Gestae* is promoting."[37] Dawson's decision to translate ἐξουσία as "freedom to act" is not accompanied by discussion of the term's more common or nuanced uses, especially as it relates to delegation, authority, and permission. She understands "freedom" in the sense of "Christian freedom," a concept she distills especially from Pauline literature but exposits primarily with examples and language from the modern world after the American and French Revolutions, especially examples from the twentieth century such as Mahatma Gandhi and Nelson Mandela. Her assertion that "ἐλευθερία and *libertas* had become rallying political catchcries in the Greek and Roman worlds" stands without citations or contextualization.[38]

Certainly a thread of freedom rhetoric runs through Israelite thought and tradition: specifically, in the postexilic periods, in the sense of independent rule of the land traditionally considered Israelite, with Jerusalem as its capital. Counter to Dawson's thesis, this should not be couched in the language of "inalienable rights" or even individual determination, particularly since, in practice, rule from Jerusalem was certainly not a democracy even on the Athenian model, and was not always welcomed or considered legitimate by those under it. Instead of "freedom to act" on an individual level, Mark's use of ἐξουσία rather indicates freedom to command, depicting Jesus in a similar light to a Roman general: answerable to a higher entity in the big picture, but in practical terms the top of the local hierarchy. Jesus delegates his command to lower echelons (e.g., the two commission accounts in 3:15 and 6:7), but primarily his ἐξουσία manifests in the ability to command demons. Conceiving of the narrative in terms of *Realpolitik*, with the Kingdom of God in conflict with that of Satan, we can read the exorcisms as battle scenes of a sort, where Jesus drives out his enemy and claims further "territory." Two major examples will demonstrate.

1:21–28: The First Exorcism

This is Jesus's first narrated encounter in a synagogue, and his first encounter with the demonic since his temptation in the wilderness in v. 13. The concept of ἐξουσία interprets both relationships: Jesus proves the superiority and worthiness of his teaching by means of his command over the demon. Significantly, Mark has not yet outlined the content of Jesus's teaching: the interest here is not in his message but in his identity. Therefore, while the teaching is certainly novel—the crowd declares it so in v. 27—the ἐξουσία of both vv. 22 and 27 validates it rather than derives from it. France argues the opposite: "The general statement that his ἐξουσία differentiated his teaching ... suggests that he is already expressing some of the radical ideas, boldly contradicting accepted halakhic teaching, that will appear later [in the Gospel]."[39] However, at this point Jesus is not encountering explicit resistance from the synagogue leaders, as he will later on. It is not an error as such to read teachings from later in the narrative back into ch. 1, but France is getting ahead of the flow of the story. At this point the emphasis is on Jesus's own ἐξουσία and its effect on how his teaching is received, not the content or independent ἐξουσία of the teaching.[40]

Joel Marcus observes that the use of ἐξουσία in connection to kings (including divine ones) in Hellenistic texts leads to its use in apocalyptic texts and "is particularly associated with God's reassertion of his royal authority in the end-time."[41] Likewise, Collins understands v. 22 in reference to Jesus's baptism and therefore messiahship, pointing out the use of ἐξουσία in Greek versions of Daniel.⁴² Myers, on the other hand, appeals to the prophetic tradition, identifying Jesus with Elisha through the demon's address to him as the "holy one of God" (see 2 Kgs 4:9).⁴³ The two approaches are certainly not mutually exclusive, but Myers's omission of the apocalyptic in interpreting ἐξουσία in this pericope, though in line with his relatively humanistic Christology,⁴⁴ masks the political possibilities. Jesus can interpret the tradition, and he can do so because of the same authorization that gives him power over enemy forces. In that sense, ἐξουσία in Mark corresponds more closely to the Latin *imperium*, specifically as applied to Pompey by Cicero in *Pro lex Manilia* as the senate's designated general, than to *auctoritas* (despite the cognate in English), which denotes personal influence and charisma rather than command.⁴⁵

2:1-12: The Paralytic

Here Mark expands on the Christology of 1:21-28 by setting up a similar situation. By this point in his ministry, as 1:28 and 32-34 attest, Jesus clearly has a reputation for healing: although he begins the scene by teaching the crowd (v. 2; ἐλάλει αὐτοῖς τὸν λόγον), at least some respond by requesting a healing. In contrast to the exorcism in ch. 1, Jesus uses this opportunity not to bolster his teaching but to directly reveal to the crowd and scribes something about his own identity.

This is the first occurrence of the title Son of Man in this Gospel. Previously the voice from heaven has declared Jesus to be God's son (1:11), and although this passage is far separated, the title is certainly meant in reference and contrast to that claim. The intended audience is likely already familiar with what Mark calls "the word," including popular titles for Jesus and at least local understandings of them, so it would not be fair to imagine a surprised reaction to the shift in nomenclature. Nor should we belabor the phrase's meaning or lack of it in Semitic dialects versus Greek, except to say that its use as a title for the Messiah is unique to the Jesus tradition.⁴⁶ Nonetheless, we should still expect that the audience would notice the contrast. That drives up the stakes for interpreting ἐξουσία (2:10) compared to ch. 1. Jesus is again demonstrating his authority by means of an incidental miraculous act, but here he is claiming authority using a significant and undoubtedly apocalyptic and eschatological title. More significantly, he is making explicit the nature of the authority that already bolstered his teaching in ch. 1: the right to act as God's direct proxy.

Although Mark has already introduced the theme of conflict between Jesus and the synagogue authorities, this is the first time they directly challenge him, and in this passage the scribes have a reasonable complaint. Unlike in 1:21-28, Jesus is not merely displacing the scribes on their own turf—he is fulfilling a role that in their understanding is explicitly and exclusively reserved for God.⁴⁷ Even taking the passive construction at face value—Jesus does not directly forgive the man's sins, but informs him that they are forgiven (presumably *by* God)—the scribes would be reasonably taken aback by the hubris of a man who is not a priest or recognized prophet acting as a divine mouthpiece. Jesus's use of the Son of Man title comes more into focus, then: by alluding to Daniel's heavenly, apocalyptic savior, he declares *by what right* he speaks for God. Thus, in this passage the title and the term ἐξουσία are conceptually inseparable and together declare Jesus to be the direct agent of God.

The use of ἐξουσία in these two examples, again, recalls the role of a general, client ruler, or governor: the local representative of the ultimate rulership, exercising his authority to interpret and settle legal matters (in the case of Jesus, to teach on the tradition and forgive sins), and enforcing and legitimizing that authority by driving out enemy combatants. Although it does not contain the precise vocabulary, the Beelzebul controversy (3:20–27) explicitly addresses both the issue of Jesus's authorizing superior (God or Beelzebul) and the fact that Satan—"the ruler of demons"—is an enemy combatant. Although Jesus uses the metaphor of burglary, it is important to recall that plunder (here in its verbal form, διαρπάζω) was a major source of income for armies. The divine source of his authority will again come into question when the priests challenge him—and back down from the fight—in 11:27–33.

ἐξουσία in the Synoptic Tradition

With only a few exceptions, Matthew and Luke do not alter Mark's use of ἐξουσία. They both contain the comparison between Jesus's teaching and the scribes/Pharisees (Mark 1:21–22//Matt 7:29//Luke 4:31–32), although Matthew takes this occurrence out of the synagogue and places it at the end of the Sermon on the Mount. However, where Mark continues this pericope with an exorcism and the declaration, "A new teaching! He commands even the unclean spirits with authority and they obey him," Matthew omits the exorcism altogether, and Luke alters the line to remove the statement about the teaching, but retains the second ἐξουσία.

The subsequent evangelists apparently had some trouble with Mark's double delegations to the disciples (3:14, which introduces the list of the Twelve, and 6:7, which introduces the instructions for their mission). Matthew combines the two pericopes to make a single one in ch. 10, and Luke omits the delegation of authority from the choosing of the Twelve in ch. 6. Further, both omit the parable of the doorkeeper (Mark 13:34), or else drastically extend it into the parable of the talents/pounds (Matt 25:14–30//Luke 19:11–27). In Matthew's case, the word ἐξουσία disappears. Luke uses it in his extended parable, but not in parallel with Mark (Luke 19:17).

There are likewise minimal added uses of ἐξουσία in the later Synoptics, mostly on the part of Luke. Luke adds it to Satan's offer of kingdoms in the extended temptation scene (Luke 4:6), and Matthew adds it to the teaching on forgiveness (Matt 9:8), making clear that the Matthean use of "son of man" includes the Semitic meaning found in Ezekiel, "human." Both later Synoptics include the non-Markan story of the centurion's slave, in which the centurion declares himself to be, like Jesus, both under authority and in possession of it (Matt 8:9//Luke 7:8). Luke extends a line in the arrest scene to accuse the chief priests, and so on, of being under "authority of darkness" (Luke 22:53, cf. Mark 14:49//Matt 26:55).

Luke generally evinces an interest in more "historical" issues such as accurate accounts of rulers, judicial proceedings, and titles. In that vein, he includes reference to the ἐξουσία of the governor in the priests' plot against Jesus (Luke 20:20) and also brings Herod and his ἐξουσία (NRSV: jurisdiction) into the trial before Pilate (Luke

23:7). He also refers to "the authorities" in the warning of persecution, where Mark and Matthew do not include such vocabulary (Luke 12:11, cf. Mark 13:11//Matt 10:19).

Besides the Matthean take on the phrase "son of man," generally the later Synoptics' usages of ἐξουσία do not differ from Mark's in meaning, and neither of the later authors demonstrates a markedly different Christology by means of this vocabulary. The centurion's slave narrative, for example, shows that both Matthew and Luke understand Jesus to be God's agent. At most, the use of ἐξουσία in Luke 12:11; 20:20; and 23:7 points to a more technical understanding of the word, but this simply indicates Luke's more accurate portrayal of government, rather than a different understanding of what ἐξουσία entails in relation to Jesus. Matthew explicitly states at the end of his Gospel that "all authority in heaven and on earth" has been given to the resurrected Jesus (Matt 28:18), but this does not necessarily represent a departure from Mark's Christology as much as from its stated ecclesiology. The largest difference between Mark on the one hand and Matthew and Luke on the other is Mark's targeted use of ἐξουσία to refer only to Jesus.

Summary

Mark's use of ἐξουσία is fairly consistent with the word's history and general usage. It carries a strong sense of delegation and corresponding power. The source of Jesus's ἐξουσία, however, is never made explicit. For the reader this is obviously God, as the controversy in 11:27–33 strongly implies. However, the word ἐξουσία does not appear at the baptism or the transfiguration, nor at any point during the trial and passion, all points where an explicit statement of Jesus's divine commission might be appropriate. The meaning of ἐξουσία can overlap with that of δύναμις, but passages containing similar themes—particularly healing stories—may be distinguished in terms of emphasis by their use of one or the other. As in 1:22, 27 and 2:10, at times the fact of Jesus's ability to perform what the text would call δυνάμεις (works of power) is less important than the evidence that such actions provide of his divine commission.

κύριος

In general usage, κύριος (both the adjective and the noun, whose morphology in the nominative is the same) appears complementary to ἐξουσία: if the latter is authority, the former is or describes the one bearing it.[48] Although there is quite a bit of overlap, an important distinction is possible: where εξουσία often connotes authority that has been granted or designated by a higher office—either an institution or an individual—κύριος can carry a stronger sense of *natural* authority, granted by law in a cosmic sense, or natural order, as opposed to legislation or direct designation by another body.

As an adjective it can denote ability, ownership, or control: in the *Agamemnon* the Chorus declares, κύριός εἰμι, "I have authority," or "I am entitled," in reference to the gods-given ability to understand and interpret portents.[49] In reference to objects or ideas it can refer to legality, sovereignty, or superiority.[50] As a noun it denotes a lord or master in legal, social, and cosmic senses. Foerster notes that it can be used interchangeably with δεσπότης, especially in reference to one who owns a slave, but also that when the two are contrasted, κύριος often denotes the favored or more legitimate option (but see Mark 10:42—in compound with the intensifying κατα, the verbal form suggests oppressiveness).[51] Beginning in the later Hellenistic period the noun and the vocative address, κύριε, become more common in reference to gods and rulers (especially divinized rulers). Foerster argues that in most cases that are Hellenistic and later, this translates an "indigenous" (i.e., non-Greek) approach to the divine/human relationship, which in his estimation is characterized by a more direct "lordship" of the god over the individual.[52] In the LXX it appears in place of the tetragrammaton (e.g., Gen 31:3; Num 8:1; 1 Sam 2:7, etc.).

The noun κύριος appears only sixteen times in Mark, compared to dozens each in the other three Gospels—in fact, it has a smaller presence in Mark than in almost any other text in the New Testament, accounting for size. This dearth, and Mark's apparent lack of systematic treatment of the title, has led some scholars to discount its importance as a Markan Christological title. Kingsbury states, "The most one can say is that it functions in some few passages as an auxiliary christological title."[53] Collins addresses it only in comments on individual occurrences, and not every single one. She gives no systematic analysis of it.[54] Thus, in scholarship it is at the same time taken for granted and deemed irrelevant.

Taking on this lack of scholarly interest, Daniel Johansson examines several Markan occurrences of κύριος and concludes that the text assigns it to both Jesus and God, and contains intentionally ambiguous uses as a means of linking the two.[55] The key point for Johansson's argument is Mark 1:2–3, the amalgamate citation of scripture that establishes John the Baptist as the text's Elijah figure, preparing the way for the one who is coming. The referent of κύριος in this passage has been a subject of debate. Robert Gundry, representing the majority, asserts that it is Jesus, on the grounds that Jesus is the one for whom John is preparing the way.[56] A few scholars, on the argument that κύριος is not a Christological title in Mark and that it is the normal translation of the tetragrammaton in the LXX, argue that here it must refer to God.[57] Marcus's more nuanced reading, that the scripture citation portrays "an extraordinary intimacy between Jesus and God" by equating both of their "ways,"[58] still reads κύριος in 1:2–3 as referring to God, even though he allows that in other parts of the Gospel it refers to Jesus.

Johansson, however, suggests that the citation of prophecy in Mark 1 must be read *both* in the context of the narrative at hand (making Jesus the referent of κύριος because it is he that John precedes) *and* in the original scriptural context (making God the referent).[59] This double reference is more obvious in the next passage that Johansson analyzes, 5:19.[60] Here Jesus instructs the exorcized Gerasene to go and tell "how much ὁ κύριος has done for you," and the man goes throughout the Decapolis proclaiming "how much Jesus had done for him," identical in Greek aside from the pronouns and subjects. On the surface it appears that Jesus is referring to God, and the Gerasene man and the narrator attribute his restoration to Jesus instead. Collins reads it this way, drawing an analogy between this passage and 1:40–45, where Jesus commands the former leper to perform the proper rituals in the temple, and instead the man goes around preaching Jesus.[61] But Johansson posits that "the best solution is perhaps to distinguish between what the characters in the story would perceive and what the audience is supposed to understand." Thus he agrees that "at the narrative level" the above reading is likely, but argues that by creating that juxtaposition, Mark "[links] Jesus not only to the work of God so that there is a unity of act between God and Jesus ..., but also to the title κύριος so that God and Jesus are united under this designation."[62]

The application of the title κύριος to both Jesus and God appears in all levels of the Synoptic tradition and in Paul. This presents a potential problem for Johansson's case. This may be an indication that, even from the earliest detectable stages of the Jesus tradition, there was syncretization of Jesus with God, on a model similar to Hellenistic identification of kings with gods (e.g., Alexander and the Seleucid kings with Dionysus). I discuss such matters in Chapter 6.

Hierarchy in God's Kingdom

Mark advocates a cosmic hierarchy that will be and is becoming realized in the Kingdom of God. God is at the top, invisible but active. Next, God's agent, Jesus, does the dirty work of rulership, both in his pre-crucifixion activity and in the military imagery of his later glorification. The elect follow, both in this schema and in their literal activity relative to Jesus. Among the elect, there seem to be two tiers: those who both follow and understand (e.g., Bartimaeus and the woman with the alabaster jar), and those who attempt to follow but do not understand, but nonetheless seem to enjoy Jesus's favor—that is, the Twelve and the women in ch. 16. The elite of the present world order occupy what we might call a "border region" of the Kingdom of God—depending on how they use their wealth (e.g., the rich man of 10:17–31) and respond to God's call (e.g., the parable of the tenants in 12:1–12) they might be in the Kingdom or out of it. In particular, the Jerusalem authorities lose their traditional status as elect in favor of those who follow Jesus. Finally, Satan and his demonic servants form an oppositional power to the Kingdom of God.

Further, with a close look it is not clear that Mark fully rejects "earthly" status markers at the level of the elect. Passages often marshalled to defend that interpretation can be interpreted in other ways. For example, Myers interprets the exchange between Jesus and the Syro-Phoenician woman (7:24–30) as representing the equal inclusion of non-Judeans in Jesus's project.[63] While it is surely the case that the woman's witty (and, in terms of gender stratification, quite daring and unexpected) riposte gains her the same miracle that Jesus granted to Jairus the synagogue leader (5:35–43), she does not actually debate the terms of his initial refusal. She does not insist that she, as either a woman or a Gentile, deserves an equal seat at the table with the "children," merely that she be given access to what is left over when the children have had their fill.[64]

Continuing on the subject of women, Liew observes that there is no narrative in which Mark's Jesus explicitly calls a woman away from home and family to follow him[65]—women such as Salome and Mary Magdalene are present, at least in the Passion narrative, but they do not rate a mention in the rest of the text as companions of Jesus, let alone inclusion among his closest circle. Horsley declares that women "at the climax of the story [the crucifixion] appear prominently as the only figures who have faithfully persisted in 'following' and 'serving.' "[66] Yet he does not address the fact that the women's final act at the tomb is to run away in fear, just as the Twelve did in Gethsemane.[67] The bleeding woman and woman with the alabaster jar grasp Jesus's identity and purpose without prompting (5:25–34; 14:3–9), and perhaps Horsley's argument would be stronger if it focused on them instead of the named women. However, Bartimaeus (10:46–52) plays a similar role. In that case, the unnamed women become less of a pro-woman statement making up for the relative unimportance of women in Jesus's inner circle, and rather a part of Mark's larger suspicion of the inner circle itself, outside of gender concerns.

The leadership of Mark's community is a common topic in discussions of the Markan disciples. Horsley argues that Mark's treatment of the disciples indicates a push toward a movement that is "egalitarian, with no heads who enjoy veneration, power, and privilege."[68] Myers is less romantic, admitting that "Mark's alternative [social order] is not leaderlessness, but leadership accountable to the 'least' in the community."[69] In fact, Mark does not at all envision the overthrow of the contemporary social structure *as such*, but he dramatically revises its qualifications. There are clearly leaders in Mark's narrative. The young man at the tomb, the woman who anoints Jesus at Bethany, the widow giving her tithe, Simon of Cyrene, and Joseph of Arimathea all play stereotypical "leader" roles: they direct or exemplify behavior, give instructions, and plan ahead for the future. There are also clearly outcasts, such as most of the wealthy, and anyone who does not follow Jesus. In the middle, as I have noted, neither exemplary leaders nor rejected outright, are those who follow Jesus in his travels but do not understand him.

In addition, those at the top of the hierarchy enjoy privileges. Following the parable of the lamp, 4:24–25 states this principle clearly: one who has more will receive more, and one who has little will be further bereft. This, in a very small nutshell, is the debt system of the first-century Levant,[70] and Jesus here applies it as a foundational aspect of the Kingdom of God. At Jesus's anointing, v. 14:9 refocuses the story from one about Jesus (the named character) to one about the (unnamed) woman. Despite her anonymity, Mark envisions her as a part of the tradition worthy of high honor. Her far-reaching fame[71] recalls Greek and Roman epigraphical practices, erecting monuments or striking coins in honor of benefactors. Here and in servant passages such as 8:34–37 and 10:42–45, Mark has taken a major aspect of the elite Roman value system—the point of magnanimity is that one must give resources in order to receive sociopolitical influence, which will bring more resources—and intensified it: one must give everything in order to receive a place in the kingdom. In the Kingdom of God the currency at issue is not just material wealth, and in fact Mark's Jesus demands dissociation not only from wealth but also from one's own sense of self-preservation. Once again, the one who espouses these values is promised rewards, and the one who fails faces punishment. The instruction to take up one's cross (8:34–38) ends with an image of Jesus at court, praising his allies before the sovereign and disavowing his enemies. The reader might be reminded of Herod Antipas's unsuccessful petition to Caligula, where the poor reference from his brother results in his exile, rather than the royal title he went to Rome seeking (Jos. *Ant.* 18.1.1).

The hierarchy of the kingdom is structured similarly, or even identically, to that of the "world." God is at the top, deputizing Jesus as his agent, and the human elect make up the remaining ranks. On the other side, the earthly elite who reject Jesus and his teachings join Satan and the demonic realm as God's opposition. Mark's values are differently focused—prizing behavior oriented toward the well-being of the community over wealth and social status—but it is a hierarchy all the same. Aphorisms such as "the last will be first," as well as the requirement of service rather than "lording it over" (κατακυριεύουσιν [10:42]), do not negate the existence of status, but rather grant status to those who do not seek it at the expense of others.

Conclusion

It is common to attribute the rebellion of the first century to economic dissatisfaction, disenfranchised and exploited natives against a foreign elite power. The natural conclusion of that argument, in a post-Marxist world, is that those on the side of rebellion fought for an egalitarian and less (if not necessarily un-) stratified society. One major support for this view is Josephus's statement that the rebels burned the records office in an attempt to make debts impossible to collect and thus empower the nonelite to fight (*War* 2.17.6). Josephus's phrasing is more cynical, however. In *War*, this is not something that the indebted masses do to their own benefit, but that elite and even aristocratic actors do as a strategy to gain popular support. Josephus's consistent reference to the rebels as tyrants is not to be trusted, but some prominent leaders of rebellious factions were aristocrats or otherwise in positions of power. Even Simon bar Giora, who seems not to have been connected to any aristocratic or priestly house, cannot confidently be characterized as a social reformer.[72]

I have avoided claiming that people living under the stratified, oligarchic governments of the ancient Mediterranean and Near East *could not* have imagined any other way. It is common to say that only 1 percent of ancient Greek and Roman writing has survived, and, besides the lost writings, what of the conversations that were never written down? In short, we have painfully little context for what possibilities ancient Mediterranean people might have imagined for themselves. Nonetheless, whether someone in ancient Judea or Galilee *could have* argued for an anarchic or communist structure of government two millennia ahead of Marx and the Spanish Revolution, the author of Mark did not. From the structure of the cosmos to the organization of communities, the Gospel of Mark assumes, defines, and constructs stratifications. Jesus explicitly displays ἐξουσία, the semantic field of which heavily leans toward granted or delegated power. More specifically, there is never a suggestion in the Gospel, even by hostile characters, that Jesus might *not* be a delegate—the only question is of whom. In turn, Jesus himself delegates, and shows through his teachings and actions that those who follow him likewise operate from stratified positions within the Kingdom of God.

Notes

1. Cf. Livy. In 1.18 the Roman senators are reluctant to crown a Sabine but cannot decide against a man of Numa's character. In 1.39.5–6 the historian denies that Servius was a slave in favor of the view that he was the son of a conquered noblewoman whom the Roman queen rescued from servitude and brought into the Roman court. Although Livy disagrees with Cicero on both accounts, the larger point remains: that Rome's early and best kings need not have been Romans. With that in mind it is notable that Rome's first and exemplary bad king, Tarquinius, was the son of a king and not a foreigner.
2. "Yet our own ancestors, rustics though they even then were, saw that kingly virtue and wisdom, not royal ancestry, were the qualities to be sought" (Cic. Rep. 2.12 [Keyes, LCL]).
3. *RGDA* 5. This and other translations of the *RGDA* from Alison E. Cooley, *Res Gestae Divi Augusti: Text, Translation, and Commentary* (Cambridge: Cambridge University Press, 2009).
4. Cic., *Inv.* 2.53; Pl. *Rep.* 427e.
5. Galinsky, *Augustan Culture*, 84–8.
6. Livy Pr. 11–12 (Foster, LCL).
7. Shemaryahu Talmon, "The Concepts of Māšîaḥ and Messianism in Early Judaism," in *The Messiah: Developments in Earliest Judaism and Christianity*, ed. James H. Charlesworth (Minneapolis, MN: Fortress Press, 1992), 87–8.
8. Talmon, "Concepts," 79–80.
9. Talmon, "Concepts," 87.
10. Talmon reads this as two figures, a priestly and a kingly Messiah, respectively, but this is not a unanimous interpretation. Talmon, "Concepts," 104; cf. Grabbe, *Judaic Religion*, 274.
11. Horsley (" 'Messianic' Figures and Movements in First-Century Palestine," in *The Messiah. Developments in Earliest Judaism and Christianity*, ed. James H. Charlesworth [Minneapolis, MN: Fortress Press, 1992], 276–95) resists calling these figures "messianic," preferring "prophetic," on the basis that Josephus uses the latter term but not the former. As the current argument is concerned with the ideal qualities and roles of a ruler, rather than titles as such, we may allow for a broad definition of "messianic." Further, Horsley does well to remind us that the literary evidence cannot fully illuminate popular sentiment (278–9, 286).
12. R. T. France, *The Gospel of Mark: A Commentary on the Greek Text*, NIGTC (Grand Rapids, MI: Eerdmans, 2002), 628.
13. France (*Divine Government*, 91), referencing David R. Catchpole ("The Answer of Jesus to Caiaphas [Matt xxvi.64]," *NTS* 17 [1971]: 226): "It is a way of accepting the words used, but dissociating oneself from the way the speaker is likely to have interpreted them."
14. E.g., Robert H. Gundry, *Mark: A Commentary on His Apology for the Cross* (Grand Rapids, MI: Eerdmans, 1993), 932–3; Bas M. F. van Iersel, *Mark: A Reader-Response Commentary*, trans. W. H. Bisscheroux (London: T&T Clark, 2004), 459.
15. Collins, *Mark*, 713. Cf. Joel Marcus, *Mark 8–16: A New Translation with Introduction and Commentary*, AB 27a (New Haven, CT: Yale University Press, 2009), 1033, where both Pilate's statement and Jesus's appear sarcastic: "*You* are the King of the Jews?" "*You* are saying it" (emphasis original).

16. E.g., Jos. *Ant.* 17.10.8; *War* 2.4.3.
17. Lk 23:1–3 is more explicit on this point. See also the governor's neutrality in the proceedings in Acts 24, Paul's trial before Felix.
18. I have written on the comparison between Mark's Jesus and Mark's Herod in more detail in Margaret Froelich, "Kings of the Jews: Herodian Collaboration with Rome through a Markan Lens," in *Greco-Roman and Jewish Tributaries to the New Testament: Festschrift in Honor of Gregory J. Riley*, ed. Christopher S. Crawford, CSNTCO 4 (Claremont, CA: Claremont Press, 2019), 27–36.
19. Jos. *Ant.* 18.7.1–2.
20. See Collins, *Mark*, 303, for a brief discussion both of Antipas and of the use of βασιλεὺς in Mark 6.
21. There can be a difficult balancing act between avoiding historical confusion and remaining true to Mark's text. In my discussion I refer to the tetrarch as Antipas or Herod Antipas when discussing historical events, in order to keep him separate from the rest of the dynasty. However, as long as such confusion is unlikely, I use the moniker Herod when discussing the character in the Gospel. For a more detailed discussion of the historical uses of Herod and Antipas for the same figure, see Gabriella Gelardini, "The Contest for a Royal Title: Herod versus Jesus in the *Gospel According to Mark* (6,14–29; 15,6–15)," *Annali Di Storia Dell'esegesi* 28, no. 2 (2011): 95–9.
22. See Collins, *Mark*, 309–10, who cites, among other things, Herodotus's account of Xerxes's fatal gift to Artaÿnte. This tale also includes an incestuous scandal and a plotting wife at a birthday party (Hdt. 9.108–13).
23. Mark McVann, "The 'Passion' of John the Baptist and Jesus before Pilate: Mark's Warnings about Kings and Governors," *BTB* 38, no. 4 (2008): 152–7; Collins, *Mark*, 303–15; S. Nortje, "John the Baptist and the Resurrection Traditions in the Gospels," *Neotestamentica* 23 (1989): 349–58.
24. Court tale: Martin Dibelius, *Die urchristliche Überlieferung von Johannes dem Täufer* (Göttingen: Vandenhoeck & Ruprecht, 1911), 80; Theissen, *The Gospels in Context*, 81n53. Martyrdom: Klaus Berger, *Formgeschichte des neuen Testaments* (Heidelberg: Quelle & Meyer, 1984), 334 (he classifies it as *both* a martyrdom *and* a court tale). Legend about John: Rudolf Bultmann, *The History of the Synoptic Tradition*, trans. John Marsh (New York: Harper & Row, 1963), 301–2.
25. LSJ, *s.v.* κράτος. This noun does not appear in Mark, and the verbal form, κρατέω, is used in generic senses.
26. For a discussion of Mark's Herod as a tyrant, without reference to the comparison to Jesus through kingship vocabulary, see Abraham Smith, "Tyranny Exposed: Mark's Typological Characterization of Herod Antipas (Mark 6:14–29)," *BibInt* 14 (2006): 259–93, https://doi.org/10.1163/156851506776722994.
27. Broadhead, *Naming Jesus*, 114.
28. Christoph Burger, *Jesus als Davidssohn*, FRLANT 98 (Göttingen: Vandenhoeck & Ruprecht, 1970), 42–6.
29. In support of their synonymity, see FerdinandHahn, *Christologische Hoheitstitel: Ihre Geschichte im frühen Christentum*, FRLANT 83 (Göttingen: Vandenhoeck & Ruprecht, 1963), 156–8. Notable exceptions are Simon bar Kochba and Cyrus (Isa 45:1).
30. Myers, *Strong Man*, 39.
31. Aes. *Fab.* 103.1.
32. Thuc. 1.38.

33. See Werner Foerster, "ἔξεστιν, κτλ," TDNT 2:560-75; Moisés Silva, NIDOTTE, "ἐξουσία, κτλ," NIDOTTE 2:216-21; Henry George Liddell and Robert Scott, "ἐξουσ-ία," LSJ 599.
34. Foerster, TDNT 2:562.
35. DH 11.32.
36. Silva, NIDOTTE 2:218.
37. Anne Dawson, *Freedom as Liberating Power: A Socio-Political Reading of the ἐξουσία Texts in the Gospel of Mark*, NTOA 44 (Freiburg, Schweiz; Universitätsverlag, 2000), 1, 11.
38. Dawson, *Freedom*, 2-3. See Chapter 2 of this study regarding *libertas* and ἐλευθερία in political and military contexts in the Hellenistic and Roman east.
39. France, *Mark*, 102.
40. Cf. France, *Mark*, 102-3, where he argues that the scribes represent the "old régime" being displaced by the "fresh new teaching of Jesus."
41. Marcus, *Mark 1-8*, 191.
42. Collins, *Mark*, 164-5n48.
43. Myers, *Strong Man*, 142.
44. See Myers, *Strong Man*, 444-6, where Myers chooses primarily earthly titles to describe Mark's Jesus.
45. Galinsky, *Augustan Culture*, 14.
46. For brief discussions of the history of ὁ υἱὸς τοῦ ἀνθρώπου and its scholarship, see Collins, *Mark*, 186-9; Mogens Müller, *The Expression "Son of Man" and the Development of Christology: A History of Interpretation*, Copenhagen International Seminar (London: Routledge, 2012), ch. 1.
47. Collins (*Mark*, 185, see also n. 26) cites Ps 130:4 to demonstrate the scribal position on Jesus's declaration.
48. Werner Foerster and Gottfried Quell, "κύριος, κτλ," TDNT 3:1039-98.
49. Aesch. *Ag.* 104-7.
50. Liddell and Scott, "κύριος," LSJ 1013.
51. Foerster, TDNT 3:1044.
52. Foerster, TDNT 3:1052.
53. Jack Dean Kingsbury, *The Christology of Mark's Gospel* (Philadelphia, PA: Fortress Press, 1983), 110.
54. Collins, *Mark*, 518, 547, 705.
55. Daniel Johansson, "*Kyrios* in the Gospel of Mark," *JSNT* 33 (2010): 101-24, https://doi.org/10.1177/0142064X10380130.
56. Gundry, *Mark*, 35-6.
57. E.g., Klyne Snodgrass, "Streams of Tradition Emerging from Isaiah 40:1-5 and Their Adaptation in the New Testament," *JSNT* 8 (1980): 34; Dieter Lührmann, *Das Markusevangelium*, HNT 3 (Tübingen: Mohr [Siebeck], 1987), 34. The *ABD* entry for "LORD" reads, in its entirety, "See NAMES OF GOD (OT); YAHWEH (DEITY)."
58. Marcus, *Mark 1-8*, 147-8.
59. Johansson, "*Kyrios*," 104-5. One might also note, though Johansson does not, that while John precedes and prepares the way for Jesus, in the rest of the Gospel and most clearly in 1:15, Jesus performs the exact same function for the Kingdom of God. Just as κύριος refers simultaneously to Jesus and God, ἄγγελος refers both to John and Jesus.
60. Johansson, "*Kyrios*," 105-6.
61. Collins, *Mark*, 273.

62. Johansson, "*Kyrios*," 106.
63. Myers, *Strong Man*, 204.
64. See Liew's incisive interpretation of this pericope in Liew, *Politics of Parousia*, 135–7, where he suggests that Jesus grants her daughter healing because he is impressed not with the woman's argument but with her acquiescence to his marginalization of her. The story of the Gerasene demoniac and Jesus's occasional returns to the Decapolis are better evidence for Mark's Gentile inclusion. The relationship between those elements of Mark and the Syro-Phoenician woman is worth investigating in more detail than this study allows for.
65. Liew, *Politics of Parousia*, 134.
66. Horsley, *Hearing the Whole Story*, 203.
67. Liew, review of *Hearing the Whole Story* (by Horsley); Robert H. Gundry, "Richard A. Horsley's *Hearing the Whole Story*: A Critical Review of Its Postcolonial Slant," *JSNT* 26 (2003): 143.
68. Horsley, *Hearing the Whole Story*, 96.
69. Myers, *Strong Man,* 204.
70. See Shimon Applebaum, "Economic Life in Palestine," in *The Jewish People in the First Century: Historical Geography, Political History, Social, Cultural and Religious Life and Institutions*, ed. Shemuel Safrai and Menahem Stern, vol. 2, CRINT (Philadelphia, PA: Fortress Press, 1976), 631–700; Ekkehard Stegemann and Wolfgang Stegemann, *The Jesus Movement: A Social History of Its First Century*, trans. O. C. Dean, Jr. (Minneapolis, MN: Fortress Press, 1999); Horsley, *Hearing the Whole Story*, 31–6.
71. See the comparison between the Anointing Woman and Euryclea of Hom. *Od.* 19 in Dennis R. MacDonald, *The Gospels and Homer: Imitations of Greek Epic in Mark and Luke-Acts* (Lanham, MD: Rowman & Littlefield, 2015), 305.
72. Gideon Fuks, "Some Remarks on Simon Bar Giora," *Scripta Classica Israelica* 8–9 (1988): 113–15.

4

Military and Conquest

Much of the recoverable history of the ancient Near East and Mediterranean is a history of international relations and of war. Conquests and their various fallouts punctuate Israelite history. Greek, Roman, Hebrew, and Mesopotamian literature all center the etiologies of their peoples on historic, legendary, and cosmic battles. Cultural and governmental transitions in the ancient world (not too differently from our own time) often came about by means of or in concert with violent regime changes and shifts in imperial power. Mark's Gospel emerged in one such transitional period, after the end of Seleucid dominance of the eastern Mediterranean and in the middle of Rome's process of solidifying its own control in the same regions. This chapter examines the transition from Seleucid to Roman hegemony, including the transition from Seleucid to Hasmonean control in Israel, for what this history says about the expectations and norms surrounding international relations in the first century CE. Having established that historical background, I will then address how it manifests in the Gospel of Mark and how the Kingdom of God and the kingship of Jesus align with broader military ideologies.

Rome's Place in the Mediterranean History of War

An image of Rome as unique on the global and historical stage is not limited to Roman self-portrayal. In recent decades, as nineteenth- and twentieth-century lionization of Roman imperialism is being met with increasing skepticism, several of the postcolonialist and empire-critical New Testament scholars cited here frame the Roman empire as exclusively, excessively, and uniquely violent in its expansion and hegemony. Horsley states, "The politics of Roman Palestine was set up and maintained by imperial violence. In Galilee during the century before the mission of Jesus, the people suffered repeated conquest, with the slaughter of people and the destruction of villages leaving collective trauma in their wake."[1] This is despite considerably more nuance in his closer treatments of Judean and Galilean history in the same book. My intent is not to contradict the basic facts of these claims—Roman hegemony was ultimately maintained through the potential for if not always actual military force, and always with the benefit of the Roman elite as its primary impetus (on the Roman side). However, such a one-dimensional portrayal of the history inhibits clearer understanding of resistance to Rome and the alternatives that resistors might have imagined.

Therefore, I will briefly demonstrate several points. First, that Rome did not adhere to a consistent policy of expansion either over time or in the diverse regions of its activity. Next, that its strategies, policies, and individual actions were intelligible to the populations of the regions where it expanded, and in general were no different from those enacted by local kings and previous large empires, especially in the east. Finally, that in the Hellenistic east, Roman expansion might be better understood as a complex and long-running process of mutual assistance between Rome and its allies, increasingly in Rome's favor, rather than deliberate "world conquest" per se, no matter the globalizing emphasis of backward-looking Augustan propaganda.

Although the image of Rome as uniquely aggressive and brutal among Mediterranean states continues to circulate in biblical studies, it has been convincingly debunked by Arthur M. Eckstein, as well as earlier work by scholars such as Erich Stephen Gruen and Robert Kallet-Marx.[2] Eckstein interprets Roman history through the lens of political Realism, which he summarizes as the principle that "the explanation of much of the international behavior of states, both today and in the past, lies in their understandable self-seeking within a condition of violence and potential violence."[3] In situations without a meaningful central authority and enforceable international law, individual states may or may not engage in international violence depending on their own decision-makers and their power relative to neighboring states. Therefore, all states must at all times be prepared for their neighbors to make war. Such pressures are recursive and result in fluid, often tense, and sometimes unpredictable interstate relations.[4]

Applying this theory to antiquity, Eckstein observes that the Mediterranean world of the second and third centuries BCE was a multipolar anarchy, that is, "a world containing a plurality of powerful states, contending with each other for hegemony, within a situation where international law was minimal and in any case unenforceable."[5] His study finds that all of the major and minor powers under this system engaged in similar warlike and expansionist behavior, at levels commensurate with their relative power. Gruen and Kallet-Marx, writing twenty and ten years before Eckstein, respectively, likewise characterize Roman militarism in the East as a response to the militarism of surrounding powers. All three interpreters agree that the particular success of Roman expansion cannot be attributed to any uniquely warlike qualities of Roman culture: Hannibal, Andriscus, and Mithridates were no less bellicose and no more responding to perceived international pressures than their Roman counterparts.

Expansion in the Second and First Centuries BCE

An overview of Roman involvement in the Hellenistic world will demonstrate these points. This is not meant to be a comprehensive history, as several of the works cited serve that purpose admirably. Instead, it is a brief survey of important military and political actions in the second and first centuries BCE meant to contextualize and add nuance to perceptions of Roman militarism.

By the second century, Rome's economic and political interests had expanded into Greece, Macedonia, and Asia Minor. Local government structures were, for the most part, unimpeded by Rome,[6] and Roman military action was often, if not always, at the behest and/or to the aid of an ally. In the 210s, Philip V had sought to take advantage of Rome's defeat by Hannibal at Lake Trasimene and marched on the Illyrian coast, intent on expanding Macedonia's control westward while Rome was licking its wounds.[7] Rome's response, to ally with the Aetolian League in a war against Philip in Greece, marks what might be considered the beginning of Roman expansion east. Polybius thinks so—he sets 217 as the beginning of συμπλοκή ("interconnectedness") between the eastern and western Mediterranean, the point at which "two systems gradually began to merge into the one large and unified Mediterranean world that existed in Polybius' own time."[8] The war with Andriscus in the 140s was the culmination of more than half a century of mutual aggression between Rome and Antigonid Macedonia for the sake of influence in Greece. By the middle of the second century BCE, although Macedonia (divided now into four administrative regions) paid tribute to Rome, it apparently otherwise ruled itself,[9] a situation that, despite scholarly assumption otherwise, is not evidenced to have significantly altered after the 140s.[10]

The definitions of *imperium* and *provincia* in this period are loose and more conceptual than legal or territorial.[11] Rome benefited from the cooperation of its allies, the forthcomingness of its tributaries, and the security of both, but it did not exert direct control except in rare cases. In fact, much of Rome's military involvement in the east in the second century can be attributed to requests by allies. Andriscus (who styled himself Philip) had conquered Macedonia with Thracian funding and was threatening Thessaly when that city sent envoys to the Achaeans for help.[12] Rome declined to get involved until the Achaeans were unsuccessful against this expansionism.[13] Roman treaties with Greek and other eastern areas during the Late Republic are standardized, suggesting Roman advantage, but in all known cases were initiated by the other parties. Kallet-Marx expresses doubt as to the real benefit of these treaties to the Greek states who requested them, but they must have had some perceived advantage, even if it went no further than perception.[14]

The organizational and administrative practices that move Rome closer to what would be recognizable as an "empire" began in the late second and early first centuries BCE. After a period of, perhaps, inattention in Asia Minor and Syria, Rome began to act on "a nascent sense of imperial responsibility in the East," possibly triggered by a lack of eastern aid for its own German campaigns.[15] Conflicts among the Seleucid kings were proving destabilizing, allowing piracy to flourish and keeping Rome's allies busy on their home turf. By the 90s Mithridates and his allies were unseating Roman-backed kings across the north and east of the Anatolian peninsula,[16] forcing war.

Sulla's successes against Mithridates and Tigranes did not result in any new foreign policy per se, but the number of cities and regions under the direct or client control of Rome was now far greater than those that were not. This included direct taxation in Greece.[17] Nevertheless, Mithridates was not defeated and resurfaced in the 70s. Against multiple fronts, political complications, and the fluctuating popularity of generals already in the field, the senate passed the *lex Manilia* to give Pompey full control (*imperium*) over the armies in the east and the campaigns against Pontus and Armenia.[18] Pompey exercised the right to conquer and to "liberate" cities at his discretion, both as reward or punishment for aid to Rome or its enemies, and also as a political tool: his liberation of Phanagorea did not allow the city any particular privileges or favor from Rome, but kept it out of the hands of enemy kings.[19] He founded the first Roman colony in the east, Nicopolis in Armenia Minor, and populated it with his veterans.[20]

Warfare and Expansionism in Hellenistic Israel

1 Maccabees, most likely from the early first century BCE,[21] retells the campaigns, politics, and reigns of the Hasmonean dynasty up to John Hyrcanus. Jonathan Goldstein refers to it as "pro-Hasmonean propaganda."[22] This assertion is backed up in part by the characterization of the Hasmonean leaders as biblical conquerors and their conquests as righteous and pious (e.g., 1 Macc 2:42),[23] the casting of the Hasmoneans' enemies as "Kittim" (1:1) and other legendary rivals of Israel, and the portrayal of the Hasmoneans as leaders of a unified Israel against the "gentiles" and "renegade" or "lawless" Judeans (υἱοὶ παράνομοι; 1:11). Note the similarities between this characterization of the Hasmoneans, based in Hebrew tradition and scripture, and the appeals to Roman gods and tradition in Virgil and other Augustan writers.

Historically, the picture is rather more complicated. Josephus's *War* begins with a dispute between two priestly families, Onias versus the sons of Tobias, which is the setup that attracts the attention of Antiochus IV toward Jerusalem (*War* 1.2.1). 1 Maccabees is without this account and does not give a reason for Antiochus's sack of Jerusalem except plunder (1 Macc 1:20–23). In yet another version, 2 Maccabees accuses the brother of Onias—not the sons of Tobias as in Josephus—of first contact with Antiochus and of introducing Hellenism to Israel (2 Macc 2:7–17; 1 Macc 1:11 attributes Hellenization to anonymous "lawless sons"). In this text Antiochus, who is violent and bloodthirsty in Josephus and 1 Maccabees, begins as sympathetic figure who mourns the murder of Onias (2 Macc 4:35–38) and sacks Jerusalem on a misunderstanding (2 Macc 5:11).

Already, regardless of the reliability of any one of these texts, the often irreconcilable differences between the accounts hint at disunities and varying agendas among Jews/Judeans during the late Hellenistic and early Roman periods. They all find agreement, however, regarding the methods and strategies of expansion. Setting aside the biblical ideology apparent in 1 Maccabees, the Hasmonean conquests can be examined under the same light as the Roman ones, writ small. The Hasmoneans, like the Romans, the Seleucids, Mithridates, and so on, were expansionist. Under cover of prophecies and messianic expectations for the restoration of unified Israel, Mattathias and his descendants not only drove back Syrian armies from Jerusalem and Judea but also conquered territory in and around Samaria, Galilee, and Idumea.[24] They were not always welcome or viewed as liberators. In an ironic reflection of Antiochus's Hellenizing policies, the Hasmoneans mandated Judean practices—including forced circumcisions—throughout the regions they controlled. Likewise, the rulers of the Herodian dynasty used military means to expand and exert control over the regions they ruled, and rewarded loyalty and aid with their favor (e.g., Jos. *War* 1.19.4; *Ant.* 15.5).[25]

Generals and Military Leadership

Pompey

Gnaeus Pompeius is the quintessential Roman general (barring, perhaps, Julius Caesar himself), just as Augustus is its quintessential emperor. In his four-decade career as a commanding officer, Pompey changed the literal and figurative shape of the Republic. His long career in some of the most important military actions in Roman history guaranteed his place in a variety of literature, and he is a fitting case study for Roman ideals surrounding military command, and the ways in which Roman authors discussed their generals.

Pompey made his name in Sulla's second civil war. At the age of twenty-three he mustered his own army, without any official appointment, and joined Sulla's cause. If our sources are accurate, he did not suffer any military losses until the Sertorian war. By then, at the age of thirty, he already had a formidable and decorated military career, had celebrated a triumph (Plut. *Pomp.* 14), and possibly had turned down the opportunity to join the senate, offered despite his being too young (14.6).

After ridding the Mediterranean of a major piracy problem, Pompey was sent to Asia to assist Roman allies against the expansions of Tigranes and Mithridates. This assignment, called the Manilian Law after the senator who put it forward, in some ways marks the beginning of the eastern Roman empire as an administrative reality. With Asia, Pontus, Bithynia, and Cappadocia secured, Pompey then moved south into Syria, eventually seizing Jerusalem in an end-run around a civil war between Hasmonean leaders in 63 BCE. Thus Pompey brought more territory than ever under direct and indirect Roman control, ostensibly as a means of guaranteeing stability for allies in the east.

The Manilian Law granted Pompey extreme power. Besides his own army, it gave him control of the armies of the three other generals who had been fighting Mithridates, as well as unlimited access to the Roman treasury. It also granted him *imperium* in the east, in this case the ability to install and depose client rulers, create direct provinces and appoint their administrators, and set tributes. In short, for all practical purposes Pompey *was* Rome in the east during the 60s BCE.

Ancient portrayals of Pompey shed light on contemporary ideas about the roles and qualities of a general. Plutarch's description of his early career mentions not only his determination and skill but also his lack of personal ambition (Plut. *Pomp.* 8.4; 13.5; with a brief interruption for a triumph at ch. 14), his loyalty (13.1–2), and his temperance (18.2). Plutarch briefly describes several cases in which the young Pompey is accused of cruelty or ill treatment of prisoners (10.3–4), but immediately dismisses their apparent source as pro-Julian propaganda and comments that as Sulla's general, Pompey should be expected to deal harshly with Sulla's enemies (10.5). The very next episode, intended as a counterpoint to the accusations, is an account of Pompey showing particular mercy to an enemy and his city, going so far as to seal up his own soldiers' weapons (10.6–7). Ultimately, Pompey's downfall in Plutarch is not because of any moral failing but a strategic miscalculation: allowing himself to be separated from his navy at Pharsalis (76.2–3).

For more abject praise of Pompey we look to Cicero's oration in favor of the Manilian Law. After a long description of the circumstances of the war, arguing the need for a change in Roman strategy in the east, Cicero begins declaiming on qualities necessary in the ideal general, and then describing the ways in which Pompey meets them. First he lists "knowledge of warfare, skill [*virtus*], charisma [*auctoritas*], and luck" (Cic. *Leg. man.* 10.28); a page or so later are duty, courage, and wisdom (11.29); and yet later temperance and trustworthiness (13.36). To illustrate his point Cicero lists many of Pompey's conquests and successful campaigns and compares him favorably against deliberately unnamed previous generals who raided Italian cities and villages (as opposed to those of foreign rivals) and misused official funds (13.37–39).

From the other perspective, in his *Pharsalia*, the poet Lucan laments the horrors of Caesar's civil war, with ambivalence toward both of its main combatants. In the first book, he decries Pompey's old age, accusing him of going soft in the face of fame and comfort (Luc. 1.121–43). Caesar's speech against Pompey (1.299–351) is more acerbic: "Shall Pompey forsooth be glutted by his vile and venal minions with despotic power renewed so often without a break? … Shall Pompey cling forever to the posts he has once usurped?" (1.315, 317 [Duff, LCL]).

As with kings, the opposite of a good general is a despotic, excessive one, and writers uphold Pompey as an example of this, too. The beginning of Lucan's second book (up to line 233) describes the bloodthirst of Marius and Sulla, who both brought violence to the streets of Rome. However, a good general also makes use of violence when it is necessary or justified. Implicit in Lucan, and in some of the praises and critiques that I have already cited, is the value difference between wars and violence against foreigners and those against allies and especially fellow Romans. Plutarch narrates some of the "best" Romans and Greeks lamenting the greed and violence of the civil war between Caesar and Pompey, with the caveat that if their own conquests and honors weren't enough for these two accomplished generals and their followers, they could always satisfy their need for victory on the Parthians and the Germans, rather than turning it inward (Plut. *Pomp.* 70.1–2). There are, at all times in Roman, Greek, and Judean estimation, those who are naturally enemies and against whom war is always and easily justified.

Peace and War in Rome

The *Pax Romana*, the centuries-long "Roman peace" first attributed to Augustus, is not so much a fiction as very narrowly defined. Octavian's defeat of Antony at Actium effectively marked the end of seventy years of nearly constant warfare, including multiple civil wars. The occasional violent succession dispute notwithstanding, the internal regions of the Roman empire, particularly Italy, enjoyed widespread peace and the resulting prosperity until the death of Marcus Aurelius in 180 CE.

However, peace for Italy and the internal provinces was concurrent with war and military occupation farther afield. Wars conducted by Romans against other Romans were replaced, largely, by expansionist action and revolts in Thrace, Gaul, Germany, Judea, and other frontier regions. The bulk of the direct Roman action in the first century CE was in Spain and Germany.[26] In the east, client kingdoms stood in between Rome and the Parthians, resulting in less direct Roman military intervention in those regions. Thus, to make a relevant example, there was very little activity of legions in or around Judea from the Herodian period until the start of the Judean War. The local armies were Herodian, recruited from Sebaste and Caesarea Maritima and primarily made up of ethnic Judeans, Samaritans, and Syrians.[27]

Against this backdrop—the end of internal warfare and the expansion and security credited to peripheral warfare—it is apparent that peace, for imperial Rome, was less the absence of war than a sign of its success. Whatever the granular realities of diplomacy with so many neighbors, in Roman iconography and literature of the early empire, the ideal diplomatic relationship is successful war or its avoidance by superior might, not statecraft and compromise. Horace's *Carmen Saeculare*, commissioned by Augustus for performance in 17 BCE, lauds Roman peace in part by expressing the terror and submission of Roman enemies (Hor. *Carm. Saec.* 53–56). Here, also, the jibes at aging Pompey are relevant—after decades of successful military leadership, his life in comfort before the war against Caesar is portrayed as softening and even corrupting him, not as a reward he has earned. He is a military man, and without constantly renewed military glory he becomes a joke.

The imagery and ideology of war in the imperial period focuses on defense and conquest on the peripheries of the empire. The Flavian response to success in Judea in the first century is a prime example of the ways in which Roman military success in the frontier regions was marshalled to emphasize peace in Italy and the nearer provinces, and to solidify Roman identity versus foreigners. The famous *Judaea capta* coins represent Judea as a subjugated figure, often a woman, kneeling or otherwise on the ground, often with a soldier, the emperor, or a suit of armor towering over her.[28] Similarly, the Arch of Titus depicts the sack of the Jerusalem temple and the transport of its treasures to Rome. Titus preceded his return to Rome with marches through cities in Syria, displaying Judean captives (Jos. *War* 7.5.1–2). At the triumph that he shared with Vespasian, captives as well as spoils were paraded through the city, and the finale was the execution of the captured Judean general Simon (7.5.4–6). Afterward, Vespasian built a temple to Pax as a goddess, storing there, among other things, treasures from the Jerusalem temple (7.5.8). Here is a direct visual, ritual, and persistent linking of internal Roman peace to the subjugation of peripheral defiance. Even more important is Judea's status as a province, and the fact of diaspora communities in most of the empire's major cities, including Rome itself—the pomp and circumstance of Roman victory at Jerusalem not only served as a locus for Roman identity versus the eastern foreigner but also as a warning against internal resistance.

Battlefield Gods

One common refrain in scholarly treatments of Jesus's exorcisms and healings is that they represent "spiritual" conflict or take place in the "spiritual realm," with the strong implication that this is different from everyday life despite the very physical effects they have on the people in Mark's narrative. One remedy to this anachronism is an understanding of the larger tradition of divine action in war.

Greek and Roman Examples

The Greek (and by extension the Roman) mythological tradition is full of battlefield gods—particularly Ares but also including Pan, Aphrodite, and others. By the early empire, stories of Olympian-style gods physically participating in contemporary battles diminish, and the emphasis instead turns to gods' favor for armies or specific commanders or to the martial victories of deified rulers. Even in Homeric and other mythological literature, the gods rarely, if ever, fight as *armies*. A single deity, or a pair or small group, will join a human army already in the process of battle—and may or may not choose the ultimately winning side. The *Iliad*, of course, is the most famous example, with major and minor deities making numerous appearances on the battlefield, but it is not alone.

Of particular interest is the failed Gallic invasion of Greece in the third century BCE after a disastrous attempt on Delphi. According to the second-century CE author Pausanias, after a less than completely successful march from the southern Balkans and around Thermopylae, the Gallic army of Brennus came to Delphi, where Apollo had promised, through his oracle, to defend what was his (10.22.12). This divine defense (10.23.1–10) began with a day of earthquakes and lightning storms, followed by the apparitions of dead heroes during the battle. At night the attackers were beset by snow and lethal rock falls. Fleeing battle after Brennus was injured, the Gauls were overtaken by delusions and fear that Pausanias attributes to both Pan and Apollo, though primarily the latter. Other accounts of the battle likewise credit Apollo with the rout of the Gauls, including mentions of epiphanies of Apollo as well as other deities during the fighting.[29]

This account is illuminating for Mark, particularly the sea miracles (4:35–41; 6:47–52) and ch. 13, because it demonstrates material divine help by means of natural disaster, mental influence comparable to some of Mark's demon-possession narratives, and, in some accounts, the actual appearance of the god to fight in the battle. Importantly, in this account no gods appear on the Gallic side, nor is there any indication that the gods and spirits that do appear are fighting anyone other than the human Gallic army. There is no spiritual analogue of the battle, only the battle itself, with human, dead, and divine combatants. Apollo saves, and there is no question of his salvation being metaphorical or somehow relegated to the "spiritual realm."

Battlefield aid in stories such as this one is part and parcel of the god's role as protector of the sanctuary and/or the city. In *Iliad* 22.166–336, Hector's defeat at the hands of Achilles only comes after he has lost the aid of the gods. In fact, a large portion of the drama of that epic has to do with which army or warrior particular gods have chosen to protect, and the fact that neither side can win until one side's gods withdraw their protection. More contemporaneously with Mark, Roman authors of the empire and the late Republic take for granted the protective benefits of divine favor. Rome adopted foreign cults, most famously that of Magna Mater, during times of war and other crises. The practice of *evocatio*, calling a tutelary god away from a city to allow for its capture or destruction, appears in several ancient authors, especially in relation to the sack of Carthage, such as in Macrobius's description (*Sat.* 3.9.7-8) and a reference in Horace (*Odes* 2.25-28). Pliny suggests this was a common practice (*Nat.* 28.18-19), although it appears in the accounts of relatively few sieges. John Kloppenborg has proposed that the *evocatio* is a helpful referent for understanding Mark's treatment of the temple and thus the dating of the Gospel.[30]

Judean Backgrounds

The near eastern tradition likewise accounts for battlefield gods, but by the end of the Hellenistic period, Judean literature had developed a discourse of divine armies—angelic and demonic—that fought alongside or even in the stead of human combatants. Aleksander Michelak connects the often complex angelologies of Second Temple, early Christian, and Rabbinic literature with earlier Hebrew accounts of the divine council and of God as one who musters and commands armies.[31] The title Lord of Hosts (יהוה צבאות) is frequent in Hebrew literature, including in contexts that preclude a human (Israelite) army. Isa 10:21-23, for example, refers to God by that title but declares that Israel will be reduced to remnants, and likewise Judah in 2 Kgs 19:31. Correspondingly, God appears at the head of a divine army in Ps 68, and even more explicitly in Deut 33:2-3.

Daniel gives personalities to two of these divine soldiers. Gabriel first appears in ch. 8 to interpret Daniel's vision of the rams, and again in ch. 9 to give the prophecy of seventy weeks. The unnamed angel of the apocalypse in chs. 10-12 interacts with Daniel similarly to Gabriel in the previous encounters, leading some interpreters to conclude that they are the same being.[32] Gabriel's function in Daniel and later literature is primarily as a messenger and deliverer of oracles, but his name seems to point to a martial personality.[33] If he is the angel in chs. 10-12, he identifies himself as one of two heavenly commanders against Persia and Greece in v. 10:21. Michael also appears in these chapters, though not in person to Daniel. The revelatory angel names him as the other commander against the Persian and Greek princes (10:21), and in 12:1-3 declares that Michael will finish the war between the kings of the south and north, and usher in the resurrection and the eschaton. Note here that unlike in 1 Enoch (below), but like Apollo at Delphi, the angelic commanders march against earthly kingdoms, who may or may not have their own divine commanders or regiments.

The Book of Watchers, the first thirty-five chapters of 1 Enoch, has an even more developed angelology, steeped in military imagery and language. The opening theophany depicts God as a cosmic conqueror, marching down from heaven with his army (1:4) and subduing not only enemies but nature itself (1:1-9). Given that introduction, it is perhaps justifiable to read the regimented obedience of nature in chs. 2-5 through a military lens, which in turn has implications for the reference to the flood narrative in ch. 10—the earth itself and its elements can serve in God's army, as they serve in Apollo's.

More importantly, the angels in the text appear in military roles. Of the two hundred that swear to rebel against God's command, nineteen are named as "chiefs of tens" (6:7-8). Compare, for example, to the lists of commands in Exod 18:25 and Deut 1:15. Certainly the title evokes a military structure even without specific scriptural citations, but the wording fits in with the larger theme of scripture-inspired language throughout the text of 1 Enoch. On the other side, the obedient angels—in this text Michael, Gabriel, Uriel, and Raphael (9:1)—are not portrayed as commanders of units, but the text does juxtapose them against the military Watchers and casts them as those in charge of defeating the rebels.

Chapter 10 is especially relevant for the military imagery of the Book of Watchers and its ideology of war. God charges the loyal angels with capturing and imprisoning the rebels (a common fate of enemy officers, in this case particularly since the text does not seem to allow execution as an option), and specifically sends Gabriel to set the children of the Watchers against each other in battle until they wipe themselves out (10:8-13). The last verses of ch. 10 (17-22) promise peace and prosperity for the righteous following this war against the Watchers and their children, again categorizing peace as an outcome of successful war, as in some of the Roman texts we have seen.

Markan Militarism

Although there are few narrative texts describing it, exorcism was a common practice in the ancient Mediterranean. The *Greek Magical Papyri* (*PGM*), a series of composite texts spanning at least the second and third centuries CE, give instructions for ridding a client of various ailments, influences, and spirits, as do the Qumran scrolls. In the first century, Josephus mentions the exorcist Eleazar (*Ant.* 8.2.5) as part of a discussion of Solomon's magical skill and tradition. One interesting aspect of this account is its management of credulity: Josephus cites Eleazar as a proof of Solomon and the continued relevance and power of Solomon's work, and Eleazar, according to Josephus, proved his own efficacy by commanding a demon to upset a bucket of water after it had been cast out. Thus we see that exorcism and therefore the idea of the demonic were commonplace, requiring no explanation, but that the exorcist himself might still require proof against charlatanism. Whether the audience might have questioned the existence of the demon and the very premise of the exorcism, like a modern reader might, is not clear from the passage.

One ongoing problem in the interpretation of Jesus's exorcisms is the argument that Gospel reports do not resemble the majority of extra-biblical exorcism accounts or formulas brought into comparison. That is, there is no recitation of hymns, psalms, or spells; Jesus does not explicitly marshal the power of any other deity or spirit in order to cast out demons; and there are no traces of sympathetic or apotropaic objects or activities. Jesus speaks, and demons respond.[34]

A partial solution to this is to excise our vocabulary of the term "report." The Gospels are neither eyewitness accounts nor magical manuals. Portrayals of exorcisms are part of the character- and world-building work of the narratives, and the Gospel authors are all invested in Jesus as something more than just an exorcist. Some commentators have explained the lack of "magic" in Jesus's exorcisms in precisely that way: an indication that Jesus is more powerful and, perhaps, more divine than the average sorcerer.[35] In Mark, the close connection of the word ἐξουσία with exorcism, made explicit in 1:27, suggests that for the purposes of the narrative, the exorcisms are important primarily as expressions of Jesus's commission, not as activity in their own right.

Further, it is possible and even necessary to question the very basis of the problem. Graham Twelftree has shown that the ancient evidence allows for a wider range of exorcism types than scholars often assume, including simple vocal outcastings like Jesus's, with no apparent use of magical objects or extended rituals.[36] Even the *PGM*, with its reputation for sometimes unbelievable complexity, contains relatively simple exorcisms comprising mainly or only vocal incantations.[37]

For the most part, ancient exorcisms do not seem to be explicitly associated with war. That is, incantations do not make use of battlefield imagery, ritual actions do not imitate combat (cf. *PGM* 4.1248–52, which prescribes the use of a branch to represent a scourge), and the conflict is treated as between individuals: the possessing spirit, the exorcist, and the patient/client are all singular in most texts. In some contexts the incantation might call on more than one deity, but nothing resembling an army. So, the presence of exorcisms in Mark does not on its own speak to any martial theme.

However, if a martial theme has already been identified—which I have argued it has, with the conflict between the kingdoms of God and Satan as a particular example—applying that lens to the exorcism scenes and related interactions can produce fruitful interpretations. Again, the vocabulary of authority is important here. Not only does the word ἐξουσία only appear in relation to Jesus, nearly half of its occurrences (all of the pre-Jerusalem occurrences, before ch. 11) are in the context of exorcism, and others, such as 2:10, are connected to healings—and Mark differentiates healing from exorcism but often pairs them. If Jesus's ἐξουσία is part of his characterization within the rulership structure of the Kingdom of God, then the exorcisms can be interpreted as the actions of a ruler.

At this point we should also recall the history of the angelic and demonic in Judea and the Near East. Even if post-Hasmonean exorcisms do not display clear-cut military themes, exorcism as a category is only a small part of the wider mythic structure of angels and demons, which is explicitly and perhaps fundamentally military before, during, and long after this period.

A helpful contribution to this question is Horsley's inclusion of anthropological studies on illness and madness in colonized and postcolonial cultures. He cites several examples from the modern world where forms of illness, madness, or demonic activity function as resistance to domination by outside political powers. Applying these insights to Hellenistic and Roman Israel, he identifies the conflicts between Jesus and various satanic or demonic agents as a narrative reflection of Roman dominance over the people of the region.[38] In that reading, and considering a postwar date for Mark, it is difficult not to see the echoes of military action in Mark's exorcism narratives—Simon bar Giora's rebellion failed, but Jesus's conquest succeeds.

Eschatological Violence

The worldview inherent to Mark is violent. Opposition on the highest cosmic level, between God and Satan, plays out in daily life as factionalism, bodily and mental illness, and economic inequality. Other texts from the Hasmonean and early Roman periods, including many of the Qumran texts, also attest to similar dualistic, conflict-heavy worldviews. Eschatological violence—that is, cosmic warfare that may or may not be mirrored temporally, and/or divine judgment of individuals for reward or punishment in the afterlife—is a feature of many, though not all, of the texts commonly identified as apocalypses. The overarching message of such themes is that God is the ultimate ruler of the universe and exerts or will exert his power over all things, to the destruction of any resistance.

Mark exhibits this view repeatedly. The exorcisms, as well as the Beelzebul controversy in ch. 3, show the dualistic opposition between Satan and God. Jesus's preaching in Galilee is often accompanied by healings and exorcisms (e.g., 1:32-34; 3:3-12). Eschatological judgment for the individual is also a recurring theme. The call to repent in preparation for (or at) the "arrival" of the Kingdom of God (1:15) carries an implicit warning for the one who does not repent. That warning becomes explicit in 9:42-48, where Jesus names the consequences for not entering the kingdom.

Chapter 13, even if it does not meet the formal requirements of the "apocalypse" genre,[39] certainly qualifies as apocalyptic in the minds of most interpreters, and is the section of Mark that most explicitly frames Jesus's activity and message in terms of war and conquest.

The chapter begins with Jesus's prediction of the destruction of the temple, taken by most interpreters as *ex eventu* prophecy. In *War*, Josephus relates that initially the temple burned (6.4), but after Titus had taken control of Jerusalem he ordered the whole city demolished, including the temple (7.1). Regardless of historical accuracy, Mark 13's imagery of a city's most glorious buildings reduced to rubble is almost unmistakably warlike, particularly in the context of first-century Jerusalem.[40]

Jesus's "birthpangs" prophecy in 13:3-8 warns the disciples of "wars and rumors of wars," with formulaic language about nations and kingdoms (ἔθνος and βασιλεία). He also warns of "many" coming "in my name," a reference to the many prophets, rebels, and apocalyptic preachers that arose in prewar Judea. In a particularly tragic episode in *War*, a "false prophet" convinces a number of people to flee into the temple and onto its walls, where they are trapped as the building burns and Roman soldiers move through (6.5.2). The reference to famines has generic as well as historical basis (Jos. *War* 6.3.3). Although food shortages might be caused by siege, burning of fields, or loss of labor power to war, they are also a natural occurrence, and paired with earthquakes here highlight the cosmic relevance of the battles to come. Passages associating natural disasters, agricultural failure, and cosmic signs with war abound in Hebrew prophetic literature, as well as Second Temple apocalyptic literature such as 1 Enoch and 2 Baruch.

From this wide view, Jesus then narrows down to individuals, who he says will face judicial persecutions. As a specifically Christian problem, these will become wider known in the second and third centuries. In the first century, Nero's persecution of the early 60s comes to mind, and we might speculate on what stories (even first- or second-hand accounts) the author could know of executions among Jesus's close circle. However, these are not the only possible reference points. The familial conflicts of v. 12 are, like the famines in the previous passage, both stereotypical language (e.g., 2 Esd 5:9; 6:24) and traceable to events associated with the Judean War (Jos. *War* 4.3.2). Loyalty and disloyalty are, of course, volatile subjects especially during times of war. The last line of this passage, promising salvation to those who endure, recalls ubiquitous attitudes honoring combatants who refuse to surrender, and looks forward to the eschatological features of the chapter.

The "desolating sacrilege" of v. 14 is often brought forward as evidence for prewar composition. There is no record of Titus erecting or attempting to erect anything in the temple, but the problem had come up under both Caligula and Nero. The phrasing itself is a citation of LXX Dan 12:11, which most likely finds clarification in 1 Macc 1:54, when Antiochus erects an unidentified statue or altar on the Jerusalem altar.[41] Mark's use of Son of Man already indicates familiarity with Daniel, so the citation here may simply be an attempt to further align the text with recognized prophecy, even if there has not (yet, for the author) been such a sacrilege. It is just as possible, however, that the author applies Daniel's language to something less obvious. The aside to the reader would support such an interpretation. In that case the possibilities are numerous. Both the fire and the later demolition might be candidates, although the verb ἑστηκότα seems to preclude them, if we are to take it literally and not as part of the Danielic imagery. Josephus has the Roman soldiers offer sacrifices at the temple gates after the fire (*War* 6.6.1), shortly before Titus gives a speech near the temple (6.6.2).[42] If either of these episodes is historical, it might serve. Looking away from Jerusalem, we might consider Titus's shows and executions in Caesarea (7.3.1), the siege of Masada, or some event that was not otherwise recorded.

The injunction to flight in vv. 14–16 is an important part of Mark's response to the war and attitude toward suffering. The three passion predictions emphasize the *necessity* of Jesus's suffering and death on the cross. Likewise, 10:30–40 predict the suffering of James and John, but do not indicate any special reward it might earn them (certainly not the one they ask for). Here, Jesus explicitly tells followers to seek safety without hesitation. This passage frames Jesus followers as noncombatants, helpless against the destruction about to come down on them. The woe for pregnant and nursing mothers and the general lament for the coming suffering argue against the kind of celebration of martyrdom apparent in Acts and other second-century and later texts, but this passage also describes a different kind of suffering. These are not the individual judicial persecutions of vv. 9–13 (which likewise predict suffering but do not glorify it), this is flight in the face of oncoming armies. Whatever loyalty one might demonstrate by speaking boldly before judges and kings, one should *survive* this particular cataclysm.

Importantly, v. 20 makes it clear that God is in control of the disaster, but will allow it to happen. The whole passage is reminiscent of wartime prophecy, in which God causes or allows destruction in order to create room for a new, more pious generation. The warning against false prophets and messiahs again recalls the many prophets and splinter leaders that appeared in the region during Roman rule.

So far, the prophecy has indicated earthly sufferings, events that are stereotypically associated with war and also were experienced in various ways during the Roman conflict. The earthquakes of v. 8 are perhaps the exception, but in many ancient worldviews, natural disasters were closely associated with political and social upheaval. Verse 24 indicates a shift: after all of the foregoing things, the truly cosmic implications of the struggle will become apparent. It is important here to remember that for most ancient Mediterranean people, the cosmos was a unified system—the activity of the divine did not take place in a "spiritual realm" separate from human reality. While, from a postcolonial perspective, such cosmic dramas are expressions of desire and fantasy,[43] we should not necessarily take that language in the vernacular sense of idle imagination or "wishful thinking." The witness of Paul (e.g., 1 Thess 4:13-17) indicates that at least some Jesus followers awaited literal cosmic salvation.

Mark's chronology is urgent. Verse 24 places the destruction of the heavens "after the troubles," and depending on when in the 70s the Gospel was composed, that either means "very soon now" or "any minute." Verse 26 points us back to Daniel, and the full passage to which Mark alludes is telling:

> I saw a vision during the night,
> and behold, one like a human being [ὡς υἱὸς ἀνθρώπου] was coming
> on the clouds of heaven,
> and one like an ancient of days was with him,
> and those placed at his disposal were beside him.
>
> And authority was given to him,
> and all nations of the earth and all peoples,
> and all glory serving him;
> And his authority is eternal,
> such that might never be taken away,
> and his kingdom,
> such that might never be corrupted. (Dan 7:13-14 [LXX])

The Son of Man, who must suffer, according to Mark 8:31; 9:31; and 10:33-34, is now the eschatological and eternal ruler over the whole earth. Mark adjusts Daniel's image, but does not significantly change it. In Mark 13, the Son of Man comes "with great power and glory"—μετὰ δυνάμεως πολλῆς καὶ δόξης—and with a cadre of angels who will seek out the elect from across the world and gather them together. The text does not indicate what happens next; we might assume that Mark's early audience had an idea about where they were to be gathered *to*. Regardless, the Son of Man (i.e., Jesus) is shown in this passage to be the eschatological hero.

Compared to ch. 13, the passage in ch. 14 ("you will see the Son of Man seated at the right hand of power and coming with the clouds of heaven") is more explicit in its identification of Jesus as the Son of Man, but in either place, it should be apparent to the reader that Jesus uses that title for himself. The high priest's question preceding the ch. 14 saying makes that the only place in Mark where Jesus claims the title Messiah fully and without qualification. The image of "sitting at the right hand" in 14:62 is unequivocally royal: Jesus appears as the second-in-command to the monarch, like Titus to Vespasian.

There is a point of translation that I am not aware of having been made before: the military connotations of δύναμις in 13:25–26. There are, in fact, three occurrences of the word that deserve attention here. The more general use will be treated in Chapter 6.

The word δύναμις occurs twice in ch. 13. The usage in 13:25, "the powers in the heavens will be shaken," corresponds to that at 6:14 ("powers at work through him"). Both use the plural form in the sense of independent entities or forces. However, in the context of ch. 13, which envisions cosmic war, v. 13:25 reflects a cosmology found throughout ancient Mediterranean literature and important for the development of Christian as well as Gnostic eschatology: there are entities that rule the heavens and the world, who might be favorably or disfavorably disposed toward humanity depending on individual traditions. Within the New Testament there are similar usages at Rom 8:38 and Eph 6:12. In the context of military and political chaos, it is easy to envision or represent these powers as enemy combatants.

Immediately following, 13:26 repeats the vocabulary but changes its sense: "they will see the Son of Man coming in the clouds with great power and glory." To interpret this passage, we look to a similar one earlier. The use of δύναμις at 9:1 is new so far in Mark. For the first time it does not refer to Jesus or to any wondrous event. It is usually translated similarly to the NRSV rendering: "the Kingdom of God has come with power." Collins translates ἐν δυνάμει "with power" but also suggests "powerfully" in her comments.[44] Non-source-critical discussion of this saying focuses on whether it refers to the parousia, the crucifixion, or even the transfiguration.[45]

Lacking in discussion of this passage is a thorough consideration of the military implications of the Kingdom of God. To put it bluntly, there is no reason, linguistic or thematic, why one option for understanding this saying cannot be "the Kingdom of God has come with an army." Authors use δύναμις in the sense of an armed force at least from the classical period on; while it is not the most common usage, it is far from minor.[46] Military or political writings such as those by Demosthenes (e.g., *Ex.* 21.3; Dem. 4.28; Dem. 19.264) or Xenophon (e.g., *Ana.* 1.1.6) are obvious references, but closer to Mark in time or context are similar usages in Josephus (e.g., *War* 1.3.7) and the LXX translation of the Hebrew title Lord of Hosts (יהוה צבאות), κύριος τῶν δυνάμεων (e.g., 2 Sam 6:2; 2 Kgs 19:31).

Verse 13:27 confirms this sense. As we have seen, angels in Hebrew tradition originated with military roles and maintained them long past this period. Immediately on the heels of the shaking of "the powers" in the heavens (v. 25), the image of the Son of Man coming and sending out his angels certainly allows us to picture this apocalyptic general with a heavenly army at his back. The mission in ch. 13 leans more toward search and rescue than conquest, though we might ask what shook the powers in the first place.

In light of a military translation of δύναμις for these verses, the case is even stronger for a military understanding of other aspects of the Gospel. In Mark's narrative, the kingdom of Satan is the opposition to the kingdom of God, and thus Jesus's and the disciples' (i.e., his appointed commanders') exorcisms can be understood as skirmishes for territory prefacing the final siege of ch. 13.

The Triumphal Entry (11:1-11)

The entry into Jerusalem is one of the most famous pre-crucifixion images of Jesus's activity. Popular interpretation emphasizes the joy of the crowd and the oxymoronic humility of God's Son parading through the streets to great fanfare, riding a less-than-glorious donkey. Whether or not to glean the symbolism of the Roman triumph ritual has been a debate in Markan scholarship at least since the 1990s. The scene contains a few basic elements of the triumph—that is, a person riding into a city while the populace hails him as a conqueror. However, it is missing others, most conspicuously not only the conquest itself but also the spoils, representation of the vanquished foe, and the humiliation and (often) execution of a defeated general or king.

The usual explanation for the lack of a war having been won is simple enough: this is a pretriumph, looking forward to Jesus as the eschatological king after the resurrection. In that case, depending on the interpreters' theological emphasis, the enemy in question might be Rome, the Jerusalem temple cult (often with more or less explicit supercessionism), or even Satan or Death themselves. The irony that Jesus, who triumphs in ch. 11, will be executed as a (crowned) rebel in ch. 15 further remedies the problem of missing details, and drives the poignancy of his entry into Jerusalem, a clever interplay on Mark's part that Allan T. Georgia has capably teased open.[47]

The triumph ritual itself is not necessarily simple to reconstruct. The basic outline of the parade is straightforward: the spoils of war, including captives and accompanied by dancers and other performers, preceded the triumphator, who was decked out in martial and/or kingly splendor with his face painted red. Following him came any Romans whom he had freed in the process of the victory, and then finally the soldiers themselves. The parade moved from the Campus Martius, through the Triumphal Gate, across the Circus Maximus and the forum to end at the Capitoline Hill, where prisoners were usually executed and the triumphator or others performed sacrifices to Jupiter Capitolinum.[48] Beyond that, however, it is difficult to say much with certainty. For one thing, as Mary Beard is quick to point out, a thousand years of ritual practice cannot have been completely uniform[49]—at what point in the development of the triumph any one of these elements might have come into practice, and what pieces might have been lost, not to mention variations of individual occasions, are all lost to us.

As a subject of description, the triumph also serves as a locus for more abstract discussions of Roman identity, including the decay of society and the glory of the Good Old Days. Pliny the Elder takes a moment in his discussion of pearls to describe some of the ostentatious fineries supposedly on display at Pompey's triumph after his defeat of Mithridates, including a bust of the general constructed out of pearls. Pliny's offense at the "triumph of luxury" is palpable (Plin. *Nat.* 37.6). Similarly, Dionysius of Halicarnassus describes Romulus's triumph in splendorous terms, complete with the display of captured treasure, public feasting, and songs of celebration, but nonetheless goes on to lament that "modern" triumphs (i.e., first century BCE, and almost certainly with at least partial reference to Pompey's) overindulge in theatrics and have become more about the ostentatious display of wealth than the honorable celebration of valor (Dion. Hal. *Ant. Rom.* 2.34). The possibility that more than a century of retelling has exaggerated Pompey's display is beside Pliny's point, but relevant to mine.

The purpose of a triumph, or of a παρουσία into a conquered city, is to demonstrate the might of the conqueror and the new status of the conquered. This is not a one-time announcement, but one that the conqueror reiterates in art, coinage, plaques and inscriptions, architecture (and sometimes large-scale urban layout changes), administrative appointments, and many other ways. The triumph is neither the conquest nor the rule of the conquered, but its ritualization. The repetition of the triumph in art, oral repetition, and literature likewise repeats and refreshes the ritual.

The triumph, as part of the larger genre of victorious entries into (usually conquered) cities was as much about the subsequent telling of the ritual as its enactment. The sheer magnitude of Pompey's triumph, as it survives in first- and second-century CE authors, approaches the unbelievable. Plutarch says that the parade was carried over to a second day in order to display it all, and even then there was enough left over for a whole separate triumph (Plut. *Pomp.* 45.1). It is not important whether Plutarch and Pliny are correct in their details—the story itself is important, not necessarily for Pompey's own status but as a representation of Roman conquest and identity. The passage in Pliny, already cited, is a moment for him to lament the loss of what he views as the quintessentially Roman ideals of austerity and personal humility—a common complaint in the late republic and early empire. The spoils signify a double standard: both Roman abundance as the result of the conquest and the decadent and therefore justifiably defeated east, a trope at least as old as the Persian Wars that in both Greek and Roman usage emphasizes the superior values of the west.[50]

What does this mean for Jesus? Some authors have treated Vespasian and Titus's triumph as the most relevant comparison for the Jerusalem entry.[51] This event took place in 71—after the main victories of the war but before the fall of Masada—and therefore most likely preceded the authorship of Mark. However, locating the author of the Gospel in Judea or Galilee, rather than Rome, complicates the literary relationship. Further, there are no details of that triumph, besides the double triumphators, that sets it appreciably apart from any other. In fact, Josephus's description (*War* 7.5.3-7) echoes descriptions of Pompey's, which were certainly in circulation around the same time and might believably have had an effect on the planning of the actual event in 71, and well as subsequent descriptions of it.

While it is difficult to name any specific Roman texts or tales the author of Mark might have known, the text shows familiarity with Roman language and ideas, and so it is appropriate to discuss ch. 11 with reference to triumphs (and παρουσίαι) as a category rather than to any specific occasion. In that case, the elements of the ritual most relevant to Mark are the procession into the city, both of the conqueror and the captives, the approach to the temple of Jupiter, and the execution of the captives. Another possible touchpoint is the mockery of the triumphator by his soldiers, attested in Pompey's case but not Vespasian and Titus's, nor in Dio's account of Augustus's triumph in 29 BCE (Dio 51.21.5-7).

Georgia argues that Mark's Jerusalem entry and passion narrative imitate the triumph "not in terms of a *narrative* parallel, but with respect to the *ritual* movements, symbolic categories, and performative logic employed in the Roman triumph."[52] The distinction between narrative and ritual here, for Georgia, excuses Mark of any inaccuracy or deviation in representing a triumph per se and focuses our attention on the purpose of the event, both in Rome and for Mark. The triumph enacts the victory for those unable to witness it firsthand.[53] For the Roman populace (both in the city at the live event and, through art, coinage, literature, and so on, to the wider empire) this comes after the fact a confirmation and demonstration of what has most likely been circulating by word of mouth. In Mark, for the fictional residents of Jerusalem as well as for Mark's reader, the performance comes before the victory, staging the eschaton for those awaiting it.

Georgia's analysis focuses on Jesus as both victor and captive, and as victor *because* of his captivity and death. He unfortunately does not develop the role of Jerusalem in this ritual logic. The city, in fact, allows us to zoom out even further, without losing sight of the specifically Roman triumph, to a wider view of postbattle processional entries. Quintus Curtius Rufus's description of Alexander's entry into Babylon (Curt. 5.1.17–23) hits many of the same marks as descriptions of Roman triumphs, in nearly the same order:[54] the defeated (in this case surrendering) general and his army head up a procession that includes precious gifts to Alexander, priests and musicians celebrating his arrival, Babylonian townspeople, the Macedonian army, and finally Alexander himself. The whole affair takes place on a richly decorated parade route, surrounded by the residents of the city.[55] The difference, of course, is that instead of returning home to announce his great victory over the foreigner, Alexander is taking over the reign of Babylon as a liberator from Persian rule. Here again, as in Roman expansionist texts, we see the logic of conquest as liberation. Alexander does not return Babylon to its own rule, except inasmuch as he makes it the capital of his own expansionist empire. And yet Alexander's rule, at least as far as our surviving sources are concerned, is freedom, if it replaces Persian "despotism."[56]

Given the time period and the context, it is possible to read in Mark 11 both an entry into a liberated city and an announcement of victory afar. The episode comes after Jesus's work in Galilee, where he was repeatedly on the "front lines" of battle against demons. Jerusalem's place as the center of the Judean world allows us to see this entry as a triumph in the Roman sense: Jesus has defeated the enemies on the peripheries, and all that remains for him is to announce his victory to the home populace and carry out the necessary sacrifices. On the other hand, Jesus's conflicts with the priesthood, and especially Mark's treatment of them and other leadership factions as corrupt and wealth-driven, recall Alexandrian and earlier Greek liberations of cities from the "decadent" and "despotic" Persians.

There is even a third facet. Mark's subtle and not-so-subtle devaluations of the temple throughout the Gospel cast a more violent shadow on Jesus's entry in ch. 11. Although the populace celebrates him, his visit to the temple in ch. 11 will end in a small-scale sack, and the final omen accompanying his death in ch. 15 will be the actual damage of the building. Here Jesus reflects less the celebratory Pompey and Alexander, and more the inimical Antiochus (1 Macc 1:21–23) and Titus (Jos. *War* 6.8–10), not to mention Nebuchadnezzar, looting Jerusalem and the temple.

This is a complex comparison, made even more layered with the addition of Jesus's paradoxically glorifying death. The sacrificial victim as the king is, of course, a core subject of Christian theology and art down the centuries.

Conclusion

From a modern perspective, there is not much military about Jesus's activity in Mark. He preaches to crowds in synagogues and out in the open; he heals injuries and diseases, and casts out demons; he proclaims the arrival of the Kingdom of God, which will put an end to the activities of Satan and the abuses of a religious elite. Finally, he is arrested, beaten, and executed via a method known for its intense cruelty and humiliation. These are hardly the activities of a warrior. However, if we put aside the lens of religion and immerse ourselves in the historical context of first-century Judea and the Roman empire, new meanings take shape. In the ancient Mediterranean, there are few examples of wholly peaceful expansion. Kings and kingdoms do not "arrive" without military implications, either to enact or defend from violent conquest. Rulers gain and maintain their seats with the backing of armies. Emperors (or senate bodies) deploy generals and client kings to be the local enforcers of imperial power. Crucifixion is a punishment for rebels and revolutionaries. The movement of soldiers, reward of allies, punishment of enemies, and raiding of cities are normal operations of kingdoms and their rulers, and these activities are reflected over and over again in the Gospel of Mark.

Notes

1. Richard A. Horsley, *Jesus and the Politics of Roman Palestine* (Columbia: University of South Carolina Press, 2014), 54.
2. Arthur M. Eckstein, *Mediterranean Anarchy, Interstate War, and the Rise of Rome*, HCS 48 (Berkeley: University of California Press, 2006), https://doi.org/10.1525/california/9780520246188.001.0001; Erich Stephen Gruen, *The Hellenistic World and the Coming of Rome*, 1st pbk printing (Berkeley: University of California Press, 1986); Robert M. Kallet-Marx, *Hegemony to Empire: The Development of the Roman Imperium in the East from 148 to 62 B.C.*, HCS 15 (Berkeley: University of California Press, 1995).
3. Eckstein, *Mediterranean Anarchy*, 12.
4. Readers familiar with the ancient Mediterranean but unfamiliar with Realism will find chapter two of Eckstein's *Mediterranean Anarchy* helpful in its entirety.
5. Eckstein, *Mediterranean Anarchy*, 1.
6. Kallet-Marx, *Hegemony to Empire*, 15–16.
7. Arthur M. Eckstein, "Macedonia and Rome, 221–146 BC," in *A Companion to Ancient Macedonia*, ed. Joseph Roisman and Ian Worthington, BCAW (Chichester: Wiley-Blackwell, 2010), 229–34.
8. Eckstein, "Macedonia and Rome," 230. See Polyb. *Hist.* 4.28.
9. Livy 45.18, but see the discussion of freedom in the next section.
10. Kallet-Marx, *Hegemony to Empire*, 12–15; Gruen, *Hellenistic World*, 433–4.
11. See esp. Kallet-Mark, *Hegemony to Empire*, 18–29.
12. Polyb. *Hist.* 36.10.
13. Kallet-Marx, *Hegemony to Empire*, 31–4.
14. Kallet-Marx, *Hegemony to Empire*, 191–3.

15. Kallet-Marx, *Hegemony to Empire*, 230–1.
16. App. *Mith.* 10, 13, 58. Kallet-Marx (*Hegemony to Empire*, 252–3) questions the historicity of Rome's warmongering tactics in App. *Mith.* 11, in part on the grounds that Rome was at the time embroiled in war in Italy and not well equipped for major campaigns in Asia Minor.
17. Kallet-Marx, *Hegemony to Empire*, 265, 279.
18. See Cic. *Leg. man.*
19. Kallet-Marx, *Hegemony to Empire*, 326.
20. Dio 36.50.3; App. *Mith.* 105, 115.
21. Jonathan A. Goldstein, ed., *I Maccabees: A New Translation, with Introduction and Commentary*, AB 41 (Garden City, NY: Doubleday, 1976), 62–4.
22. Goldstein, *1 Maccabees*, 64. For Goldstein's discussion of various propagandistic aspects of the text, 73–84.
23. Katell Berthelot, "The Biblical Conquest of the Promised Land and the Hasmonean Wars According to 1 and 2 Maccabees," in *The Books of the Maccabees: History, Theology, Ideology. Papers of the Second International Conference on the Deuterocanonical Books, Pápa, Hungary, 9–11 June, 2005*, ed. Géza Xeravits and József Zsengellér, JSJSup 118 (Leiden: Brill, 2007), 45–60.
24. Torleif Elgvin, "Hasmonean State Ideology, Wars and Expansionism," in *Encountering Violence in the Bible*, ed. Markus Zehnder and Hallvard Hagelia, BMW 55 (Sheffield: Sheffield Phoenix Press, 2013), 52–67.
25. Peter Schäfer, *The History of the Jews in the Greco-Roman World: The Jews of Palestine from Alexander the Great to the Arab Conquest*, rev. ed. (London: Routledge, 2003), 65–80.
26. Christopher J. Dart, "Frontiers, Security, and Military Policy," in *A Companion to the Flavian Age of Imperial Rome*, ed. Andrew Zissos, Blackwell Companions to the Ancient World (Chichester: Wiley-Blackwell, 2016), 209.
27. Zeichmann, *Roman Army*, 3–4.
28. Michael Kochenash, "Cornelius's Obeisance to Peter (Acts 10:25–26) and Judaea Capta Coins," *CBQ* 81, no. 4 (2019): 630–5. This section of the article describes not only the coins but also other Julio-Claudian and Flavian iconography depicting the subjugation of enemies or Rome's fatherly, protective role over provinces.
29. Craige Champion, "The Soteria at Delphi: Aetolian Propaganda in the Epigraphical Record," *AJP* 116, no. 2 (1995): 213–20.
30. John S. Kloppenborg, "Evocatio Deorum and the Date of Mark," *JBL* 124, no. 3 (2005): 419–50.
31. Aleksander R. Michalak, *Angels as Warriors in Late Second Temple Jewish Literature*, WUNT 2. Reihe 330 (Tübingen, Germany: Mohr Siebeck, 2012), 16–30.
32. Michalak, *Angels as Warriors*, 124–5.
33. John J. Collins, *Daniel: A Commentary on the Book of Daniel*, ed. Frank Moore Cross, Hermeneia (Minneapolis, MN: Fortress Press, 1993), 336.
34. See Collins, *Mark*, 165–70.
35. E.g., Paul J. Achtemeier, *Mark*, 2nd ed., Proclamation Commentaries (Philadelphia, PA: Fortress Press, 1986), 85–91.
36. Graham H. Twelftree, "Jesus the Exorcist and Ancient Magic," in *A Kind of Magic: Understanding Magic in the New Testament and Its Religious Environment*, ed. Michael Labahn and Bert Jan Lietaert Peerbolte, LNTS 306 (London: T&T Clark, 2007), 63–74.
37. Twelftree, "Jesus the Exorcist," 69–74.

38. Cheryl Pero, *Liberation from Empire: Demonic Possession and Exorcism in the Gospel of Mark*, StBibLit 150 (New York: Peter Lang, 2013). Horsley, *Politics*, 80–107.
39. John J. Collins, *The Apocalyptic Imagination: An Introduction to Jewish Apocalyptic Literature*, 3rd ed. (Grand Rapids, MI: Eerdmans, 2016), 12–51.
40. Rome was not in the habit of utterly destroying the cities it conquered. Carthage and Corinth are special and famous cases, and exceptions that prove the rule. In *War*, Josephus insists that Titus did not initially plan the temple's destruction, but had his hand forced by the rebels (6.4.1). We should be attentive to the historian's pro-Roman stance, but the outline is believable. Even if Titus did plan from the outset to raze the city, it was still an unusual occurrence, and this has implications both for the dating of Mark and for an understanding of the intensity of the imagery in ch. 13.
41. Collins, *Daniel*, 357, 385.
42. John Kloppenborg has also seen the possibility of Titus as the sacrilege, pointing to the masculine participle ἑστηκότα rather than neuter ἑστηκός to agree with βδέλυγμα. However, he quickly retracts the possibility, on the grounds of historical unlikelihood that may or may not be appropriate for interpreting Mark. Kloppenborg, "Evocatio Deorum," 423–4.
43. Liew, *Politics of Parousia*, 60.
44. Collins, *Mark*, 396, cf. 413.
45. See the discussions of this passage in Collins, *Mark*, 412–13; France, *Mark*, 343–6; and the discussion of Mark 13:30 in George Raymond Beasley-Murray, *Jesus and the Last Days: The Interpretation of the Olivet Discourse* (Peabody, MA: Hendrickson, 1993), 443–9.
46. Hyp. 5.3; Xen. *Ana*. 1.1.6.
47. Allan T. Georgia, "Translating the Triumph: Reading Mark's Cruci•xion Narrative against a Roman Ritual of Power," *JSNT* 36, no. 1 (September 2013): 17–38, https://doi.org/10.1177/0142064X13495132.
48. Mary Beard, *The Roman Triumph* (Cambridge, MA: Belknap Press of Harvard University Press, 2009), 81–2.
49. Beard, *Roman Triumph*, 82–3.
50. For esp. Plato and Xenophon on Persian "softness," see Pierre Briant, "The Greeks and 'Persian Decadence,'" in *Greeks and Barbarians*, ed. Thomas Harrison, ERAW (New York: Routledge, 2002), 193–210. For an example of this trope weaponized against the Seleucids as both easterners (especially from a Roman standpoint) and monarchs, see Fotini Hadjittofi, "Midas, the Golden Age Trope, and Hellenistic Kingship in Ovid's Metamorphoses," *American Journal of Philology* 139, no. 2 (2018): 277–309, https://doi.org/10.1353/ajp.2018.0014.
51. E.g., Georgia, "Translating the Triumph," 18; Gelardini, *Christus Militans*, 886–94.
52. Georgia, "Translating the Triumph," 18, emphasis original.
53. Georgia, "Translating the Triumph," 23; Beard, *Roman Triumph*, 4.
54. As Curtius was writing in the early to mid-first century CE, perhaps from Rome, he was surely aware of the tradition of Pompey's triumph and of triumphs in general.
55. There is a final and likely coincidental parallelism between Mark's narrative and Curtius's: Curtius specifies that Alexander tours the buildings and temples of Babylon the day after the parade. Jesus, likewise, enters Jerusalem and only takes a quick look around before leaving and visiting the temple the next day.
56. See also Jos. *Ant*. 11.8.4 on Alexander's entry into Jerusalem, and *Diod*. 37.26, on Mithridates's celebratory and even divine welcomes to cities throughout Asia after defeating the Romans.

5

Salvation

The Gospel of Mark never affords Jesus the title "savior." That is, the nouns σωτήρ and σωτηρία make no appearances in the text. However, the verb σῴζω occurs eleven times (3:4; 5:23, 28, 34; 6:56; 8:35; 10:26, 52; 13:13, 20; 15:30–31). This chapter will investigate the cosmic, political, apocalyptic, and spiritual possibilities for understanding the concept of salvation in Mark, in the context not only of the culturally hybridized Mediterranean east but also with specific reference to war.

Salvation in Hellenistic and Roman Culture

The constellation of words related to σῴζω has at least as broad a usage in Greek as do the words related to "save" in English. They refer to rescue from battle or other dangers, pardon from the death penalty, keeping or regaining possessions, cure from disease, preservation of a city or way of living, or the activity of a god to turn aside fate.[1] In Jewish, Christian, Gnostic, and philosophical texts dealing with the afterlife or eschatological salvation it is used in a cosmic, eschatological, or personally spiritual sense, but that usage does not take on its fullest life until after the first century CE.

The semantic field of "rescue" or "preservation" is important throughout the Hellenistic and early Roman periods. The title σωτήρ is very common for gods, Zeus in particular but not exclusively, and is attested for a number of Hellenistic rulers, notably Ptolemy I and Antiochus I, as well as Roman emperors.[2] Neither Augustus nor Ptolemy I are known for saving anyone's eternal soul, so their roles as saviors must have referred to more mundane rescues.

In the case of Augustus, salvation is primarily from war, as he is credited with beginning the *pax Romana* upon his victory at Actium. The early chapters of the *Res gestae divi Augusti* catalog the ways in which he brought salvation to Rome, although it uses the vocabulary of freedom rather than salvation, when vocabulary is at issue (see below). In that text and others, Augustus ended civil war, was successful in foreign wars, defeated pirates, and gave money and grain to the people—often from his own pocket.

Freedom

The practice of warfare and expansion in the Mediterranean during these centuries was standardized and taken for granted. Not all governments were expansionist, and not all expansionists sought to move beyond relatively small regions, but the control and protection of territory, the striking of mutually beneficial alliances, the "enslavement" (by tribute or direct control) of conquered cities, and the rewarding of allies or other politically beneficial parties were ubiquitous features of the military-political landscape. Further, Roman and Judean expansion show similar appeals to divine mandate, ancient tradition, and just action. While the brutality of Rome's armies should not be diminished, it also should not be treated as special except in its scope. At the same time, an accurate understanding of Roman expansion and domination must not overemphasize this brutality. The territorial, political, and economic benefits of Roman protection for the elites of its provinces and allied states should all be taken into account.

The terms *libertas* and ἐλευθερία, as well as their sentiments, are common in texts dealing with Roman wars. They are generally rendered into English as "freedom," "independence," or "liberty." In practical terms, these simply refer to the status of a city or state's administration relative to the administration of Rome or other expansionist states.[3] On their own they do not illuminate the kind of life residents of a state might experience, the socioeconomic structures they might participate in, or even under whose administration—local or foreign—any group or individual resident might most thrive. "Enslavement" of a city is not the same as the capture of enemy combatants or defeated noncombatants for sale in the slave trade.[4] Enslavement or liberation of a city might have little or no practical effect on the lives of nonelites, except perhaps where the change, addition, or abolishment of tribute would alter the ways in which the elite exacted revenues from the majority's labor.

Linda Zollschan identifies five aspects that, in various combinations, tend to characterize republican Roman declarations of independence for city-states under its influence: "Specifically they granted autonomy and the right to live according to one's laws, immunity from tribute (*immuntas*), the withdrawal of troops or garrisons, freedom from monarchy, and the introduction of a republic or democracy." These aspects are not always seen all together.[5] For example, Livy (45.18.1–2) indicates the possibility of declaring cities "freed" when they were still under at least some kind of influence from outside monarchy. In fact, Livy's account of the Macedonian settlement (esp. 45.29.4–14) indicates quite a high level of Roman interference in the laws and administration of the region, from taxation to marriage restrictions to mining and logging activities. Using this passage as an exemplar, it seems that the primary benefit of *libertas* to cities and their leaderships was Roman protection from war and support against political opponents.[6]

Judaic Soteriology

In Jewish texts, salvation outside of mundane activity (e.g., rescuing a person from a life-endangering situation or protecting livestock from predators) is primarily attributed to God. Earlier Hebrew texts have no sense of an afterlife, but the prophets begin to discuss the salvation, destruction, or renewal of Israel as a whole, often but not always in anthropomorphic terms. This sense of national salvation (or not) from foreign conquerors eventually developed into ideas about eschatological destruction and renewal.[7]

By the time Rome became involved in the region, philosophical ideas about the eternity of the soul had made their way into Judaic thought, resulting in the development of traditions about individual afterlives, resurrection, and reincarnation. The Pharisees, as I have already discussed, apparently ascribed to these kinds of eschatology, and they are also visible in Josephus (e.g., *War* 3.8.1-7), Philo (e.g., *Leg. Alleg.* 3.161), and many Second Temple texts. The judgment of the dead is common in texts of this long period (e.g., Dan 12: 2-3; 1 En 22) and has parallels in both Greek and Egyptian literature. Paul's version of the resurrection, that the righteous will be resurrected in spirit but not bodily (1 Cor 15), is also reflected in Jubilees, which seems to indicate that the unrighteous will have no afterlife at all (Jub. 23:22-31).

Although the explicit vocabulary of salvation does not appear there, 1 Macc 14 describes Simon in terms familiar from Greek and Roman praise of kings and generals, many of whom were awarded with the title σωτήρ. The eulogy in vv. 4-15 is also highly reminiscent of prophetic and psalmic passages describing the benefactions of God: cessation of war, rescue of captives, agricultural bounty, and restoration of the temple and cult. Messianic ideology in general, of which Hasmonean propaganda partook, is a rare if not singular strain of Judean tradition attributing salvation to a figure other than God (although the messiah never operates apart from God).

Salvation in Mark

In this brief overview, I will identify two different types of salvation in Mark: bodily and eschatological. Before the eschaton, Jesus offers salvation from disease and injury, natural disaster, hunger, and possession by demons. After, citizenship in the Kingdom of God allows one to avoid eternal punishment and gain eternal life and unspecified "treasure in heaven." I will also cover the question of ransom, an aspect of Mark's soteriology with explicitly military connotations.

Bodily Salvation

The first act of salvation in Mark is the exorcism in Capernaum (1:21-28)—a man is possessed by an evil spirit and Jesus casts it out. We do not hear what the effects of the possession are or anything about the man. The purpose of this passage is not to highlight the saving act as such but the demonstration of ἐξουσία, as discussed in Chapter 3. Immediately afterward he heals Simon's mother-in-law (1:29–31) and then goes out and does widespread healing and exorcisms in the community (32–34). Salvation, so far and consistently throughout the text, is salvation from sickness and possession (which causes particular kinds of what a modern reader would call sickness).

Chapter 2 gives us a new kind of salvation: the forgiveness of sins (2:1–11). We have already encountered sin as a concept at the beginning of ch. 1, and the equation of forgiveness with salvation is made clear in 2:17, where healing of sickness is used as an analogy. So far the Gospel has not made clear the nature of sin, nor the consequences for one whose sins are not forgiven. The list of sins in Mark 7:21–22 ranges from extreme (murder) to everyday (folly), and likewise, the declaration of 1:15 assumes without qualification that all people have sinned. Augustus claims that after the civil war he pardoned all citizens who asked, and in the cases of foreign wars, pardoned all enemy combatants when he felt it was safe to do so (*RGDA* 3.1–2).

The parables of ch. 4 do not mention salvation, but the consistent metaphor of agricultural abundance promises some benefit that comes from the Kingdom of God. Again, neither Jesus nor the narrator specify what that benefit is, even when explaining the parable of the sower (vv. 10–20). The kingdom itself seems to be the benefit, especially in the parables of the growing seed (vv. 26–29) and the mustard seed (vv. 30–32).

Following the parables are four salvific acts that are more intense than what we have seen so far, and that together give a dramatic demonstration of Jesus's power and add to the list of things one needs salvation from. The calming of the storm in 4:35–41 is the first showcase of Jesus's cosmic efficacy (and puts him in the category of the famous seafaring gods, Castor and Polydeuces). The exorcism outside of Gerasa (5:1–20) is an especially detailed and dramatic example of an activity he has been performing since the beginning of the Gospel, but the addition of Legion—an explicitly military and explicitly Roman term in this period—points to one of the things that Jesus saves from: military occupation.

Like the previous pericope, the healing of the bleeding woman (5:21–43) is a reiteration of a power we know Jesus has, made more dramatic and given more interpretive content through its details. The chronic and long-term nature of the woman's illness and the comment about how much money she has spent on failed treatments both highlight the level of Jesus's healing power. The story of Jairus's daughter, which frames it, adds revivification—salvation from death, not only sickness—to his repertoire. Perhaps significantly, these two linked healings demonstrate reversals of two significant types of ritual pollution: uterine bleeding and corpse contamination.[8]

For the rest of the Galilee narrative, Jesus continues to offer salvation through healings and exorcisms. These are punctuated by the two feeding miracles (6:30–43; 8:1–9), which save from hunger. Thus far, Mark's Jesus saves in bodily (i.e., material and social) ways: from illness (including demon possession, which affects the body), environmental dangers, armies (i.e., Legion), and starvation. He also undoes or delegitimizes ritual impurity, which has social consequences (besides ch. 5, see 7:1–23), though he does not reject the concept wholesale (1:40–44).

Eschatological Salvation

The first reference to eschatological salvation occurs in 8:34–38. In this short speech full of paradoxes and conditional language, Jesus hints at both an afterlife and an eschatological judgment. This sits in between the first passion prediction (8:31–32) and the revelation of Jesus as a divine being (9:1–8), confirming his identity as God's son and delegate, intertwining his eschatological functions with his death and resurrection, and directly connecting salvation to all of these. Here the text is more explicit about how one gains salvation: by following and giving up one's life.

A discourse on belonging begins at 9:33. It begins with the disciples arguing over who is the greatest and a repeat of the requirement of servant leadership from ch. 8. The section on the outsider exorcist, beginning at v. 38, widens the definition of "insider" to "anyone who is not against us" (v. 40)—that is, those who are not actively opposed to the Kingdom of God are de facto within it. Matthew (12:30) and Luke (11:23) flip the saying around, so that on the surface Mark's kingdom seems more inclusive. However, the section beginning at 9:42 will show that just as insidership is as simple as offering compassion to a fellow insider, that status can quickly be revoked, and for the first time expresses consequences for those outside the kingdom. Initially, in v. 42, it is consequences for impeding believers ("it is better for you if a great millstone is hung around your neck and you were cast into the sea"), in contrast to v. 41 ("The one who gives you a drink of water in my name because you are of Christ, truly I say to you that he will not lose his reward"). Then the discourse quickly turns to the possibility of betrayal from inside, using the metaphor of the body, reminiscent of Paul's "members of Christ" metaphor in 1 Corinthians. Feet, hands, and eyes that "cause to stumble" must be amputated, lest the rest of the body be thrown "into Gehenna."

Neither Jesus nor Mark are more specific. The use of σκανδαλίζω and related words in relation to the punishment of and temptation to sin is common in the LXX and later Greek translations of Hebrew literature,[9] and Gehenna as a site of eternal punishment either in the afterlife or after the eschatological judgment is similarly endemic to the period.[10] Therefore we can expect that Mark's author did not consider them novel ideas that needed explication. The description of eternal torment that makes even nonexistence seem like a better deal is probably also not new information so much as dramatic emphasis.

Likewise, and throughout the rest of Mark, there is very little information about what the post-eschatological "reward" might be. Jesus's rebuke of the Sadducees regarding marriage (12:18–27) acknowledges the resurrection and seems to define it in some eschatological or metaphysical way ("they are like angels in heaven"), rather than as a physical resurrection or simple reincarnation, but gives no other details. Chapter 13 ends with the return of the Son of Man, without any description of a post-eschatological kingdom. Chapter 10 again emphasizes the importance of "entering" the Kingdom of God (vv. 14–15, 24–27), and Jesus tells the rich man that by selling what he owns he will amass "treasure in heaven" (v. 21). Verse 30 also promises "a hundredfold" of whatever his followers have left behind, but adds the enigmatic μετὰ διωγμῶν, "with persecutions." Looking ahead to the promise to James and John, that they will "drink the cup" and "be baptized with the baptism" of Jesus (v. 39), and again to ch. 13 and the warnings of judicial and military danger, it becomes clear that despite his campaign of healing and exorcism, Jesus is not offering an existence truly free from suffering, at least in the current (pre-eschatological) age.

Ransom

One of the most explicit declarations of Jesus as savior in Mark is 10:45: "For the Son of Man did not come to be served but to serve, and to give his life as a ransom for many." The word normally translated here as "ransom" is λύτρον, which can have a general meaning referring to a price or recompense, and appears in the Oxyrhynchus papyri in the context of slave manumission. It is used in the LXX variously and mostly in legal and cultic contexts, for payments to the temple or priesthood (e.g., Lev 27:31), recompense to a husband as a penalty for sleeping with his wife (Prov 6.35), redemption of land during jubilee years (Lev 25:24), payment to a victim's family in lieu of the death penalty (Exod 21:29; Num 35:31–34), and slave manumission (Lev 19:20). But most commonly in pre- and non-Christian literature it refers literally to ransom, securing the return of captured soldiers or other prisoners by trading money, goods, favors, or other captured soldiers. A common title for the twenty-fourth book of the *Iliad*, in which Priam pleads with Achilles for the return of Hector's body, is Ἕκτορος λύτρα, the Ransom of Hector. The word also appears frequently in Herodotus, Thucydides, and the LXX of Isa 45:13.

Interpreters of Mark most commonly look to the connotations of slave trade for understanding this passage.[11] Verses 43–45 emphasize service as the marker and responsibility of leadership among Jesus's followers. In vv. 43 and 45, the words are "servant" and "to serve" (διάκονος and διακονέω), respectively, but v. 44 explicitly states that one who wishes to be a leader or "first" (πρῶτος) among Jesus's followers must be πάντων δοῦλος, the "slave of all." In this context, however, Jesus as λύτρον is somewhat contradictory—one is supposed to submit voluntarily to "slavery" to the community, not be manumitted from it. The Pauline answer, that Jesus frees from slavery to sin so that one can willingly and joyfully become a slave of God (e.g., Rom 6:22), is possible here, but Mark does not make that interpretation obvious. Collins prefers a cultic meaning of λύτρον, citing several cultic inscriptions and the use of ἱλαστήριον (propitiatory or expiatory sacrifice) to refer to the deaths of Eleazar and the others in 4 Macc 17:22. In the LXX she prioritizes occurrences in which the λύτρον circumvents death in either a legal or cultic context, and with all of this evidence together suggests that the Markan usage indicates propitiation.[12]

Another layer becomes apparent, however, when we consider v. 10:42: "those who seem to rule the nations lord it over them, and their great ones exercise authority over them." This verse does not refer to slave owners as such, but to rulers and political leaders. The use of the intensifying κατα- in compound with the verbs κυριεύω and ἐξουσιάζω introduces a negative connotation—the leaders of the nations *over*-rule and *over*-extend their authority, and thus are no longer rulers but tyrants. Interpreting Jesus's death as a trade for prisoners of war does not invalidate other readings of λύτρον, especially not those referring to the slave trade or the death penalty—one of those fates usually awaited any soldier who was not ransomed.

Conclusion

Although Jesus is never called "savior" in the Gospel of Mark, it is clear he takes on that role. Use of the verb σῴζω and other vocabulary to refer to healing, preserving life, and eschatological salvation indicates a range of Jesus's salvific functions. Each one of these functions—healer, life-saver, warrior, ransom, and eschatological redeemer—has precedent in Greek, Roman, and/or Jewish tradition, variously attributed to kings, generals, and gods. The next chapter will go deeper into Markan theology, from the perspective that the gods were important civic actors in all ancient Mediterranean societies.

Notes

1. Foerster, "σῴζω κτλ.," TDNT 7:965–68.
2. E.g., σεβαστὸς σωτήρ. The epigraphic evidence is particularly rich (e.g., IG II² 3173). A search for σωτήρ in the Packard Humanities Institute's database of Greek inscriptions turns up roughly 5,400 results, the largest collection of which is from Asia Minor (https://inscriptions.packhum.org/).
3. Gruen, *Hellenistic World*, 145–57.
4. Individual liberty in the Roman consideration is a somewhat separate discussion. See, e.g., Mason Hammond, "Res olim dissociabiles: Principatus ac Libertas: Liberty under the Early Roman Empire," *HSCP* 67 (1963): 93–113.
5. Linda Zollschan, "Macedonian Libertas," *ClB* 78, no. 2 (2002): 176. Livy 45.18.1–2 indicates the existence of "free cities" nonetheless still under kings. For the issue of tribute from free cities, see Rainer Bernhardt, "Die Immunitas der Freistädte," *Historia* 29, no. 2 (1980): 190–207.
6. W. S. Hanson, "Forces of Change and Methods of Control," in *Dialogues in Roman Imperialism: Power, Discourse, and Discrepant Experience in the Roman Empire*, ed. D. J. Mattingly, JRASup 23 (Portsmouth, RI: JRA, 1997), 70.
7. Grabbe, *Judaic Religion*, 259. See also Lorenzo DiTommaso, "Deliverance and Justice: Soteriology in the Book of Daniel," in *This World and the World to Come: Soteriology in Early Judaism*, ed. Daniel M. Gurtner (New York: T&T Clark, 2011), 71–86, https://doi.org/10.5040/9781472551047, for a discussion of different types of soteriology in Daniel, corresponding to compositional dates.
8. The NRSV obscures the language of salvation in this pericope, consistently translating σῴζω as "to make well." See also v. 6:56.
9. Gustav Stählin, "σκάνδαλον, σκανδαλίζω," TDNT 7:339–44.
10. Duane F. Watson, "GEHENNA," ABD 2:926–28.
11. E.g., Bas M. F. van Iersel, *Mark: A Reader-Response Commentary*, trans. W. H. Bisscheroux (London: T&T Clark, 2004), 338; Carter, *Mark*, 283–6.
12. Collins, *Mark*, 501–4.

6

Jesus as the Son of God

In the twentieth century, major investigations of the title Son of God debated its origins, particularly whether it emerged from the early "Palestinian" or "Hellenistic" churches; whether it should be considered Jewish or non-Jewish; and where and when it entered the Synoptic tradition.[1] Almost entirely, investigations of the title have asked whether it is "Jewish" or "Christian"; until the early twentieth century there was little if any effort to understand possible polytheistic origins and how they might shed light on early conceptions of Jesus. As early as the 1970s, Martin Hengel made note of the Roman imperial title υἱὸς θεοῦ, the translation of *divi filius*, but rejected it as a model for the Christological title.[2] In 2000, Adela Yarbro Collins published an article that compares Jesus to various Greek and Roman mythological figures with reference to the idea of divine sonship and directly links Jesus to the Roman imperial cults.[3]

Throughout this study I have argued, explicitly and implicitly, that it does us no good to assume that a document as early as Mark will necessarily align with the worldviews and priorities of later Christianity. There is much research on the possible Judaic backgrounds of Markan theology—any good commentary can provide a summary. This chapter will instead look to some of the possible polytheistic backgrounds, not simply for literary models and analogous imagery but for the very ontology of Mark's Christological thought. The first question is not "How is Jesus (like) a god?" but rather "What does divinity mean for Jesus's earliest followers?" Thus, in this chapter I will investigate aspects of ancient polytheistic thought, as well as the idea of divine sonship and its place in Mark. This is not a departure from the previous chapters; having established that God's kingdom and Jesus's kingship follow patterns that are intelligible through contemporary political and military structures, it follows to investigate whether the divine aspects of Jesus's identity might also be understood similarly. Gods played important roles in the civic structures of all the cultures under investigation in this book. The imperial cult was an integral aspect of imperial rulership and emerged out of characteristically Hellenistic modes of ruler worship (see the summary of S. R. F. Price below). This chapter situates Mark's Jesus within that worldview.

Divinity and Divinization in the Ancient World

To discuss the ways in which Mark's Jesus is or is like a god, we must begin by defining the category of divinity in the first place, and this is no simple task. Platonic or Ciceronian systematizations of the divine do not always easily reconcile with the assumptions of civic or household cult, not to mention mysticism and the innovations of various syncretisms. Attempts to separate "Jewish" from "Greek" theologies often oversimplify the differences, particularly for the Hellenistic and Roman periods, and assume too much mutual exclusion. The following discussions of the various types of divinity in the ancient Mediterranean are necessarily noncomprehensive, but give an idea of the diversity and possibility available to Mark's author and audience.

The "Classic" Gods

When we say "the Greek [or Roman] gods," these are the ones that we first think of. Zeus, Hera, Athena, and the others—a dozen and perhaps a few more if one is well read. For most modern readers these gods are *characters*, the subjects of myth and, often less relatably, of cult. In ancient and modern discourse, their divinity is usually taken for granted—one does not need to define one's terms when saying that Zeus is a god.

Albert Henrichs identifies three qualities that are definitive of Greek gods in pre-Hellenistic cult and literature. These are immortality, anthropomorphism, and power. He differentiates true immortality from the eternal afterlife that is often attributed to heroes. Anthropomorphism, the quality of being human shaped, allowed the Greeks to experience their gods through epiphanies, either in dreams or live. Power is perhaps the most fundamental quality of Greek gods, which, as we will see, carries through all of the other ways of construing divinity in the ancient world.[4]

An examination of ancient sources shows that over quite a long period of time, these basic characteristics of the gods held true with some exceptions, especially in philosophical schools. However, I would add to Henrichs's schema that inherent in, and perhaps more fundamental than, anthropomorphism is physicality. The classical gods have different kinds of bodies than humans do, even when they look like humans, but they are never fully disembodied. One of the most dramatic examples of this principle is when Diomedes wounds Aphrodite on the battlefield (Hom. *Il* 2.335–43). By the end of the Hellenistic period, some philosophical schools had developed ideas of nonphysical deity, such as the conception of "God" as the divine mind or reason that orders the universe. But others continued to describe gods in physical, if not always anthropomorphic, terms. Cicero refers to many theologies, such as of gods as elements of nature (e.g., air), celestial bodies, and inhabiting human form (Cic. *Nat. d.* 1.10.26; 1.11.28; 2.2.6). Gods also inhabited cult statues (Livy 29.11.7–8), but we should be cautious against taking at face value the polemic of Paul (1 Cor 8:4) and other detractors that such ontology *limited* the god to the statue.

Although aniconism was a prominent value in Hebrew tradition (e.g., Deut 5:8; Hos 8:6), the God of Israel frequently appears in Hebrew literature in physical forms. In Genesis and Exodus, God performs actions that, taken literally, require a body: he walks at Gen 1:8; alights on Mount Sinai at Exod 19:20; and appears in bodily form at Exod 24:9–11. At other points, he takes the form of fire or cloud. Thus, the god of Genesis and Exodus exhibits the same basic features that Henrichs describes for the Greek gods: immortality, anthropomorphism (with my addition of physicality in general), and power.

Demigods and Heroes

In Greek culture, human ancestry did not preclude certain types of godhood. Most major figures of Greek mythology boast a divine parent or ancestor, whose inherited nature provides excellence and/or importance beyond what would normally be considered obtainable for humans. As staples of classical literature, the heroes tend to serve as larger-than-life examples of or foils for social values, and often provide etiological explanations for cities, families, cult practices, and sociopolitical formations.

As subjects of cult, the heroes occupied a liminal place in Greek culture. Death was a major source of ritual pollution, and in any case, the fact of the heroes' mortality complicated their inclusion among the gods (with literary exceptions such as Homer's Menelaus proving the rule). Nonetheless, nineteenth- and early-twentieth-century formulations of Greek cult, which drew bright lines between heavenly and earthly deities, and further separated heroes and the (nonheroic) dead from the gods, have not fully survived to the current day. Increased archaeological evidence, including inscriptions, and a wider variety of methodologies have shown a spectrum of cultic types in classical antiquity, rather than a regimented taxonomy. Practices and taboos previously considered reliant on the class of cultic subject (e.g., the idea that only sacrifices to "heavenly" deities could be consumed by human celebrants) have been shown often to have been connected to circumstance: the particular festival or reason for the sacrifice, not necessarily the god or hero to whom it was dedicated.[5] Applied to heroes, this means that while they often received cult as to the dead,[6] both the literary and especially the epigraphic evidence demonstrate hero cult with "divine" features, such as participatory sacrifices and identical vocabulary as was used in cult to the gods.[7]

A further subcategory of ancient Greek divinity is called in modern scholarship the "demigods." These are figures, especially Dionysus and Asclepius, who received mostly or entirely divine cult, but whose mythology attested human parentage. In their myths they are both mortal and immortal, having gone through some kind of death before being raised and granted immortality by the gods. Such figures set a precedent for apotheosis, which will become increasingly important in the Hellenistic and Roman periods.

Hellenistic Innovation: Ruler Cult and Divine Benefaction

The veneration of nonheroic rulers in the Greek world is first attested at Samos in the early to mid-fourth century BCE, where altars and festivals were dedicated to the Spartan general Lysandros for his successes in the Peloponnesian War. Such veneration flourished in the Hellenistic period, especially under the Seleucid kings, and eventually provided the model for veneration of the Roman emperors in the east. An innovation of this mode of worship over against the Greek tradition of hero cult was its focus on living rulers. Apotheosis was neither required nor even attested except in rare cases until the death of Julius Caesar. Although existing cults might persist for some time after their subject had died, there are no pre-Roman descriptions of postmortem appearances, and "people do not seem to have appealed to the protection of a deceased ruler."[8]

The landmark study on imperial cult and emperor worship in the Roman east is Price's *Rituals and Power*.[9] Price resists two major dichotomies of foregoing work on the emperor cults: first, the Christianizing treatment of imperial cult as either "flattery" or "sacrilege"; and, related, the Modernist notion of the separation of religion and politics. Price maintains that these and other problems with earlier scholarship have led to shallow or cynical treatments of ruler cult that ultimately do not take it seriously as cultic expression.[10]

Price understands the cult honors afforded to the emperor not simply as expressions of loyalty or even sycophancy but "as a system whose structure defines the position of the emperor." He cites Clifford Geertz and other ritualists to argue that ritual does not primarily contain or impart "encyclopedic" or ontological knowledge (knowledge of facts) or semantic knowledge (that of categories), but symbolic knowledge, which does not fit neatly into either of the former types of knowledge and is not always easily articulated. Emphasizing what a ritual of the imperial cult communicates symbolically means not asking whether or not the practitioner *really believes* that the emperor is a god (because the answer to such a question "can only be private and mental"), but rather what the ritual communicates and enforces at the social level about the world.[11]

The imperial cults included sacrifices *to* the gods *for* or *on behalf of* the emperor and sacrifices *to* the emperor independently.[12] Although the earliest examples of Hellenistic ruler cult are modeled at least conceptually on the veneration of heroes,[13] by the Roman period the emperor cults often most closely resembled divine cult, in some cases even syncretizing the ruler or members of his family with major deities.[14] Price argues, therefore, that imperial cult in the east allowed "accommodation of external authority within the traditions of the local community,"[15] a complex cultural interaction that can be described as a part of the Greek formulations of power, social and political structures, and cosmology, but not presented as a functional shorthand for them.[16]

In both the Hellenistic and Roman periods, rulers received divine honors on the basis of their benefactions. The object of worship provides or has provided a boon to the worshipper, in forms of military protection, just rule, economic prosperity, and so on. There are numerous inscriptions and other documents referring to rulers as gods and praising them for their benefactions. The fourth-century BCE hymn from the Athenian cult of Demetrius Poliorcetes reads:

> The other gods are far away or do not have ears or do not exist or do not pay any attention at all to us, but you we see present, not of wood or stone but real.[17]

A second-century CE decree from Ephesus instituting birthday celebrations for Antoninus Pius emphasizes the ruler's divinity as connected to the benefits he provides:

Since in accordance with the joint prayers of the whole world, the most divine and most pious emperor Titus Aelius Antoninus, having inherited the kingdom given to him by his divine father [Hadrian], preserves the whole human race, and since he has especially elevated the reputation of our city …

… and as much as it is possible for people to repay the benefactions of the gods, we will continue eagerly repaying them.[18]

Finally, similar texts record the decision of the province of Asia to celebrate the birthday of Augustus, using language such as "a savior who brought about an end to war and established all things"; "whereas the birthday of the god marked for the world the beginning of good tidings through his coming"; and "he has restored at least to serviceability, if not to its natural state, every form that has become imperfect and fallen into misfortune."[19] These inscriptions explicitly refer to the rulers as gods—not godlike—and describe their divinity as immediate and of cosmic significance, and in terms of the benefactions they give.

One mechanism of ruler cult was the identification of the ruler with a preexisting god. This was often managed through iconography, as Kyle Erickson demonstrates.[20] His article reviews numismatic evidence associating Seleucid kings with Ammon, Dionysus, Apollo or Helios, and/or local deities, by the depiction of the king with horns or starred halos. Cultic honors also assimilated rulers with gods. In the late fourth century BCE, Demetrius Poliorcetes was honored in Athens with a priesthood and sacrifices, with the title σωτήρ. The city further renamed the Dionysia festival "Dionysia and Demetria" and honored him with the same hospitality (ξενισμός) as Demeter and Dionysus whenever he came to the city.[21] Marc Antony also identified himself with Dionysus, so much that he took on the official title νέος διονύσος (Plut. Ant. 60.3). These are only a few examples.

Through identification with specific gods, Hellenistic rulers became associated with the particular powers and mythology of the gods, in a sense shortcutting the deification process. Dionysus's conquests in the east were a particular point of emulation for the Ptolemies and Antony.[22] The propagandistic function is obvious, but, taking Price's hint, assigning pure cynicism to this phenomenon does not help illuminate all facets of it. In fact, it may not be possible to fully understand how such claims were taken by the average participant in ruler cults.

Nonetheless, the identification between the ruler and the god was not absolute. While the evidence demonstrates a range of closeness when a ruler assimilated to a god, it is more difficult to say that there were any instances in which the *god* was assimilated to the *ruler* in the Greco-Roman context. That is, while rulers took on the iconography, titles, and sometimes very names of gods and could be worshipped alongside gods in preexisting temples or have separate cult established for them, I am not aware of a case in which a preexisting cult to a god was ceased or altered to honor the ruler alone as the god. This perhaps marks an extension of the mythological tradition that gods could take on "forms," with the innovation that the god was not limited to any one form and could exist in multiple places at once. Antony may have been Dionysus, but Dionysus was not Antony.

Apotheosis

Dramatic apotheosis or ascension narratives are available throughout Greek literature and mythology. Ganymede is a famous example of a mortal granted immortality and life with the gods, and Homer, Hesiod, and later classical writers attest to a number of others. Interestingly, these accounts are less common in the ruler cults. The comet at Julius Caesar's funeral games, the *sidus iulium*, is a particularly alluring example, but there is no such postmortem sign for Augustus. Suetonius, who fills the life of the princeps with omen after omen, does not suggest any indication of apotheosis for Augustus, or at least stops short of narrating any postmortem signs.

In fact, several prominent ascension narratives from or important in the Hellenistic period emerge from Judean contexts. Apart from Jesus, there were also ascension traditions associated with Moses, Elijah, and Enoch. Philo of Alexandria's preexistent, angelic Moses is steeped in Platonic and Egyptian thought,[23] but the lawgiver's presence at Jesus's transfiguration in Mark 9 suggests more widespread recognition of a related or similar tradition.[24] Elijah's narratives in 1 Kings portray him as the model prophet, a channel for God's word and power and a thorn in the side of rulers who would go against God's will. His thrilling and cinematic ascension in 2 Kgs 2:1–12 became, by the Second Temple period, the basis for his role as the eschatological harbinger.[25] Enoch's mysterious nondeath in Gen 5:24 became the basis for an entire mythology surrounding the otherwise indistinct character, centered especially in the Enochic literature.[26]

Summary

All of these examples demonstrate that in the thought worlds of Roman, Jewish, and Greek people in these periods there were multiple ways to conceive of godhood. In most nonphilosophical contexts we should not look for systematic, internally consistent, and well-defined categories. Instead, we should recognize that all of these ideas were current, and that individuals could hold any of them, and might express multiple and even contradicting ideas in various contexts.

The Divinity of Jesus

Daniel Johansson's 2010 article is an accessible stepping stone into the debate on Mark's Christology.[27] Although his stated intent is not to focus on the title Son of God, it is nonetheless a major point of comparison between scholars. Beginning more or less at Wrede, Johansson demonstrates that the majority of scholars, though not all, have considered the title to be one of several indications of Jesus's divinity, for some value of "divinity." Since about the 1970s the trend has shifted, by Johansson's analysis, to Christologies that emphasize Jesus's role as God's agent rather than a divine being in his own right, primarily with renewed interest in Jewish messianic ideas and the concept of "kingship."

Johansson's article and the scholarship as he represents it all come down to various kinds of dichotomous thinking. Does Mark present a divine *or* human Jesus? Is the Gospel's Christology best understood as Hellenistic *or* Jewish? Johansson himself presents the scholarship on Mark's Jesus as espousing either high or low Christology, where any interpretation of Jesus as divine in any sense is considered high.[28] Such rigid categories are prescriptive and do not take into account the many possibilities for understanding divinity in the post-Alexandrian east. Additionally, for many scholars (and especially those in the first half of the twentieth century), "Hellenistic" indicates a θεῖος ἀνήρ concept, a human person endowed with divine powers that usually manifest in healings and miraculous deeds. Even since the concept of θεῖος ἀνήρ as a title has been debunked, it has stubbornly remained a touchpoint of Markan interpretation, usually with a caveat along the lines of this, by Heikki Räisänen:

> On the other hand, the phenomenon to which the term refers in modern study was not unusual, i.e., a person to whom supernatural powers were ascribed, whether gifts of healing or miraculous foreknowledge. Empedocles, Pythagoras, Apollonius of Tyana and Moses all appear in this role in ancient tradition.[29]

A fundamental problem with approaching Mark's Christology from a θεῖος ἀνήρ framework—either a strict one as developed through the first half of the twentieth century or a looser, more broad one as advocated by Räisänen and Broadhead,[30] is that this framework emphasizes the ἀνήρ (or ἄνθρωπος), relegating the θεῖος to a mere adjective: a hyperbolic statement of wonder or an indicator of divine favor. Modern discussions of the figures that scholarship admits to the ranks of the θεῖοι ἄνδρες tend to emphasize their humanity, even if they receive cult.[31] Scholarship that begins with the idea of Jesus as θεῖος ἀνήρ—even if its purpose is to develop a more descriptive and observational use of the term—implicitly precludes consideration of Jesus as simply divine.

Absent a birth narrative, and considering the appearance of Jesus's family in ch. 6, Mark would seem to support this interpretation. However, I submit that it is an anachronistic distinction. As I discussed earlier, the categories "divine" and "human" bled into each other considerably in Classical and Archaic hero worship. The changes of the Hellenistic period—the rationalizing and often monotheizing tendencies of the philosophers, the expansion of ruler cult throughout Greek and Roman cultures, and the proliferation of the mystery cults—complicate those differences even further. It cannot be so simple as humans made of meat and gods made of godstuff (or fire, or nothing at all), or humans mortal and gods immortal. Both of these distinctions, though present, are repeatedly transgressed in literature and cult throughout Greek antiquity and have quite different significance in some of the neighboring cultures. Jesus is certainly human in the Gospel of Mark, but, as we saw in the inscriptions in the previous section, in the world of the first century that does not preclude him from being a god.

Son of God

Through comparison with the Hellenistic and Roman ruler cults, it is possible to view the divine sonship of Jesus as a question of his status and function, rather than of his ontological, "genetic" nature. In other words, whether Jesus is divine or human becomes something of a nonsensical distinction: the two are not mutually exclusive in the Hellenistic period, and it is primarily only philosophers and later Christians who bother themselves with parsing them. The cult of Asclepius is not overburdened with questions of ontology, and neither is Paul (insofar as he does not seem concerned with the nature of the pre-crucified Jesus at all in any of his surviving letters). Perhaps, then, we might unburden Mark.

This functional model of deity—divinity expressed through benefactions, not necessarily ontology[32]—accords well with the Gospel of Mark. It is repeatedly stated that Jesus brings benefactions, by "proclaiming" (1:38) the arrival of the βασιλεία; by forgiving sins and thus redeeming sinners (2:10, 17); by healing and casting out demons (5:19; 7:37); and by eschatological salvation (13:13, 27). None of these, except perhaps the exorcisms (3:11), are directly connected with the title Son of God (2:10 connects forgiveness with the title Son of Man), but the use of Jesus's sonship to frame the text (1:11; 15:39) renders the entire Gospel a development of it. Jesus's human family is showcased at Mark 3:31–35 and 6:3, first in his rejection of them in favor of his followers and then as a repudiation of his power. Thus, Mark's repetition of Jesus's divine sonship, directly expressed by God and demonstrated through Jesus's exercise of his authority, is narratively and conceptually in conflict with the fact of his earthly family. The reader is expected to prioritize the functional over the ontological.

Famously, υἱός θεοῦ and its variants appear in the eastern imperial cults translating *divi filius*. The passive voice and institutional connotation of *divi* ("divinized" as opposed to "divine" or "god"), at home and even necessary in its Roman senatorial context, is not reflected in the Greek for reasons that have more to do with pre-Roman eastern and Hellenistic ruler and hero cult than with linguistic limitations.[33] In either language the title indicates something about its bearer's place in society and the cosmos. Octavian's use of the title was an integral part of his campaign for legitimation against Marc Antony:[34] emphasis on *divus* (as opposed to simply *Iulii filius* or similar) takes the status of Octavian/Augustus beyond just the rightful heir of Julius Caesar, and the title as a whole helps to cement the legitimacy of the Julian line as cosmically ordained and hereditary rulers of Rome. Although the *Res gestae* and other Latin pro-Augustan texts tend to emphasize Augustus's deference to the senate's authority, the language of deification and the promulgation of imperial cult in Italy and abroad correspond with propagandist efforts, such as Virgil's *Aeneid*, to portray Julio-Claudian emperors as inheriting a divine mandate, fulfilment of which would bring peace and prosperity to the whole world.

Tae Hun Kim has suggested that *divi filius*/υἱός θεοῦ was not a persistent title in the imperial cults, applicable to any emperor, but was a specific designation used by and for Augustus himself.[35] This seems to be a rather limited conclusion. In the Ephesian inscription cited above, Hadrian is the "divine father" of Antoninus Pius, and sources name Tiberius θεοῦ Σεβαστοῦ υἱός and similar titles. Other Julio-Claudian emperors likewise appear in literary and epigraphical sources with implicit or explicit variations on the title.³⁶ Even if no other emperors after Augustus take the title verbatim, it is clearly common for the sentiment to remain, especially in connection with the emperor's stewardship of the state and benefactions to humankind. For Jesus, then, his designation as Son of God—even if he himself avoids it in the narrative—indicates his position in the political and cosmic worldview of the early Roman empire. Jesus is the Son of God because of the authority God has imparted to him, in the same way that Augustus is *divi filius* and ὁ υἱὸς τοῦ θεοῦ because of his adoption by Julius Caesar. This delegation of authority is announced three times in the Gospel: privately to Jesus at the baptism (1:9–11), to the inner circle at the transfiguration (9:2–8), and publicly by means of divine omens at the crucifixion (15:33, 38). Jesus, surpassing Augustus, is the benefactor who inaugurates the new, salvific world order: not the *pax Romana*, but the *pax Dei* or even *pax Christi*, ἡ βασιλεία τοῦ θεοῦ. Chapter 13, which includes a less dramatic version of the cosmic destruction that will later drive the Revelation to John, notably does not explicitly promise an eternal paradise, only the cessation of war after the Son of Man's victorious arrival (13:20, 27)—one of the major accomplishments attributed to and claimed by Augustus.

Jesus and Cosmic Power

In the context of Judean and Galilean culture, Jesus as a divine being cannot equate to Jesus as capital-G God in the way that Antony claimed to be Dionysus. Even allowing for heavy Hellenistic and Roman influence, it is natural and even expected for the divine benefactor who walks upon the earth to represent or be otherwise legitimized by greater powers or institutions. I have already mentioned Augustus's genuflections to the senate in the *Res gestae divi Augusti,* and the title Son of God is a direct expression of this dependence. Further, the roles of major patron deities in rulership (e.g., Jupiter Capitolinus in the Roman context or Serapis in the Ptolemaic) and the various modes of association between rulers and their tutelary gods also demonstrate the importance of this structure. In Mark, Jesus's dominion is mediated as authority—something granted to him. Likewise, his power, as I will demonstrate through an examination of the use of the word δύναμις in the Gospel, is not an integral part of him but another example of his status as an agent.

δύναμις

Previous chapters examined Mark's strategic use of vocabulary to characterize Jesus's rulership. A further example is δύναμις. Compared with ἐξουσία, δύναμις and its verbal form, δύναμαι, are far earlier attested (both appear in Homer) and more basic to the language. Functionally, this has led to a complex and wide-ranging semantic field, not all of which is relevant to the present purpose. The meaning of δύναμαι ranges from the simplest statement of ability (English "can") to a referent to wealth, might, will, or even equivalence. The noun δύναμις is similarly broad, with roughly the same generic and therefore ubiquitously applicable sense of the English "power" or "force," and plays a crucial role in the Greek philosophical development of God.[37] Silva suggests that the earliest usage of the word group referred to physical strength, and subsequent usages proliferated from that concept.[38] While δύναμις can overlap with ἐξουσία in the sense of legal rights and actuated ability, New Testament authors tend to use it in less mundane senses. It appears as a circumlocution for God in Mark 14:62 ("you will see the Son of Man sitting at the right hand of power") and is connected to the general resurrection at 12:24, in the hypothetical dispute over the marriage in the resurrection ("you know neither the scriptures nor the power of God"). Jesus's miracles are sometimes called δυνάμεις (often translated "mighty deeds"; e.g., Mark 6:2). In Paul it appears alongside ἐξουσία and related words in reference to cosmic powers (e.g., Rom 8:38).

The word δύναμις appears ten times in the Gospel of Mark: four in reference to miraculous acts or exorcism (5:30; 6:2, 5; and 9:39); and the other six in various eschatological or theological contexts (6:14; 9:1; 12:24; 13:25, 26; and 14:62). A striking quality of the δύναμις by which Jesus operates in Mark is that he is not in control of it. In the story of the bleeding woman, he is apparently even unaware of where his power has gone and why (5:30). In fact, the use of δύναμις for this healing—rather than ἐξουσία as in chs. 1 and 2, highlights the fact that there is no conflict of teaching or theological interpretation at stake here, nor is the emphasis on Jesus merely as God's agent. Rather, the focus is on the *fact* of the healing power. In this case not to put forward or cement his claim as the legitimate agent and interpreter of God, as ἐξουσία is used in other passages, but primarily to show him as the vehicle of God's benefactions. Within the New Testament, the most obvious comparisons are two episodes in Acts: in ch. 5, word of Peter's healings becomes so widespread that people begin placing their ill along the street in the hopes that they might fall under just his shadow (5:12–16); in ch. 19, pieces of cloth that have come into contact with Paul's skin heal people of various ailments (19:12).[39] In these pericopes, neither Peter nor Paul should be understood as the source of the healing power, merely its conduit.

The characterization of Jesus's δύναμις as external is similar to the portrayal of his ἐξουσία, so much so that the source of Jesus's δύναμις is also a topic of discussion (like his ἐξουσία at 3:19–35). At 6:14, however, there is no obvious challenge—as in Nazareth (6:1–6; see the next section), the *fact* of Jesus's miraculous deeds is not in question. The verse simply lists several rumors Herod has heard about its source. Further, there is no explicit question of these acts being Satanic, unlike the question of his ἐξουσία in the Beelzebul controversy. The question is which prophet—that is, which agent of God—he represents. The statement that "these powers are at work in him" (ἐνεργοῦσιν αἱ δυνάμεις ἐν αὐτῷ) indicates an assumption that the δύναμις is not intrinsic to Jesus but rather has possessed him, or indicates the work of another entity through him. This finds confirmation at 9:39, with the other exorcist, where we learn that Jesus does not even need to formally delegate in order for his δύναμις to work through others. His rebuke to the disciples—"anyone not against us is for us"—suggests an outside source of δύναμις that operates independently from Jesus, even when he is its primary representative.

A few specific usages of δύναμις are worth closer consideration.

6:2 and 5: The Rejection at Nazareth

In Nazareth, Jesus encounters popular resistance for the first time. In both of these verses δυνάμεις refers to healings and is often translated "deeds of power." Verse 2 is a statement of wonder by the unspecified locals: "What δυνάμεις come from his hands!" Verse 5 repeats the vocabulary but this time in the negative: Jesus *cannot* do any δυνάμεις there besides a few cures. The doubling of δύνα- in this verse—οὐκ ἐδύνατο ἐκεῖ ποιῆσαι οὐδεμίαν δύναμιν—demonstrates the versatility of the root and its fundamental place in the language, but is most likely not rhetorically significant as repetition except perhaps for emphasis. However, the statement of inability is intriguing. Matthew and Luke did not preserve the verb δύναμαι in their treatments of the scene: Matt 13:58 reads οὐκ ἐποίησεν and Luke alters the scene significantly, omitting this portion of it.

The next verse, Jesus's wonder at Nazareth's ἀπιστία, informs the common understanding of this passage.[40] In the opposite situation from 5:30, Jesus's power does not flow, although he wishes it to. The rest of the verse, however, seems to contradict itself: "Jesus *could not* perform any δυνάμεις, *except* that he laid his hands on a few people and healed them." The question of Jesus's ability or inability is transformed to one of criteria: Why could he heal *only* these few people and no others? Again, comparison to ch. 5 is apt. Verse 5:34 credits the woman's healing to her faith, and in Nazareth it is the general lack of faith that prevents him, so it follows that perhaps these few that he does heal are those with faith.

The meaning of πίστις here requires careful thought. Verse 2 surely indicates belief—the townspeople are marveling at the wondrous deeds that Jesus has already performed, not challenging their veracity. The questions in this verse address the *source*, a problem that has already come up: the inquiry "From where does he have these things?" reflects the accusation of 3:22: Satan is an option. In this case, πίστις must indicate trust. The townspeople comment disparagingly on Jesus's family and social standing, not in an attempt to cast doubt on the fact of his healings and teachings, but to discredit their source and Jesus himself by attacking his identity.[41] Those few healed ones that previously tangled up our reading of 6:5 are, perhaps, the few in Nazareth that take him at his word. Jesus's δύναμις does not turn on or off according to the *belief* of the potential recipient, but seems to reward those who trust or are loyal to the source of his power.

Summary

The usages that refer to Jesus as the possessor, enactor, or conduit of δύναμις make it clear that while the term is not interchangeable with ἐξουσία, it plays a similar role. Neither are inherent to Jesus. By definition and especially considering the priests' challenge to his authority (11:28–33), ἐξουσία must be granted by someone higher. Mark's use of δύναμις in connection to Jesus functions similarly. Although God is never explicitly named as the source, the Gospel's theology understands God to be in control of history and the cosmos. However, the Beelzebul controversy (3:20–27) and the questions of the Nazarenes (6:2) allow the reader to imagine multiple, competing sources of power and authority, even if one is unquestionably dominant, reflecting the unstable political situation of Judea and Galilee. Further, both Jesus's ἐξουσία and his δύναμις are transferrable. He is able to commission others to both teach and heal/exorcise under his aegis, others may at least perform healings and exorcisms through invocation of his name, and those who are loyal to him, expressed in terms of πίστις, receive his benefactions.

Conclusion

Ruler cult, though for the most part successfully kept out of Jerusalem, was a major aspect of culture throughout the eastern Mediterranean during the Hellenistic and Roman periods. The so-called gentile cities of Galilee participated in imperial worship, and even the Jerusalem priesthood conceded to offer sacrifices on behalf of Roman rulers. Since this book has been reading Mark's Kingdom of God and Jesus's role as God's royal agent through the lens of the local cultural-political context, it is natural to look to the imperial cults and investigate whether they might offer any insight into Mark's Jesus. In practice, divinity in the ancient world was complex and rarely systematized, and by the late Hellenistic and early Roman periods was as much a matter of social status and magnanimity as it is of divine birth. Thus, Mark's Jesus, already a king who rules as the agent of God, can be called the Son of God, a title that denotes both divinity and rulership. Like the objects of ruler cult, Mark's Jesus is imagined in relation to God, the ultimate source of Jesus's benefactions. The lack of a birth narrative is no impediment to the divinity of Mark's Jesus; the imperial throne (and therefore the imperial divinity) was often handed down by adoption, sometimes at the expense of natural sons, and although Augustus would eventually gain a birth narrative (Suet. *Aug.* 94), other emperors did not.

Notes

1. For the most important contributions through the first half of the twentieth century, see van Iersel, *Der Sohn*, 3–26. See also Hahn, *Christologische Hoheitstitel*, 280–333. For more recent work, see Yolanda Dreyer, *Institutionalization of Authority and the Naming of Jesus* (Eugene, OR: Pickwick, 2012).
2. Martin Hengel, *The Son of God: The Origin of Christology and the History of Jewish-Hellenistic Religion*, trans. John Bowden (Philadelphia, PA: Fortress Press, 1976), 23–30.
3. Adela Yarbro Collins, "Mark and His Readers: The Son of God among Greeks and Romans," *HTR* 93 (2000): 85–100.
4. Albert Henrichs, "What Is a Greek God?," in *The Gods of Ancient Greece*, ed. Jan N. Bremmer and Andrew Erskine, Identities and Transformations (Edinburgh: Edinburgh University Press, 2010), 19–40, http://www.jstor.org/stable/10.3366/j.ctt1r236p.8. In this brief essay, Henrichs focuses on the major gods (Athena, Apollo, Zeus, etc.) and does not discuss the extent to which these categories,

especially anthropomorphism, might be the same or different for more minor deities, such as the gods of rivers.
5. Scott Scullion, "Olympian and Chthonian," *ClAnt* 13 (1994): 75–119.
6. Walter Burkert, *Greek Religion*, trans. John Raffan (Cambridge, MA: Harvard University Press, 1985), 203.
7. Gunnel Ekroth, *The Sacrificial Rituals of Greek Hero-Cults in the Archaic to the Early Hellenistic Period* (Liége: Presses universitaires de Liège, 2002), http://books.openedition.org/pulg/490.
8. Angelos Chaniotis, "The Divinity of Hellenistic Rulers," in *A Companion to the Hellenistic World*, ed. Andrew Erskine, BCAW (Malden, MA: Blackwell, 2003), 432–3. Cf. the establishment of a temple for the deceased Seleucus in App. *Syr.* 63.
9. S. R. F. Price, *Rituals and Power: The Roman Imperial Cult in Asia Minor* (Cambridge: Cambridge University Press, 1984).
10. Price, *Rituals and Power*, 11–16.
11. Price, *Rituals and Power*, 7–11.
12. Price, *Rituals and Power*, 210–20
13. Price, *Rituals and Power*, 29.
14. Price, *Rituals and Power*, 217.
15. Price, *Rituals and Power*, 238; see also 25–32.
16. Price, *Rituals and Power*, 234–48.
17. Douris *FGrH* 76 F13. Translation from Price, *Rituals and Power*, 38. See the fuller discussion of this hymn in Chaniotis, "Divinity," 431–2.
18. *OGIS* 493 1.16–23; 38–42.
19. *OGIS* 458. Translation from Price, *Rituals and Power*, 54–5.
20. Kyle Erickson, "Another Century of Gods? A Re-Evaluation of Seleucid Ruler Cult," *ClQ* 68, no. 1 (2018): 97–111.
21. M. David Litwa, *We Are Being Transformed: Deification in Paul's Soteriology*, BZNW 187 (Berlin: De Gruyter, 2012), 71–4; Plut. *Dem.* 10.4, 12.1.
22. Litwa, *We Are Being Transformed*, 77–8, 83.
23. M. David Litwa, *Posthuman Transformation in Ancient Mediterranean Thought: Becoming Angels and Demons* (Cambridge: Cambridge University Press, 2021), 74–93, https://doi.org/ 10.1017/9781108921572.
24. For the purposes of this book I primarily focus on figures that receive cult or other forms of widespread recognition or veneration. Thus I do not address the traditions of individual mystery initiation or mystic ascension attested in Greek, Second Temple, and rabbinic thought, although they are a necessary part of the wider discussion on theology in the ancient Mediterranean. Jewish aspects of these phenomena are addressed in the first two chapters of Kimberly Stratton and Andrea Lieber, eds., *Crossing Boundaries in Early Judaism and Christianity: Ambiguities, Complexities, and Half-Forgotten Adversaries. Essays in Honor of Alan F. Segal*, JSJSup 177 (Leiden: Brill, 2016), by John J. Collins and Jonah Chanan Steinberg respectively.
25. J. Edward Wright, "Whither Elijah? The Ascension of Elijah in Biblical and Extrabiblical Traditions," in *Things Revealed: Studies in Early Jewish and Christian Literature in Honor of Michael E. Stone*, ed. Esther G. Chazon, David Satran, and Ruth A. Clements, JSJSup 89 (Leiden: Brill, 2004), 123–38; Sigurd Grindheim, "Sirach and Mark 8:27–9:13: Elijah and the Eschaton," in *Reading Mark in Context: Jesus and Second Temple Judaism*, ed. Ben C. Blackwell, John K. Goodrich, and Jason Maston (Grand Rapids, MI: Zondervan, 2018), 130–6.

26. John Reeves and Annette Yoshiko Reed, *Enoch from Antiquity to the Middle Ages, Volume I: Sources From Judaism, Christianity, and Islam, Enoch from Antiquity to the Middle Ages, Volume I* (Oxford: Oxford University Press, 2018).
27. Daniel Johansson, "The Identity of Jesus in the Gospel of Mark: Past and Present Proposals," *CBR* 9, no. 3 (2010): 364–93.
28. Johanssen, "Identity of Jesus," 365.
29. Heikki Räisänen, *The "Messianic Secret" in Mark*, trans. Christopher Tuckett, SNTW (Edinburgh: T&T Clark, 2003), 64.
30. Edwin K. Broadhead, *Teaching with Authority: Miracles and Christology in the Gospel of Mark*, JSNTSup 74 (Sheffield: JSOT Press, 1992), 21.
31. Besides Broadhead and Räisänen, see Carl R. Holladay, *Theios Aner in Hellenistic Judaism: A Critique of the Use of This Category in New Testament Christology*, SBLDS 40 (Missoula, MT: Scholars Press, 1977). Gods with human parentage, such as Dionysus and Asclepius, are usually not listed as θεῖοι ἄνδρες in the scholarship.
32. But cf. John Serrati, "A Syracusan Private Altar and the Development of Ruler-Cult in Hellenistic Sicily," *Historia* 57, no. 1 (2008): 81.
33. See Price, *Rituals and Power*, 32–40.
34. Cicero refers to Antony as the priest of *divus Iulius* (Cic. *Phil.* 2.43), and Dio Cassius describes that Antony and Cleopatra attempted to elevate Cleopatra's son Ptolemy to the kingship of the eastern regions, on the argument that Ptolemy was Julius Caesar's natural son, as opposed to the adopted Octavian (Dio 49.41.1).
35. Tae Hun Kim, "The Anarthrous υἱός θεοῦ in Mark 15,39 and the Roman Imperial Cult," *Biblica* 79, no. 2 (1998): 221–41.
36. Bruce W. Winter, *Divine Honours for the Caesars: The First Christians' Responses* (Grand Rapids, MI: Eerdmans, 2015), 80–7.
37. Walter Grundmann, "δύναμαι, κτλ," TDNT 2:286–90.
38. Silva, "δύναμις," NIDOTTE 1:776.
39. For miracles and magic in the Jesus tradition, see Richard A. Horsley, *Jesus and Magic: Freeing the Gospel Stories from Modern Misconceptions* (Eugene, OR: Cascade Books, 2014); Howard Clark Kee, *Miracle in the Early Christian World: A Study in Sociohistorical Method* (New Haven, CT: Yale University Press, 1983); Howard Clark Kee, *Medicine, Miracle and Magic in New Testament Times*, SNTSMS 55 (Cambridge: Cambridge University Press, 1986); Michael Labahn and L. J. Lietaert Peerbolte, eds., *A Kind of Magic: Understanding Magic in the New Testament and Its Religious Environment*, LBS 306 (London: T&T Clark, 2007).
40. See Collins, *Mark*, 292; France, *Mark*, 244; Marcus, *Mark 1–8*, 379–80.
41. There are various ways to read "the carpenter, the son of Mary" (6:3). Most commentators note the relatively low social standing of a manual laborer, and several point out that referring to Jesus with a matronymic rather than a patronymic might indicate an accusation of illegitimacy. See Collins, *Mark*, 290; Myers, *Strong Man*, 212.

7

The Values of Empire

New Testament scholarship has long seen a fundamental conflict between early Christianity's apocalyptic, eschatological thrust and the idea of ethics in the sense of organizing and operating in a society. Torah lays out commands for cultic, civic, judicial, and even agricultural life, and New Testament texts variously ignore and abrogate Mosaic law, or reinterpret it in ways that seem to emphasize the individual's spiritual state rather than community functioning or ritual concerns. Community or ecclesial rules such as those in the Pastoral epistles and the Didache are often understood as evidence of composition later in the first century or into the early second, once expectations for an immediate eschaton had died down.

One reason for this difference between the Hebrew scriptures and the Christian ones is simple historical circumstances. The Torah represents the process, or the remembered and reconstructed process, of administering a nation—it is a law code with genetic resemblance to the law codes of other Near Eastern kingdoms and cities. First-century Jesus followers, as minority collectives within the cities and districts of the Roman empire, were in no position to develop or enforce a legal code. Proponents of the idea that the Gospels or Jesus himself meant to promote an entirely new social and administrative structure, such as Ched Myers and Richard Horsley, have put forward no evidence that such a society was ever actually practiced on even the village scale.

That is not to say that there are no ethics in the New Testament. Besides Jesus's major sermons in Matthew and Luke, Paul promotes and in a few specific cases prescribes modes of behavior even in as relatively early an epistle as 1 Corinthians. Controversies such as whether to eat meat sacrificed in temples outside of Jerusalem (1 Cor 8–10; Rev 2:14) are the iceberg's tip hinting at larger issues of community segregation and everyday interaction with outsiders.[1] Paul's treatment of the topic does actually constitute an ethical discussion about handling disagreements within the community as well as the rights and treatment of apostles. The fact that those kinds of discussions are few and scattered in the preserved first-century texts does not mean they were not happening, simply that they were rarely canonized.

It is perhaps better to say, as some have, that early Jesus texts as a collective focus more squarely on *values* than *ethics*. That is, as Paul argues in Romans, the emphasis is on one's acceptance or rejection of certain ideals or states, and behavior does not need to be prescribed because one's commitment at the outset will determine one's actions. Using that approach, we can examine the values of Mark not exclusively by looking for things that Jesus says his followers should or should not do (although there are plenty of those moments) but by also being attentive to the motivations and relationships that the text treats as good or bad. By comparing such patterns in Mark to similar investigations of some Roman imperial literature, we can discuss whether and to what extent Mark promotes different values and ethics than the Romans did.

Here is a good place to remind my reader of James C. Scott. A common strategy in empire-critical work is to take both Mark's (or whichever NT author's) portrayal of the Kingdom of God *and* its (or the modern author's) portrayal of Rome at face value, and to judge from there that Mark espouses more admirable values than the Romans did. This, however, begs the question. By applying an infrapolitical lens we can get a more scientific result. Within the Roman empire, Mark represents a certain private (or hidden) transcript. However, the Gospel positions itself as the public transcript for the Kingdom of God. When making comparisons, therefore, we should compare similar types of text—in this case, pro-regime writings—and treat them similarly. It is important to specify that at the beginning of this process I am investigating what values and ethics the target authors, including Mark, *profess*, not necessarily which ones either Rome or the Kingdom of God lives up to.

Greco-Roman Ideals and Values

Virtue in Greek and Roman culture was a complex equation of interrelated social, economic, behavioral, and inborn qualities. The Latin *virtus* and Greek ἀρετή both have their conceptual beginnings on the battlefield, denoting courage and physical or strategic prowess, before expanding out into much wider aspects of life. In the highly stratified world of the early Roman Mediterranean, status and expectations of behavior were considered linked and were also connected to appearance, ancestry, ethnicity, and gender. Traits such as courage, intelligence, piety, and wisdom were expected among elite males and deemed impressive, or sometimes impudent, in anybody else. On the flip side, status itself was a virtue that was due honor and privilege, especially from those of lesser status. Roman culture had particularly subdivided and precise stratification, marked by intricate and highly visual signals such as dress and class-assigned seating in public places,[2] but stark divisions between elite and nonelite were also present in contemporary Greek and Judean cultures.

Honor and Shame

Honor is a complex system of social organization that intertwines with and mutually enforces the values of a culture. Diachronically, Robert Oprisko defines honor as "the category of related processes that structure social reality by inscribing value onto persons and groups" and "a process of altering social reality through the medium of value."[3] In the ancient Mediterranean, honor particularly but not exclusively turned on expressions and recognitions of socioeconomic status. It is expressed in vocabulary such as τιμή, *honor*, and כבד, but analysis of its dynamics cannot be limited to word studies.

Oprisko's definitions of honor are helpful for categorizing discussions of the phenomenon in the ancient world. They are too lengthy to quote in detail here, but I will attempt a brief summary. First, *external honor* refers to the "processes of social intercourse between individuals and groups" and comprises prestige, shame, face, esteem, affiliated honor, and glory. All of these aspects preserve or change a person or group's relative status among other persons or groups. *Internal honor* refers to the processes "that occur within an individual's psyche." Oprisko subdivides internal honor into honorableness, which is the extent to which an individual or group values honor as a personal quality, right, or possession; and dignity, the development and expression of a "personal honor code" that the individual holds separately from and often as proof against wider social codes.[4]

What is missing from Oprisko's schema is a definitional distinction between the honor that a person holds, expresses, or deserves and the honor that others afford to them. These distinctions are essential in the ancient Mediterranean. In Roman, Judean, and Greek cultures, a person's honor is functionally distinct from, but in a close reciprocal relationship with, the ways that others (including nonpersonal "others," such as law and custom) acknowledge, behave toward, and contribute to it. In English, these two concepts are not expressed with different vocabulary, but with different syntax and grammar, where the verb "to honor" expresses the external response.

In ancient Mediterranean cultures, a person had a certain amount of inherent honor based on their social class, ancestry, gender, legal status, and ethnicity. At the top of the scale were high-status nonforeigner men, with women, children, and especially slaves occupying the bottom levels. Wealth afforded specific and limited amounts of social mobility, as did marriage and manumission. Behavior could also affect one's honor: notable acts of courage or cowardice, important literary or civic contributions, and correct or incorrect behavior with respect to the honor of others could affect one's esteem, which is to say, insiders' and outsiders' perceptions of one's honor.[5]

Suetonius's life of Nero is an informative example of the various facets of this dynamic in Roman culture. It begins with brief accounts of a few of his ancestors, in order "to show more clearly that though Nero degenerated from the good qualities of his ancestors, he yet reproduced the vices of each of them, as if transmitted to him by natural inheritance."[6] This immediately creates a tension between, on the one hand, the honor derived from his aristocratic birth and the noble reputations of a few of his forefathers, and, on the other hand, the shame that Suetonius ascribes to both the emperor himself and to his birth family on account of violent reputations (*Nero* 2–5). After his adoption by Claudius, his birth father's family name became a source of insult, due to the man's poor reputation and conviction of treason, and perhaps also because the name indicated a lower status than the imperial family into which Nero was adopted (5; 7.1; 41.1).

The early part of the biography, depicting Nero's youth and the good aspects of his reign, shows him amassing honor through success at sports, largesse to the people and the military, and a prodigy's skill at poetry and legal matters (7; 8.2; 10). He also demonstrated appropriate piety toward the deceased Claudius and toward Augustus (8.1; 12.4), enacted or planned measurable improvements in Roman infrastructure and law (16–17), and was known for financing impressive entertainments (11–13).

Suetonius intentionally divides the accounts of Nero's blameless (*nulla reprehensione*) and praiseworthy (*non mediocri laudi digna*) acts from his shameful and criminal ones (*probris ac sceleribus*) (19.3), a common strategy in Suetonius's writings that highlights the valuation he places on one act or another. Besides an abundance of paranoia, violence, and sexual deviancy, this section of biography also includes Nero's singing career (20–25), which was prodigious and successful, despite the weakness of his instrument (20.1). The "shame" here seems to rest on his lust for fame, which had him violating festival customs, hogging the spotlight, reveling in base flattery, and even, according to rumor, forcing women to give birth during his concerts, rather than leave before he was finished (23.2). Since self-control (*gravitas*) and temperance (*temperentia*) were important values in Roman culture, this kind of egoism would diminish, or at least not contribute to, Nero's honor.

Masculinity (*virtus*) was also a crucial aspect of honor in Roman culture, and although Suetonius does not outright label Nero as effeminate, he describes a number of traits that the Romans coded as feminine. The emperor's love of performance is among them,[7] as well as his tendency to take a submissive role during sex,[8] his love of wealthy extravagance,[9] and the way he wore his hair.[10]

As a social function, honor is tied to how well one meets or exceeds social expectations, which depend on the level of status one occupies. Nero makes for an excellent example for us because, as a man of aristocratic birth, adopted into the imperial family and eventually becoming emperor himself, he occupied the highest social level attainable by humans. Therefore he was due proper acknowledgment and deference to his status by all others, but also was responsible for maintaining types of behavior, dress and grooming, and company that Roman society deemed fitting to his station. Nero is also a clear demonstration of the privilege of wealth and status: if Suetonius's accounts of his socially deviant behavior are accurate, it is unlikely that someone of much lower status would have been able to maintain such a lifestyle for very long. Many of the things he is accused of were only or especially possible because of his status. Further, aside from material legal consequences, the reputation of a lower-status person might be damaged beyond access into many facets of elite society. After a humiliating and graceless flight from Rome at the end of his life, Nero was nonetheless afforded a rich, imperial burial. Ultimately, the worst consequence he faced for his lack of honor was an unsalvageable reputation.

With its rigid and multilayered social system, Roman society provides particularly clear examples of honor and shame, but the dynamic is not absent from eastern societies. The Homeric literature, which Greeks looked to for centuries as a standard for emulation and social values, depicts honor as a man's most important possession, more important than wealth or life, a value amply reflected in Hellenistic literature.[11] In Hebrew tradition, the Ten Commandments famously contain an emphasis on honor toward one's parents, the people most immediately above a person in social status. Josephus highlights for us the competitive nature of honor in Hellenistic and early Roman Judea when he claims that John of Gischala incited the city of Tiberias to revolt against him (Josephus) out of jealousy of his success (*Life* 122–5).

Carlin Barton and Daniel Boyarin have shown that the word *religio* was used in a variety of situations to denote behavior between entities of different social classes, including not only gods but also parents, rulers, teachers, and so on. The same was true of Greek θρησκεία, although that word was more consistently cultic than *religio*.[12] In both cases and especially the Latin, behavior toward the gods is categorized in the same schema as other social relationships, where gods occupy the top stratum. Thus, royal and imperial cults were a way of assigning even higher status to individuals or families than was normally possible for humans. Appropriate acknowledgment of this highest status included sacrifice; adherence to taboos or sacred laws; and tithes, financial donations, or other material gifts to the god or the temple.

Wealth

One of the primary indicators and vehicles of status in the Greco-Roman world was wealth. The aristocracy amassed and maintained wealth through landownership and, sometimes, war spoils. The same was true of local and provincial elites away from Rome, some of whom also had the ability to collect taxes, either in money or kind. Under Roman law, equestrian and senatorial status were only accessible to those who possessed specific levels of wealth. A long aristocratic ancestry was ideal for status, but for freeborn men, admission into or ejection from elite rank was legally a matter of wealth.

With wealth comes power. The more wealth and status a person could claim, the less power could be exerted over them by other elites and the more power they amassed over those below them in rank, especially in their immediate networks. As smallholding became less and less common, subsistence and local cooperative networks also diminished in favor of wage economies, rent farming, and debt practices that increased the control elite landowners enjoyed over local populations (see Appendix A). One of the controls put on this power was the social value of the correct use of wealth.

Euergetism, the practice of elites using personal wealth to finance infrastructure, festivals, and other civic goods, was a crucial part of the economic and governmental structures of the early empire, both in purely economic terms and socially. By paying for the construction of public buildings and infrastructure such as roads or financing local festivals, sacrifices, or games, wealthy members of the community benefited local life and commerce in observable ways, and amassed honor for themselves, some of which still survives in the form of inscriptions and literary mentions. It was also an important system for maintaining administrative power. Arjan Zuiderhoek describes how the practice of euergetism created bonds between elites and the rest of the populace by promoting trust. By spending one's own money for the benefit of the community, one demonstrated that "one cared about the community, was prepared to make sacrifices on its behalf, and could thus be trusted with social power and political office."[13] This was deeply ingrained as a responsibility of the wealthy and a source of honor in both Greek and Roman societies and is also demonstrated in Judean contexts. 1 Maccabees, for example, preserves or imagines a decree by the people of Judea declaring Simon Maccabee their ruler and high priest (14:25–49), citing military victories and effective leadership, but also "spent much of his own money" (v. 32) in raising and paying the army. The statements that he fortified various towns and cities (vv. 33–34) also include financing building projects.[14]

Once again, we can turn to Suetonius's *Nero* for concrete examples of the use and misuse of wealth in Roman consciousness. Among the first of Nero's "good" actions is his distribution of money or goods (*congiarium*) to the people, along with a financial bonus (*donativum*) to the soldiers (7.2). This he followed with a gift of four hundred sesterces to every man in Rome, salaries to cash-poor senators, and a grain allowance for the praetorians (10.1–2). He also financed entertainments such as races, plays, and gladiatorial games (11–12), at which he would sometimes distribute lavish gifts among the audience (11.2). After the great fire in 64 he paid out of his personal fortune (*easque sumptu suo*) to retrofit or rebuild buildings with firefighting measures supposedly of his own design (16.1).

On the other hand, Suetonius also shows us the limits of proper use of wealth. He accuses Nero of "riotous extravagance" (30.1 [Rolfe LCL]), spending money on gambling, gifts to friends and those to whom he owed favors, clothes, extravagant travel and leisure, and, famously, the ostentatious rebuilding of his palace after the fire (30–31). Once, his lavish spending on entertainment also displaced regular commerce, driving up grain prices (45.1). Thus, the proper use of wealth was to maintain a balance. The elite were considered responsible for improving civic life with their wealth as part of the social contract. An elite person was also expected to avoid looking or living like a lower-class person, as Suetonius demonstrates in this backhanded description of Nero's usual clothing: "He often appeared in public in a dining-robe, with a handkerchief bound about his neck, ungirt and unshod" (41 [Rolfe LCL]). However, it was at least as shameful to *over*spend. Greek and especially Roman ideals around masculinity favored a certain austerity in a person's presentation, painting excessive luxury and ostentatious display as feminine and foreign. Spending oneself into poverty through luxury was a failure of *temperentia* and a sign of weak character.

By the first century BCE, Latin writers closely associated luxury with corruption, which could manifest either as a softening to helplessness or as avaricious violence. Pliny the Elder's sneering outrage at Pompey's over-the-top triumph (*Nat.* 37.6) and Livy's prologue both embody the conviction that Roman society had fallen from its noble origins into decadence, violence, and greed.[15]

Although euergetism was a crucial aspect of the early empire's society and economy, it had its limits. Civic gifts and building projects were expected to improve the general welfare in some way. This could be directly, in the case of infrastructure like roads and aqueducts, or, as with games, festivals, and public buildings, by promoting commerce and improving the morale of the populace. At the level of individuals or families, the patron/client system functioned between the wealthy and the less wealthy, or the wealthy and what in a modern context we might call the working class: free or freed laborers, merchants, farmers, and craftsman. While it was admirable enough to assist the truly destitute, and promoted in Homer and other foundational folklore as a part of the obligation of hospitality, the fundamentally reciprocal nature of the patronage system did not promote purely altruistic giving.[16]

Judean Values

In the Judean context, there is a temptation to separate out the threads of Hebrew tradition from the foreign influences of Hellenism and Romanization. Herod's extensive building projects throughout Greece, Syria, and Asia Minor contributed to his reputation as a foreigner and a Greek and Roman sympathizer. Meanwhile, although support for one's city or household as a whole was a Roman and Hellenic value, care for the impoverished—those who could not meaningfully reciprocate—had deep roots in near eastern tradition, far more explicitly than in Greece and Rome; Ramsay MacMullen particularly highlights the Egyptian evidence.[17]

In its own right, the Hebrew tradition is vocal regarding ethical responsibility to the poor, including the destitute. Torah contains various requirements of support or agricultural leavings for the poor (Exod 23:25-27; Lev 19:9-10; 23:22; 25:35; Deut 15:7-11). The prophets often cite disregard for the poor as one of Israel's transgressions (e.g., Jer 5:28; Amos 8:4-6; Ezek 16:49) and exalt God for protecting and caring for the poor (e.g., Isa 25:4; Jer 22:16). Ben Sira even declares that charity atones for sin (3:30). Rabbinic literature after the war continued to emphasize help to the poor as a major value.[18]

Concern for the poor in Jewish literature does not necessarily translate to suspicion of wealth. There are numerous warnings against fraud, greed, and other bad-faith economic activity, but wealth is often understood to be a sign of divine favor, which can be maintained in part by just action toward the poor. The idea of retributive justice—that good or bad actions garner appropriate consequences—was widespread in the Near East and embedded in Hebrew thought. In Proverbs, verses such as 12:3, 13:25, and 14:19 contrast the righteous (in the LXX generally δίκαιος) with the unrighteous (ἀσέβειος, ἄνομος, κάκος, etc.) in terms of the wealth and power that the former enjoy as rewards. By this means, diligence and industriousness are also associated with righteousness, as qualities that bring about wealth (e.g., 10:4). These verses cannot be taken on their own, and an important caveat to them is that wealth is a reward of righteousness, but not the only one, and is not, in itself, righteous. For example, 10:4 (NRSV: "A slack hand causes poverty, but the hand of the diligent makes rich")[19] is part of a longer list of oppositions between the righteous and the unrighteous, in which memorialization, honor, and peace are also the reward to the righteous and wise. Chapter 11 continues the litany and includes several warnings on the misuse or mishandling of wealth, power, or goods (vv. 1-2, 4, 24-26, 28), as well as nods toward eschatological rather than material rewards (vv. 4, 7, 18-19, 21, 31). Verse 28 shows clearly that wealth and righteousness are not synonymous: "Those who trust in their riches will wither, but the righteous will flourish like green leaves" (NRSV). One can be wealthy and unrighteous, or poor and righteous, and justice can be marked in ways other than materially.[20]

These sentiments maintained into the Second Temple period and are evident in Ben Sira (e.g., 10:13; 27:10), which understands reward and punishment both as direct actions of God and as the natural operations of the world (which God created).[21] In that text and others, wealth is recognized as a good, or at least desirable, thing. Its desirability makes possible comparisons such as 40:25: "Gold and silver make one stand firm, but good counsel is esteemed more than either" (NRSV). In fact, the chapter goes on to declare that death is better than begging, casting what is sometimes the only avenue of survival for the destitute as a sign of covetousness and lack of intelligence (vv. 28–30). Like Proverbs, Ben Sira acknowledges that wealth enables certain kinds of sin (20:21) and that virtue and vice reside within a person, and might be influenced but is not created by their financial state.[22] There is no suggestion that the average person should not have wealth, simply that they should not value it above other good things and certainly not over the fear of God.[23]

Mark

The ethics, values, and morality of the Gospel of Mark are hardly an untapped field. My goal in the following pages will not be to bring entirely new discoveries to light, nor to make an exhaustive investigation of the topic, but to read these issues through the same lenses that I have been using throughout this study. If we begin with the assessment that Mark is about the Kingdom of God, then it makes sense to try and understand its values and ethics in civic terms. This section will investigate major aspects of Mark that express the values and ethics of the Kingdom of God.

Honor

The importance and ubiquity of honor valuation in the ancient world make it likewise an important topic for understanding Markan values. Many studies have approached the topic of honor in early Christian writings, and I will focus on three of them here. Richard Rohrbaugh's insights on the challenge-riposte dynamic illuminate some of Jesus's interactions with Pharisees and other opponents,[24] David Watson revisits the Messianic Secret through the lens of honor and shame,[25] and Adam Winn expands on Watson's conclusions through consideration of Roman political ideology.[26]

Rohrbaugh identifies the challenge-riposte as a common dynamic in ancient enactments of honor. Honor was considered a limited good. Similar to the real economy, the economy of honor, as it were, was zero-sum. A person gained honor either at the direct expense of a challenger or by rising above competitors. Therefore, challenges to one's honor were difficult to let go unanswered. Rohrbaugh sees this process at work in many of Jesus's interactions in Matthew and Luke. The temptation scene (Matt 4:1–11//Luke 4:1–13) is a classic example: Satan challenges Jesus and each time Jesus answers with a witty and knowledgeable reply, until eventually Satan runs out of challenges and leaves, losing the exchange and thus diminishing in honor.[27]

Although he does not address Mark in any detail, Rohrbaugh's conclusions are easily applicable there. "Public questions are always honor challenges,"[28] he warns. Thus Mark 2:1–11, the healing of the paralytic, takes on an enlightening element of social, not just cultic or political, competition. The fact that *Jesus* initiates the challenge—the Pharisees question "in their hearts" and thus not publicly—adds a wrinkle that is not usually a part of the discourse on this passage. Jesus deliberately sets out to gain honor at the expense of the Pharisees at this gathering. He is not defending himself, as the embattled rightful king, but stepping forward in an aggressive move to elevate his own status.

Throughout the text, Jesus does not come away from a verbal encounter without having the last word except twice. I have already discussed the exchange with the Syro-Phoenician woman (7:24–30) in terms of the Gospel's treatment of gender. In Chapter 3 I argued that the pericope does not indicate an elevation of the status of women in the Gospel. However, the element of honor adds another layer. Although, as I demonstrated before, the text does not challenge her low status as a woman and a foreigner, it does allow her to gain honor at Jesus's expense by challenging him and winning, and Jesus concedes. The other instance is in his πάτρια Nazareth. Unlike in ch. 7, Jesus does not happily concede. Here he explicitly declares himself without honor (ἄτιμος; 6:4) and is unable to enact works of power. In the very next pericope he instructs his disciples to curse such places in their own travels (6:11)—not to tolerate lack of honor in his name.

Watson applies the honor/shame dynamic to Jesus's healing miracles and the so-called Messianic Secret. He suggests that, rather than secrecy, Jesus's operative motivation for silencing demon and instructing beneficiaries to silence is refusal of earned honor. He notes that in ancient society, an act such as healing or exorcism would require reciprocal honors from its recipient, and that, in social terms, Jesus refuses to allow those who have received his patronage to fulfil their obligations as clients to honor him. However, Watson ameliorates this social conflict by positioning Jesus as a "broker"; that is, benefactions such as healing come *through* Jesus *from* God, and therefore Jesus is not the one owed honor.[29] This seems to be the case in the healing of the leper in 1:40–45, where Jesus instructs the leper to make the appropriate sacrifices in the temple;[30] and in the Gerasene demoniac, whom Jesus commands to spread the word about what "the Lord" had done for him (5:19–20).[31]

Rather than arguing that Mark rejects the honor/shame system wholesale, Watson reads the erstwhile secrecy motif as a revision or critique of it. The crucifixion in particular, widely considered the most shameful manner of death, is transformed into a critique of the honor economy in Mark.[32] The fact that the text will only allow Jesus royal imagery in ch. 15 is a support of this reading. However, it is worth recalling the long tradition of killed and/or humiliated heroes in Greek tradition, if not as much Hebrew and Roman. Enduring defeat and shame, especially for the sake of others or at the hands of a particularly violent rival, can, ironically, be a source of earned honor. In Mark this dynamic appears in 6:14–29: we are not meant to read John's death by beheading as an elevation of Herod's honor, but of John's at Herod's expense.

Winn's contribution to Watson's schema accounts for Roman dynastic sensibilities. Watson investigated the honor/shame dynamic in Greco-Roman culture generally and directly, citing many examples of rulers or heroes seeking great honor and thus interprets Jesus's inconsistent rejection of accolades as a critique of the system. Winn, however, finds direct parallels in Roman imperial narratives. He observes that Roman political ideology "necessitated certain limits to an individual's acquisition of public honors" in line with Roman suspicion of ostentation and monarchy.[33] Winn shows that multiple writings demonstrate the Augustan strategy of *recusatio*, refusing excessive honors, which was also emulated by later emperors.[34]

I have already discussed Augustus's refusal of honors and the appearance of maintaining the republic in Chapter 3.. Applying the honor/shame dynamic as a more holistic category, we can see that it is not a rejection of the system, but a balance to it, and even an ironic strategy to amass more honor. It also, as Winn notes, solves the problem of inconsistency in the Markan secrecy motif: no one expected Augustus to refuse all honors, and he did not.[35] Augustus and later emperors made use of *recusatio* in order to avoid the appearance of tyranny and, especially in the early empire, protect the appearance of the venerable republican government. That is why official cultic honors were slow to arrive in Italy, but widespread in the eastern provinces, where monarchic kingship and high honors for rulers were more culturally at home.

In Mark we see Jesus directing honor toward God, as in 1:40-45 and 5:19-20. He also refuses honor from demons, in the form of naming, whom he silences or refuses to let speak in 1:24-25; 1:34; and 3:11-12. Watson suggests that he is rejecting honors from (and thus debts of honor to) enemy combatants or rejecting titles that acknowledge his close relationship with God, as a means of sidestepping excessive honor.[36] Another possible interpretation is that he rejects titles such as "Holy One of God" (1:24) and "Son of God" (3:11) so as not to be seen to amass honor in the place of God, just as Augustus avoided amassing honor in the place of the republic.

The major episode where Jesus does not silence a demon is in ch. 5, the episode in the graveyard. There the demons address him by a title much like the two he has already rejected from demons, Son of the Most High God (υἱὲ τοῦ θεοῦ τοῦ ὑψίστου; 5:7), and instead of silencing them he asks their name. The demons' military name offers a hint for interpretation. Homeric battlefield encounters often begin with an exchange of names and ancestry, assuming that honor in battle comes from defeating an equal or superior opponent. Here, Legion recognizes that they are no match for Jesus and surrender. Jesus has gained honor, as vv. 14-20 demonstrate.

Discipleship

When a rich man asks Mark's Jesus how a person can obtain eternal life, his answer is, "Sell everything you own and follow me" (10:17-22). At the beginning of the Gospel, his first direction is "Repent!" and his second is "Follow me!" (1:15, 17). Throughout the Gospel there are commands to follow and examples of what it means to succeed or fail in that endeavor. Even Satan is invited to follow—the usual English rendering of 8:33, "Get behind me, Satan," obscures the repetition in the next verse, "If any want to become my followers" (NRSV). The verbs in both sentences are modified with ὀπίσω μου.

Investigations of discipleship in Mark have often, naturally, focused on *the disciples*, which is to say the Twelve whom Jesus calls over the course of the first three chapters and who constitute the core of his following for the rest of the narrative. Mark's intense ambivalence toward the Twelve and especially the central four (Simon, Andrew, James, and John) has driven many interpretations of the Gospel. That discussion often becomes one of belief and comprehension—the disciples fail because they embody the wrong Christology, seeing Jesus as a miracle worker or a Davidic messiah instead of the apocalyptic savior of souls. Scholars have offered several solutions to the disciples' failure. Many focus on the revelatory nature of "the cross"—that is, Jesus's death and resurrection—as the central feature of Mark's Gospel, the necessary event that illuminates Jesus's true identity and the true meaning of discipleship.[37] Others hypothesize a sectarian conflict, in which Mark represents a Galilean movement opposed to the Jerusalem church[38] or a Gentile Christianity opposed to a Jewish one.[39] Robert Tannehill's narrative evaluation of the role of the disciples argues that the reader is meant to identify with the Twelve, first as those who are called, then as those who struggle to understand, and finally by way of a negative example.[40]

I will not disagree with the basic premise of such assessments, although their various conclusions cannot always be reconciled. The twelve disciples clearly misunderstand who Jesus is and what he is there to do. Peter's challenge in 8:27–38 is difficult to interpret in any other way, not to mention the request of James and John and the subsequent argument (10:35–45). However, Suzanne Watts Henderson reminds us that "the second gospel devotes much greater attention to the *nature* of Jesus' messiahship than it does to the claim *that* Jesus is the Christ."[41] Likewise, although the theme of misunderstanding pervades Jesus's interactions with the disciples, it always rotates on the question of correct or incorrect action. Understanding Jesus means following him, and following Jesus entails a constellation of right and wrong behaviors.

Henderson divides discipleship into two types of action: presence and practice. She illustrates presence through analyses of the parable discourse in 4:1–34 and the wilderness feeding in 6:30–44; and practice through the sending in 6:7–13 and the walking on water in 6:45–52. Through the first example, she shows that "presence" is not only the passive acceptance of the Kingdom of God (the lesson of the soils), but also taking up the seed bag of the no-longer-present Christ to continue to sow, persisting through temporary failure toward the ultimate abundance of the Kingdom.[42] The feeding story shows presence to be "transformative," as the disciples move from roles as teachers and the "privileged" retinue of Jesus to active workers and servants of the Kingdom, and those trusted with the Kingdom's bounty.[43] The sending narrative of ch. 6 translates presence into practice, as the disciples (and, diachronically, Mark's readers) take on the role of successors, engaging in the exact activities that Jesus did in the first few chapters of the Gospel.[44] Finally, Henderson finds in the sea narrative that the disciples not only fail to recognize Jesus but also fall short of understanding their own role in the Kingdom. Had they understood "about the loaves," that is, that they are active and authorized successors of Jesus, with the ability to enact his power, they would have fared differently.[45]

Henderson's analysis is helpful because it understands discipleship in terms of participation in the Kingdom of God, not just through discrete behaviors such as giving to the poor or tending to the sick but as an interplay between identity and action. Although she does not take it in that direction, Henderson's framing is a good starting point for an empire-critical reading. Her somewhat spiritualized abstractions, "presence" and "practice," can be expressed more concretely through a sociopolitical lens as, perhaps, loyalty and responsibility. I do not say "citizenship," as that was a specific legal status, and loyalty and responsibility were not expected solely of legal citizens.

It is possible to read many of Jesus's interactions with his disciples and others in terms of loyalty. That the disciples follow him at all, and that they come readily when he calls them (1:16–20; 2:13–14) is indicative of their loyalty. The first mention of the Twelve as a group, 3:13–19, begins with them unquestioningly responding to his summons, and ends with a foreshadowing of Judas's disloyalty. The very next pericope, vv. 20–30, is also a teaching on loyalty. Although it begins as a statement on the weakness of Satan's kingdom, it transitions into a teaching on blasphemy against the Holy Spirit. The intensely metaphysical language masks such a reading, but v. 30 clarifies that the "Holy Spirit" in this instance refers to Jesus's authorization as God's agent, and that the specific βλασφημία against it is the slander of saying, "He has Beelzebul," in v. 22. In short, they have expressed disloyalty against Jesus by accusing him of being an agent for the enemy. Another facet of the relationship between disloyalty and enemy activity appears in ch. 8, when Jesus responds to Peter's uncomprehending insubordination by referring to him by the enemy's very name (8:32–33). By the end of the Gospel, Jesus has no followers at all—loyalty has not survived adversity, as he predicted it would not in the parable of the sower.

The next piece is responsibility. By accepting Jesus's commission, the disciples take on responsibility for his work. As Henderson observes, the feeding narratives translate the disciples' privileged position as Jesus's inner circle, his "aristocracy," into direct service of the community, a responsibility that Jesus states outright in 10:42–44. In both feeding stories they mistrust or forget Jesus's ability to provide for the populace, but also forget their own responsibility in administering the Kingdom's abundance, a responsibility of the rich in Hebrew texts. The central four also fail in their responsibility to Jesus, not to the community, in Gethsemane (14:32–42), unable to stay awake and keep watch while Jesus is in prayer.

Mark's development of suffering as an essential feature of status in the Kingdom of God starkly illustrates the link between loyalty and responsibility. Jesus's suffering sets the bar, as he tells James and John in 10:39, and the disciples eventually prove themselves incapable of facing it. This might be the answer to Mark's lack of punishment for Judas, compared to his various gory ends in later texts. Judas certainly commits what we might call high treason, handing over Jesus to his enemies (and παραδίδωμι has military uses indicating surrender or treason, e.g., Thuc. 7.86.4; Paus. 1.2.1), but the others respond by deserting. All twelve have, from a military perspective, committed capital crimes, and so it is possible that Mark does not feel the need to single out Judas's betrayal as worthy of greater punishment than Peter's.

Wealth

Perhaps the strongest case to be made that the Gospels operate under a different value system than Greco-Roman and Judean society is in their treatment of wealth. The theme is most apparent in Luke-Acts, which displays an ambivalence toward wealth, repudiating it in passages like the Sermon on the Plain (Luke 6:20–49) and the tale of the rich man and Lazarus (16:19–31), but stopping short of requisite poverty for characters such as Cornelius (Acts 10:1–33).

Mark has less of a laser focus on wealth than Luke does, but the critique of it is by no means absent or less ambivalent. The most obvious touchpoint is 10:17–31, a three-part treatment of wealth and discipleship. In the first part, Jesus directly instructs the man to give away all of his wealth (v. 21) and implies a link between such voluntary poverty and following, which is to say, loyalty. Suggestions that the command applies *only* to this (unnamed) character and is not intended to be general create a difficulty: why include it at all in that case, and why attach it to the subsequent sections that very clearly express general instruction?[46] Further, Michael Peppard connects this exchange directly to what he calls the region's "zero-sum" economic system, by means of Jesus's addition "do not defraud" to the list of commandments otherwise in the Decalogue (v. 19).[47] By pointedly referring to *how* the man must have obtained his wealth—by taking and withholding it from others—Jesus sets up the reason why the wealthy in vv. 24 and 25 have such difficulty entering the Kingdom of God. Not because material possessions are inherently unclean or sinful,[48] but because of their participation in the unjust system that made them wealthy.

Other features of the Gospel likewise suggest that possessions, in and of themselves, are not the problem. The call narratives of Simon, Andrew, James, John, and Levi (1:16–20; 2:13–14) have these five disciples at least temporarily abandon their livelihoods, but they seem to retain property and certainly maintain family ties (1:29; 2:15). Collins compares the call scene in ch. 1 to similar narratives in various philosophical writings, and while some of those include a repudiation of material wealth, it is not a ubiquitous feature. Socrates's students, for example, are not expected to live in poverty.[49]

The implication in 10:28–29 that the Twelve and possibly others have left behind their entire lives is somewhat difficult to reconcile narratively. Recipients of Jesus's benefactions in Galilee are not explicitly commanded to abandon livelihoods, possessions, or families. If Peppard's analysis is correct, we might read the command to the rich man as referring exclusively to the wealthy, and not applicable to wage-earners. We may also be seeing the author's hindsight in Peter's statement at 10:28 ("We have left everything and followed you")—from Paul we know that Peter engaged in at least some traveling evangelism, and tradition assigns similar lives to most of the original apostles. In that case it is not meant to apply to all followers of Jesus, but simply the closest ones—perhaps, outside of the narrative, a reference to a nascent professional clergy—and the promise of vv. 29 and 30 should not be read as a command.

The widow who gives two λεπτά (12:41–44) and the woman with the alabaster jar (14:3–9) complicate this discussion. Although in ch. 10 Jesus instructs the rich man to give away his wealth to the poor, in ch. 12 he praises an impoverished widow (χήρα πτωχή) for giving her entire livelihood (βίος) and in 14 he rebukes the person who suggests that the woman should have followed Jesus's own instruction from ch. 10, by selling the jar and helping the poor with the proceeds.

Susan Miller observes that Jesus addresses the remarks in ch. 10 to his disciples in (relative) private, in contrast to the previous verses, which are part of his "teaching in the temple" (v. 35) and therefore probably to a crowd. This adheres to the same pattern found in ch. 4, where Jesus moves from teaching appropriate for the public to teaching meant for insiders.[50] Thus we can afford it the same consideration as 10:28—perhaps it is a teaching meant only for certain members of the community.

In another possibility, the widow's case can be reconciled by understanding it as an observation of the action, rather than praise of it. Jesus has not commanded the widow to give her last *quadrans*—to the Jerusalem temple, no less, which he excoriated for its economic practices in the chapter before. Further, the woman seems to have no connection with Jesus whatsoever, or even awareness that she is being observed. Thus he is pointing out to his disciples a quality of the woman's character, without commenting on the ethics of the act itself. At its most basic, the contrast to the "many rich people" in v. 41 makes this moment a simple teaching in percentages and relative dedication; the temple is, for the moment, not relevant, only the fact that the widow values her devotion to God with her whole life, and the rest do so only with the bare minimum, or what they have to spare.

Like all episodes in Mark, the action of the woman with the alabaster jar can be read through multiple lenses. Warren Carter highlights many of them, particularly issues of power, gender, class, and Roman occupation.[51] In terms of wealth, the passage seems to contradict Jesus's command to the rich man in ch. 10. Far from selling this thing of great value, the woman effectively destroys it—whether she breaks the jar itself or only the seal, she uses the ointment up. Jesus responds with what Carter calls a "contextual argument,"[52] that "you will always have the poor with you and whenever you wish you can do good for them" (v. 7). The immediacy of Jesus's death momentarily overrides ethical obligations, much like his presence temporarily overrides the necessity for fasting in 2:18–20.

Interpreters tend to take this explanation for granted. Even Carter, who is otherwise alert to dynamics of power and not hesitant to name hierarchies and violence in the text, does not comment on Jesus's response except with the explanatory "[the woman's act] signifies multiple and rich dimensions of Jesus' identity and of being a follower" before going on to contrast the woman's loyal action to the betrayal of Judas.[53] Modern interpreters, by and large, have not failed to notice that Jesus sets one rule for followers and another for himself, they simply accept that it is a just double standard.[54] But double standard it is, or, perhaps more accurately, a material example of the Kingdom's hierarchy. Verse 10:21 does not say, "Sell everything you own *except what you might need for a rich and honorable burial.*" (The disciples, by leaving behind homes, family, and so on (10:28), also risk losing out on honorable funerary rites. But Jesus, in contrast to the "first will be last" teaching in 10:43–45, claims to deserve them. The narrative contrast between the woman's action and Jesus's humiliating death is poignant, but this passage complicates any schema that assigns a consistent inverse relationship between wealth (or honor) and status in the Kingdom of God.

Does Mark Overturn Majority Values?

It has been my argument throughout this book that, contrary to the readings of many empire-critical scholars, the Gospel of Mark does not include a reimagination of the basic cosmic and social structures that were common to the societies of the ancient Mediterranean. There are, likewise, many readings of Mark and indeed the rest of the New Testament—not limited to academic readings—that claim that the overturning of elite values is basic to the Christian message. I have demonstrated that the Gospel subscribes to a fundamentally stratified worldview and understands there to be hierarchies of status in the Kingdom of God. The question, then, is whether the privileges and responsibilities of status maintain in Mark's world. Does Mark overturn these Roman values, or simply repackage them?

An argument for the former is David Watson's comparison of Mark and the *Life of Aesop*, a Greek novel from the first century CE.[55] In this paper, Watson argues that both texts critique elite values. *Aesop* does so by satirizing them, making education and status the butts of jokes. Mark is no comedy, but the Gospel similarly humbles the wealthy and powerful and elevates characters who would be derided in Greek and Roman elite culture. The difference, Watson concludes, is that *Aesop* mocks but does not challenge: it puts forward no other way to organize society, and its ending can be read as vindicating elite ideas about status and *paideia*. Mark, on the other hand, challenges. According to Watson, the Gospel uses language that upends Mediterranean ideas about status and honor, and at the end greatly glorifies a crucified man—not despite his humiliating death, but in part because of it.

However, while Watson convinces that Mark "criticizes the elite value system while demanding fundamental changes in actions and attitudes toward status relations,"[56] he and many other interpreters overlook the fact that Mark *upholds the values of status and honor* by definition. Further, Adam Winn's additions to Watson's observations about honor in Mark show that the Gospel works within well-established ideas about honor and shame. In fact, the only elite value that Mark consistently rejects is wealth as a marker of or prerequisite to status. Once a person has status in the Kingdom of God, that person is due all of the normal privileges and honors appropriate to their rank, including gifts (14:3–9), fame (5:20), and influence (6:7–12).

Another difficulty comes from the problem of preserved perspectives. The vast majority of surviving Greek and Roman literature was produced by and for members of the elite class. Even texts that laud magnanimity and assistance for the poor tend to cast suspicion on the *misuse* of wealth, not wealth per se. Similarly, much pre-Roman Jewish literature emerged from the priestly class, elite if not always extravagantly wealthy, and much Second Temple and first- and second-century CE Jewish writings are eschatological, apocalyptic, and often sectarian. In any of these categories, it is difficult at best to determine how well they represent the ideals of the majority. Therefore, rather than saying that Mark overturns or maintains "Roman" ethical values, it is better to ask its relationship to *elite* values. Overall, as I have shown, it upholds the values of honor, status, community care, and loyalty, and only departs in its rejection of the inherent ethical value of wealth.

Notes

1. Margaret Froelich, "Sacrificed Meat in Corinth and Jesus Worship as a Cult among Cults," *JECH*, November 3, 2020, 1–13, https://doi.org/10.1080/2222582X.2020.1779101.
2. Joseph Hellerman's thorough summary highlights the rigidity of Roman social stratification in the late republic and early empire. Joseph H. Hellerman, *Reconstructing Honor in Roman Philippi: Carmen Christi as Cursus Pudorum* (New York: Cambridge University Press, 2005), 3–33.
3. Robert L. Oprisko, *Honor: A Phenomenology* (London: Taylor & Francis Group, 2012), 4–5.
4. Oprisko, *Honor*, 6–7.
5. Oprisko, *Honor*, 6, 88.
6. Suet. *Nero* 1.2 [Rolfe LCL].
7. Craig A. Williams, *Roman Homosexuality: Ideologies of Masculinity in Classical Antiquity*, Ideologies of Desire (Oxford: Oxford University Press, 1999), 139–40.
8. Suet. *Nero* 29; Williams, *Roman Homosexuality*, 204.
9. Colleen Conway, *Behold the Man: Jesus and Greco-Roman Masculinity* (Cary, NC: Oxford University Press, 2008), 24.
10. Suet. *Nero* 51; Kelly Olson, "Masculinity, Appearance, and Sexuality: Dandies in Roman Antiquity," *JHS* 23, no. 2 (2014): 188–9.
11. Mark T. Finney, *Honour and Conflict in the Ancient World: 1 Corinthians in Its Greco-Roman Setting*, LNTS 460 (London: T&T Clark, 2012), 17–34.
12. Carlin A. Barton and Daniel Boyarin, *Imagine No Religion: How Modern Abstractions Hide Ancient Realities* (New York: Fordham University Press, 2016).
13. Arjan Zuiderhoek, "Benefactors, Markets, and Trust in the Roman East," in *The Extramercantile Economies of Greek and Roman Cities: New Perspectives on the Economic History of Classical Antiquity*, ed. David B. Hollander, Thomas R. Blanton, and John T. Fitzgerald (London: Routledge, 2019), 55, https://doi.org/10.4324/9781351004824.
14. For a detailed analysis of this passage and its similarities with and departures from similar Greek inscriptions, see Gregg Gardner, "Jewish Leadership and Hellenistic Civic Benefaction in the Second Century B.C.E.," *JBL* 126, no. 2 (2007): 332–7, https://doi.org/10.2307/27638437.
15. For an analysis of attitudes toward luxury in late Republic and early empire writers, see Robert J. Gorman and Vanessa B. orld: A Study in Sociohistorical MethoGorman, *Corrupting Luxury in Ancient Greek Literature* (Ann Arbor: University of Michigan Press, 2014), 326–426.
16. Ramsay MacMullen, "Social Ethic Models: Roman, Greek, 'Oriental,'" *Historia* 64, no. 4 (2015): 487–510.
17. MacMullen, "Social Ethic Models," 494–7.
18. B. Z. Rosenfeld and H. Permutter, "The Attitude to Poverty and the Poor in Early Rabbinic Sources (70–250 CE)," *JSJ* 47 (2016): 411–38.
19. Contrast this with the LXX rendering, πενία ἄνδρα ταπεινοῖ, χεῖρες δὲ ἀνδρείων πλουτίζουσιν "Need makes a man impoverished, but the hands of the strong [lit. masculine] make wealthy."

20. For a close analysis of the dynamics of wealth and poverty in Proverbs, see Raymond C. Van Leeuwen, "Wealth and Poverty: System and Contradiction in Proverbs," *Hebrew Studies* 33 (1992): 25–36.
21. Bradley C. Gregory, *Like an Everlasting Signet Ring: Generosity in the Book of Sirach* (Berlin: De Gruyter, 2010), 38–44. The whole chapter is informative.
22. Gregory, *Everlasting*, 50.
23. Gregory, *Everlasting*, 29–32.
24. Richard L. Rohrbaugh, "Honor: Core Value in the Biblical World," in *Understanding the Social World of the New Testament*, ed. Dietmar Neufeld and Richard E. DeMaris (London: Routledge, 2009), 109–25, https://doi.org/10.4324/9780203865149-17.
25. David F. Watson, *Honor among Christians: The Cultural Key to the Messianic Secret* (Minneapolis, MN: Fortress Press, 2010).
26. Adam Winn, "Resisting Honor: The Markan Secrecy Motif and Roman Political Ideology," *JBL* 133, no. 3 (2014): 583–601.
27. Rohrbaugh, "Honor," 114.
28. Rohrbaugh, "Honor," 114.
29. Watson, *Honor among Christians*, 40–7.
30. Watson, *Honor among Christians*, 47–9.
31. Watson, *Honor among Christians*, 98–9.
32. Watson, *Honor among Christians*, 69.
33. Winn, "Resisting Honor," 589–90.
34. Winn, "Resisting Honor," 589–92.
35. Winn, "Resisting Honor," 600–1.
36. Watson, *Honor among Christians*, 58.
37. This is basic to Wrede's conclusions (William Wrede, *The Messianic Secret*, trans. J. C. G. Greig, Library of Theological Translations [Cambridge: James Clark, 1971], 67). For an analysis that focuses on Mark, see especially Weeden, *Mark*.
38. Werner H. Kelber, *The Kingdom in Mark: A New Place and a New Time* (Philadelphia, PA: Fortress Press, 1974), 138–44.
39. Joseph B. Tyson, "The Blindness of the Disciples in Mark," *JBL* 80, no. 3 (1961): 261–8.
40. Robert C. Tannehill, "The Disciples in Mark: The Function of a Narrative Role," *JR* 57 (1977): 386–405.
41. Suzanne Watts Henderson, *Christology and Discipleship in the Gospel of Mark*, SNTSMS 135 (Cambridge: Cambridge University Press, 2006), 11–12, emphasis original.
42. Henderson, *Christology*, 97–135.
43. Henderson, *Christology*, 169–203.
44. Henderson, *Christology*, 136–68.
45. Henderson, *Christology*, 204–37.
46. Thomas E. Schmidt, *Hostility to Wealth in the Synoptic Gospels* (London: Bloomsbury, 1987), 111.
47. Michael Peppard, "Torah for the Man Who Has Everything: 'Do Not Defraud' in Mark 10:19," *JBL* 134, no. 3 (2015): 595–604, https://doi.org/10.15699/jbl.1343.2015.3006.
48. "The fact that possessions are to be given away and not destroyed does, incidentally, forestall the conclusion that the material world is inherently evil" (Schmidt, *Hostility*, 111).
49. Collins, *Mark*, 156–60.

50. Susan Miller, *Women in Mark's Gospel*, JSNTSup 259 (London: Bloomsbury, 2004), 116.
51. Carter, *Mark*, 380–9.
52. Carter, *Mark*, 387.
53. Carter, *Mark*, 389–90.
54. Besides Carter, see, e.g., Collins, *Mark*, 640–3; Miller, *Women*, 135–7; Michele A. Connolly, *Disorderly Women and the Order of God: An Australian Feminist Reading of the Gospel of Mark* (New York: T&T Clark, 2018), 157–62, https://doi.org/10.5040/9780567674159.
55. David F. Watson, "The 'Life of Aesop' and the Gospel of Mark: Two Ancient Approaches to Elite Values," *JBL* 129, no. 4 (2010): 699–716.
56. Watson, "'Life of Aesop,'" 700.

Conclusion

This book began with the observations of liberationist, postcolonial, and empire-critical scholars that the Gospel of Mark is an example of literature of the oppressed. With wide scholarly agreement that Mark was written in the period immediately after the destruction of Jerusalem and its temple, it is important to understand the ways in which it responds to and is shaped by its historical circumstances. There are many aspects to Mark's treatment of Roman power and indigenous resistance in the 60s and 70s, but this study has focused specifically on the questions of rulership, authority, and hierarchy. It has done this by analyzing three major aspects of the Markan world: the Kingdom of God, Jesus's royalty and agency, and Jesus's divinity.

Chapter 2 examined the Kingdom of God, setting the stage with a description of the political and military circumstances of Rome's expansion into Asia, Syria, and the Levant. This chapter found that Mark reflects and portrays a complex political and social situation. The Gospel assumes and advocates for a cosmic hierarchy with God at the top, Jesus as his deputy, humanity occupying various levels in the middle, and Satan and the rest of the demons as enemy forces.

Chapter 3 narrowed the scope from the kingdom to its king. Through the interrogation of titles for Jesus and the use of the word ἐξουσία, Chapter 3 found that Mark uses such vocabulary strategically and rhetorically. The word ἐξουσία exclusively relates to Jesus throughout the Gospel, characterizing him as the agent of God and implicitly denying authority to characters or groups that do not receive it through this chain of command.

Chapter 4 turned from the ideologies of rulership to the military and war. The chapter established that militaristic expansion was a usual part of international relations in the Hellenistic and early Roman periods, including among Judeans. Portions of Mark that use military language or imagery were closely analyzed from this point of view, showing that war and militarism are just as necessary to Mark's kingdom of God as to Augustus's Rome.

Chapter 5 took up the issue of salvation. Markan salvation is comparable to the common Hellenistic ways of understanding that vocabulary, in that it envisions rescue from war, hunger, and sickness. Markan salvation is different from common usages in the text's reliance on Jewish apocalyptic literature and ideas about God's fulfilment of history. Importantly, in the present context "freedom" is a relative idea that has more to do with propagandistic portrayals of conquering and conquered than it does with individual or political liberty.

Chapter 6 moved from kings to gods, without taking a step. Like Augustus and the other Roman emperors, Jesus is divine because of the authority and power granted to him by God. The title Son of God, despite the Gospel's ambivalent treatment of it through Jesus's use of Son of Man, identifies Jesus as a ruler like the Roman emperor. Like ἐξουσία, the word δύναμις is closely connected to Jesus in Mark, not only emphasizing his benefactions but also pointing past Jesus to the sovereign above him, who is the true source of the benefactions.

Chapter 7 looked back on the preceding chapters to ask how different Mark's worldview really was. I began this book with the charge that many empire-critical authors idealize the Gospels' "anti-Roman" and "anti-imperial" rhetoric, sometimes going so far as to suggest that they were promoting (economically if not administratively) separatist communities. Chapter 7 concluded, with the help of the rest of the book, that Mark upholds the values of status and honor that were integral to Hellenistic and Roman society and rule.

The most important insights of this study for Markan scholarship have to do with Mark's ideal world. Counter to some political readings of the Gospel, especially those by Myers and Horsley, this study found that Mark does not propose or expect an egalitarian structure for the Kingdom of God. It does not advocate an ethic of nonviolence. Instead, Mark's Kingdom of God is strikingly similar to the Roman empire in structure and modus operandi. It consists of clear and rigid stratifications that are just as determinative as those of Rome, although based on different values. Those nearer the top of the hierarchy, who have eagerly accepted God's reign and live according to its rules, will ultimately reap rewards. Those who resist will be punished. The model of Jesus as the active ruler who yet claims authority from a higher divinity and from the cosmic order itself is identical to Roman propaganda such as the *Res gestae divi Augusti*, Virgil's *Aeneid*, and the writings of Suetonius.

Empire and the Death of the Hero

Chinua Achebe's *Things Fall Apart*, the first postcolonial novel, is the story of Okonkwo, the ambitious and respected leader of a fictional village in Nigeria just before and after the arrival of British colonizers. The last third of the book describes the dissolution—through a combination of coercion, force, and apparent acquiescence—of the village's traditional lifestyle and social infrastructure as English ways take hold. Okonkwo is not only unwilling to submit to the new power but also incapable of resisting it. In the end he commits suicide rather than accept the processes of colonial law, which he knows are stacked against him.

In Homer's *Iliad*, the city of Troy endures its tenth year of siege. In the story, the goal of the Achaeans camped on the beaches is not imperial conquest but cosmic justice, the rightful avenging of the Trojan prince Paris's flaunting of divinely ordained rules of hospitality. The best of the Trojans, the prince Hector, displays no motivation besides the protection of his city, and for the city's sake walks into battle against an opponent he knows outmatches him. The epic ends with the glorious funeral of Hector, Troy's last hurrah before the utter destruction every reader knows will follow.

In the Gospel of Mark, Jesus travels throughout Galilee, Judea, the Decapolis, and Syria, delivering people from under the weight of Satanic oppression. He conflicts with the local authorities in his interpretation of divine will and mandate, and runs afoul of Roman imperial control when he claims the title Messiah. He challenges the most basic meaning of the title as he goes willingly into arrest, trial, torture, and finally execution. His final breath is accompanied by a portent of Jerusalem's destruction.

These three stories are separated by millennia, and although they approach the issue of conquering power in different ways (the *Iliad*, e.g., celebrates it), the similarities of their endings are striking and surely not coincidental. Whether Achebe recognized the resistance inherent in Mark, he certainly knew both the Gospel and Homer, and Okonkwo is without a doubt a tragic non-Christ. Whatever Mark thought of the *Iliad*, it is impossible that he would be unfamiliar with its story, and his Jesus is many things but certainly an apocalyptic—and more successful—Hector, going to his death because he must.

In the earliest and latest of these three works, the dead heroes are symbols of futility. Okonkwo cannot stop his son being educated by the missionaries, and, more fundamentally, can neither take things back to the way they were before the British arrived nor compromise in his resistance. Hector cannot save his city, because Zeus has already made up his mind for its destruction, and the loss of him is Troy's loss of the war.

Mark's Jesus is different. He goes to the cross as willingly and as driven by necessity (δεῖ; e.g., 8:31) as Hector and as stubbornly as Okonkwo. Like the Trojan prince, he dies humiliated and mocked by his enemies, but even without Hector's lavish funeral games he at least receives expensive anointing and a tomb. Like Okonkwo two thousand years later he dies without friends, having to the casual observer failed in his mission. But he promises to return with a vengeance. The author and his first readers knew that Jerusalem had fallen and violent resistance had only resulted in destruction and Rome's stronger grip on Judea and Galilee. But Jesus does what Hector and Okonkwo cannot: he rises from the dead and fulfills his mission. He goes back to Galilee to usher in the Kingdom of God under the nose of the emperor.

For Mark, Jesus's mission is never the salvation of Jerusalem nor the restoration of Israel. Mark knows those things will not be done. Maybe he has seen battles or their aftermath, or watched recently captured slaves build a mountain for soldiers to march up and take an impregnable fortress. He knows that God, called out by Rome's generals, left the temple and Jerusalem to their fate. For Mark, Jesus's mission was to be the harbinger and client ruler of a different kingdom, one as inexorable and as universal as Rome, ruled over by the one true God and his true Son.

Appendix A

Judea before the War

To establish a baseline from which to discuss the portrayals of military and political leadership in Mark, this chapter will describe various aspects of the history, society, politics, and military matters of Hasmonean and Roman Judea, and other connected regions. A reading of many of the empire-critical, liberationist, and (to a lesser extent) postcolonial treatments of the Gospels and Judean history in general will leave one with a sense of an oppressed majority under constant threat by a violent, foreign minority. However, by highlighting details of the rulership, economics, and political and social divisions of the region, this appendix will challenge the sentiment of that reading, if not all of the facts.

Rulership, War, and Expansion

The importance of the eastern Mediterranean coastal regions as a gateway between Egypt and points north stretches back as far as the historical record. In their own right, Israel and Judea were militarily and politically small areas situated at a strategic point in between large and powerful empires, and this did not stop being the case after the exilic period.

For Alexander and the Diadochid dynasties, control over Syria and the larger Levantine region was imperative to maintaining dominance across the Baltic peninsula, Anatolia, Egypt, and Persia. Increased naval technology and power on all sides changed the ways in which Egypt interacted with allies and rivals, but the land bridge through Judea remained a crucial tactical holding.

Internal Judean politics come more into focus after the Hasmonean revolt. 1 Macc 7 demonstrates a clear divide among the Judean aristocracy regarding Seleucid rule—the "lawless and impious men of Israel" of v. 5 are difficult to locate with any specificity, but are certainly aristocrats who support Demetrius's reign over Judas's. Competing accounts (1 Macc, 2 Macc, and Josephus) of the impetus for the revolt and variant accounts of Judas Maccabeus's embassy to Rome[1] further demonstrate a range of attitudes toward the Hasmonean dynasty.

The history of Roman involvement in Judea nominally begins here. By all accounts, the first approach to Rome secured something like the treaty cited in 1 Macc 8:23–32. Rome had already clashed with the Seleucid empire in its defense of Egypt, so from an anti-Seleucid Judean perspective they were a useful ally: somewhat distant, but willing to make the trip, or at least had been willing for the Ptolemies, and superior to the Seleucids in military might. Likewise, if we follow the pro-Hasmonean accounts, Judas's defeat of the Seleucid general Nicanor in 161 seems to have been enough for the senate to regard him as worth a treaty. Diodorus of Cicely gives an account that suggests someone other than Judas may have convened the embassy,[2] but all the sources attest to a successful negotiation. As ever, the position of Judea over the land routes between the Seleucid and Ptolemaic empires may have played a role.

Despite the treaty, the Hasmoneans did not receive military aid from Rome against Seleucid armies. Rome seems to have remained completely uninvolved in Judean affairs until Pompey's intervention.[3] Roman contact during the Hasmonean period was limited to periodic diplomatic confirmations, with no known requests for or offers of aid on either side. The Hasmoneans instead played rival Seleucid rulers off of each other for aid and support. The Roman alliance may have contributed to those negotiations at times, but otherwise, as Seeman observes, it seems to have functioned largely as a legitimization tool: Rome was a known and feared power and recognized Hasmonean leadership as legitimate.[4]

Eventually, Hasmonean infighting concurrent with Roman consolidations of power across Cappadocia and Syria led to Pompey's intervention in Judean affairs and subjugation of Jerusalem in 63 BCE. Pompey also reduced the borders of Judea, which had been expanded under Aristobulus and Alexander Jannaeus across the Jordan and north toward Damascus, to "its own boundaries" (Jos. *Ant.* 14.4.4). Thus Samaria, Idumea, and Galilee were no longer under Judean control, and Judea itself was made tributary to Rome through Syria.

The Roman civil war and the period of the Triumvirate afforded further opportunity for the last Hasmoneans to strategize for power, but the end result was the establishment of the Herodian dynasty, beginning with Antipater, who had earlier sided with Hyrcanus of the Hasmoneans.

A full summary of the political and military saga that culminated in Herod's installation as king is not necessary here, except to say that control of the region remained as important and contentious during the triumvirate period as it had been among the Seleucids and Ptolemies. Antipater and Herod were able to leverage their good relationships with Rome, and at the height of his power Herod's territory covered Judea, Idumea, Perea, Samaria, Galilee, and Batanea—most of what would have been the Davidic kingdom of Israel, minus most of the Decapolis and plus a fair amount of territory to the north. Upon Herod's death, Rome once again divided the territory among his heirs, so that by the time of the events of Mark's Gospel, Judea, including Samaria, was fully a Roman province under the administration of a prefect, and Galilee and Perea were under the control of Herod Antipas, whose official title was tetrarch. By 66 CE and the beginning of the war, the majority of the area outside of provincial Judea was under Herod Agrippa II.

This rough and rather dry summary of three centuries' rulership in the region is intended to highlight the instability of leadership, even under Roman influence. No portion of the southern Levant during this period enjoyed a stable, long-term government, with peaceful transition of power, for more than a few decades at a time, and some cities were subject to frequent shifts and sieges.

Our ancient sources, of course, focus on the major personalities of these conflicts and power imbalances. We learn the names of the most important dynasts, as well as their close advisors, and of the kings and generals who played various roles over the centuries. It is more difficult to tell how instability at the highest levels of rulership affected the common people.

During the Hasmonean period, expansion meant forced cultural change in some cases. 1 Maccabees begins with Antiochus's cultural genocide and Mattathias's violent overturning of it. The NRSV translation of 1 Macc 2:46 perhaps overemphasizes the scope of Mattathias's actions, reading "forcibly circumcised" for the neutral LXX περιέτεμον, and adding "all" to the LXX's less explicit "the uncircumcised boys whom they found within the boundaries of Israel." By comparison, Josephus's version has Mattathias allowing the circumcision of those boys who had not undergone the ritual, by driving away Seleucid enforcers who had prevented them from doing so (*Ant.* 12.6.2). Whether Mattathias's imposed or repermitted Torah observance, Josephus claims that John Hyrcanus imposed forced circumcisions on Idumea (*Ant.* 13.9.1). Each of these episodes includes the destruction and/or erection of temples and cult images. In all of these cases, dynastic change and military expansion seem to have had real effects on the lives of nonelites, at least in terms of what practices were or were not allowed, and which gods received public cult.

Other effects are difficult to quantify. The Hasmonean and Herodian rulers mustered their armies from the cities and villages that they ruled, so frequent war and heavy losses would have social, familial, and economic impacts. There is archaeological evidence of villages that endure battles and cease habitation during the Hasmonean period,[5] and the ancient sources attest to full-scale war on various cities and citadels. However, the literary language of war is formulaic and generalizing, and these texts rarely account for the noncombatant experience of sieges, sacks, and battles in much detail.

Economics

Similarly taxation: Herod the Great and his heirs impressed the Romans in part by quickly pulling together large sums in taxes, but their methods of doing so and the everyday effects on the populace are not made explicit in our sources.

In fact, the scholarship on the economic world of early Roman Judea and surrounding regions is divided. Ancient literary sources emphasize socioeconomic divisions as well as cultural ones, painting a picture of a foreign and Roman, or local and Hellenized/Romanized, elite exploiting the majority peasantry. Some portrayals take on the kind of moralizing that is common in the Gospels, depicting wealth as inherently or closely connected to spiritual rot. Recent New Testament scholarship has combined these ancient perspectives with modern Western liberal and progressive ideologies to emphasize the damage, violence, and exploitation that empire wreaks on indigenous communities.

On the other hand, archaeological investigations show a generally stable system of local and regional districts connected to each other and the wider Mediterranean world through extensive and consistent trade. The benefits of the system surely favored the elite, but the archaeological evidence does not depict the kind of bleak situation put forth by Horsley when he says that "village communities in Galilee and Judea were disintegrating under the political and economic pressures of Roman rule."[6]

A middle way is possible. When facing the literary evidence, it is important to remember that documents like the Gospels come from relatively small communities with specific agendas regarding the social, economic, and political realities they address. We know very little about their earliest audiences and virtually nothing about their authors—we cannot and should not assume that they give an objective picture. In fact, we need to recognize that in many respects these documents do not reflect the perspectives of the majority, while also remaining cognizant of different possible levels or experiences of poverty, oppression, and colonization on various subgroups of the population, as well as the limits of modern historical and archaeological methods to illuminate these things. To complicate matters, modern categories of empire and indigeneity, developed in response to European colonialism in the modern period, do not always cleanly apply to the complex populations of the eastern Mediterranean, who had undergone and participated in colonizations and imperial expansions back and forth for millennia by this period.

Addressing the archaeological evidence, economic stability does not preclude other, less physically persistent forms of oppression or conflict. Cultural pressures between Judean and non-Judean populations might and do find some archaeological survival, but are perhaps more clearly seen in, for example, the rising emphasis on halakhic food taboo in Second Temple and New Testament literature.[7] Archaeology by no means invalidates the existence of an elite class in the region (and I am aware of no attempts to argue that it does), and the basic existence of an elite, nonlaboring class implies some level of exploitation of the nonelite class, even if it is not as abject and dramatic as some portrayals would have. Less exploitation is still exploitation. Finally, and dovetailing with my critique of the literary evidence, a group's material level of stability and power is not always the same as its perceived level, especially when we allow for factors other than strictly economic and political. Regardless of the recoverable economic situation of Roman-era Judea and Galilee, the revolt took place and the Gospels and other texts preserve ongoing dissatisfaction with the elite classes.

With those caveats in mind, I will give a brief and rough outline of the economic and administrative world of first-century Galilee, Samaria, and Judea. My main source for this outline is Anthony Keddie's *Class and Power in Roman Palestine*,[8] a recent monograph that pulls together both literary and archaeological research to attempt a complex picture of the economic world of the eastern Mediterranean.

Ancient Mediterranean society, writ large, was socially and economically stratified. It operated in large part on networks of patron/client relationships, both between individuals or families and between administrative bodies, for example, the Roman imperial house and the provinces. By the first century this system had begun a transition to greater state control, as the emperors amassed greater and greater resources,[9] although it is still very much in operation and assumed in New Testament writings (e.g., the healing of the centurion's son in Luke 7:1–10 demonstrates a relationship between a patron—the centurion—and his clients—the Judean elders who appeal to Jesus on his behalf).[10]

In Israel in particular, regional and local elites, such as the Herodian kings and the priestly aristocracy, seem to have had a greater impact on urbanization, building, and trade networks than imperial representatives did. To dispel ideas of a "consumer city" economy, in which an urban elite relied on heavy exploitation of a rural peasant class, Keddie points to a slower process of urbanization than has often been assumed, strong toparchies administered from large villages rather than more distant cities, and large amounts of production and commerce within cities.[11]

Nonetheless, landownership and therefore wealth heavily favored the elite. Most land was "royal land," that is, owned by the ruler and worked by slaves and tenant farmers for the production of royal wealth. That land tenancy was not an innovation of the Roman or even the Hellenistic period is irrelevant except ideologically—it interferes with modern portrayals of a righteously egalitarian native Judean society versus exploitative foreign empires. In fact, the main change in the Roman period seems not to have been from smallholders to landlords, but from royal ownership to (elite) private and taxed farms.[12] On its own this would not require any changes to the ways tenant farmers experienced their work, although the relationships between individual landowners and their tenants cannot always be accounted for. The main effect of this change would be increased wealth among the elites favored by these land gifts. That is a political effect as much as an economic one, as much of the change in ownership and administration of these lands took place in the shift from Hasmonean to Herodian control. Direct Roman control of estates in the region seems not to have taken place until after the first revolt.[13]

For nonelites, one major source of dissatisfaction with this system was debt. The loan system could be predatory and often involved interest, and there is papyrological evidence of contracts that hold potential future assets as collateral alongside the property initially put up to secure the loan.[14] A tenant with none of his own property could use the property of a guarantor (a demonstration, perhaps, of the patronage system at work), but in the event of nonpayment that could simply transfer the ownership of debt from the initial lender to the guarantor. Debt could also be inherited by one's surviving family, making it a generational issue and further stymying the growth of wealth among nonelites. Rent and debt forgiveness were well attested and legally regulated, and could be to the benefit of lenders where they contributed to the broader stability of income. However, the debt spiral was still a real problem, and famously a major impetus for the revolt in 66 CE.

Taxation in the Roman southern Levant was complex, involving incomes to Rome, Herodian rulers and their allied aristocracy, and the Jerusalem temple and its priesthood. The amount of taxation fluctuated both over time and with respect to land and activity types, but overall there is little information allowing researchers to assess the amount of taxes paid with much overall accuracy. Herod gained Roman favor by quickly collecting taxes (Jos. *Ant*. 14.11.2; 14.13.2), and within Judea proper the temple aristocracy seems to have been responsible for collecting direct taxes on behalf of Rome,[15] but it is unclear to what extent any of those taxes were more burdensome to the populace as a whole than what had been collected under the Hasmoneans, as suggested by trends in New Testament empire criticism.

Overall, Keddie's marriage of literary, papyrological, and archaeological evidence confirms the basic facts of the economic situation described by Horsley and others, such as a widening wealth gap, extensive tenant farming as opposed to small landholding, complex taxation, and high debt. However, it at the same time challenges many of the details, and especially challenges the idea, common in New Testament studies, that the hardships and inequality that the general populace faced were novel, appreciably worsening on the population level, and distinctly Roman. Thus, two conclusions are especially relevant to this book's major arguments. First, that leading up to the Judean War, life in Judea and Galilee was socially and economically stratified, with a consistent history of military activity and expansion; and second, that this had been the case under Roman, Idumean, Judean, and Macedonian rule and beyond.

Factions and Interests

Factionalism is an often overlooked or oversimplified factor of prewar Judea. Ancient and modern authors alike frame the war as opposition between Rome and the Judeans/Jews. In fact, the more religious translation of Ἰουδαῖος contributes to the difficulty: in modern terms, a shared ideology, much more than a shared geography, carries a sense of assumed unity, whether or not that is actually the case. Gospel interpreters who do allow for factionalism among Judeans (including Judeans not resident in Judea proper) often reduce the issue to aristocracy versus the masses—a step in the right direction, but still incomplete.

Josephus's account of the war depicts a Gordian knot of factionalism throughout the region that cannot be easily summarized. There is no "nation" in the modern sense: he treats cities individually, for the most part, as to whether and when they sided with Rome or the rebels, so that populations as near to each other as Tiberias and Sepphoris are not always in agreement. Beyond that, the populations of individual cities or towns were not unanimous, with competing movements in support of Rome or rebel leaders. To make further complications, not all of the rebel leaders were unified, and some cities put in their lot with Rome not out of acute loyalty to the empire or the Herodian dynasty but simply in an effort to maintain the status quo and seek protection from rebel armies.[16]

Because Mark does not narrate events related to the war, these dynamics are not immediately visible. However, it takes for granted disunities that modern ideas and vocabulary about religion and national belonging tend to gloss over. For a clearer picture of what is going on in the Gospel, it is necessary to set down at least a cursory understanding of some of the factions, demographics, and interests that appear within it.

Pharisees

The pre-Mishnaic sources are generally negative toward the Pharisees, more often than not portraying them as a unified bloc, with little objective description and a lot of rhetorical exploitation. We have no obvious primary sources for the Hellenistic and prewar periods. Josephus claims to have studied as a Pharisee in a passage that is self-aggrandizing to the point that it stretches belief (Jos. *Life* 1.2), but, as I will outline, represents them from the perspective of a hostile outsider. Paul likewise claims to be a Pharisee (Phil 3:5), but, as usual for Paul, is an enigma and possibly a very special case. I expect that a comprehensive understanding of the Pharisees would do more to illuminate Paul than vice versa.

Josephus's treatment of the Pharisees is infrequent, not in the least comprehensive, and mostly rhetorical. They appear in both *Antiquities* and *War* as a political party, to use an anachronistic term, generally power-hungry and despotic. He first introduces them in the reign of Alexandra, the widow of Alexander Jannaeus, who quickly becomes their pawn while they wreak tyrannical havoc on the aristocracy (*War* 1.5.2). He expands on this despotism in *Antiquities*, where he has the Pharisees assassinating those who disagree with them (*Ant.* 13.16.2). In another episode in *Antiquities*, they manipulate a group of women in Herod's court in order to subvert the king (*Ant.* 17.2.4). Later, Josephus holds Zadok the Pharisee partially responsible for founding the "fourth philosophy," on which he ultimately blames the war (18.4–10). This passage specifies that there are roughly six thousand of them and that they are (or claim to be) oneiromancers and legal experts.

The Gospels also paint the Pharisees as corrupt and concerned with their own status. In Mark, at least, they are mostly spared association with Jesus's crucifixion (except 12:13, where they seem to be acting under orders of the priests), but they are consistently opposed to his activities in Galilee and for the first half of the Gospel exist almost entirely as a foil to emphasize Jesus's popularity the righteousness of his teaching.

From Josephus, the Gospels, and Paul, a few details about the Pharisees are likely: they were not primarily aristocratic (though aristocrats were not de facto excluded), they represented a school of civic and cultic jurisprudence that was not strictly Mosaic law but had its basis in it, and they were popular among the nonaristocratic classes of Judea and Galilee. Their power seems to derive mostly from this popularity, so much that Josephus can portray them as the nearly unshiftable power behind Alexandra's throne, and in the Gospels they hold significant enough influence on the village level that Jesus must deal with them as his primary Galilean opposition.

Steve Mason attributes at least some of this popularity to their philosophy of jurisprudence. From the narratives in Josephus he gleans that the Pharisaic interpretation of the law was appreciably gentler than the Sadducean.[17] In *Antiquities* 13, during the rule of Alexandra, they are a deadly problem to the aristocracy, but an incident earlier in the book (13.10.5–6) has them recommending corporal punishment, rather than capital, on someone who has offended the king, thus situating them as demonstrably more merciful, in that situation, than the Sadducees. Their worldview, which Josephus gives in the most detail (but not much clarity) in *Ant.* 18.1.2, allowed for either resurrection or reincarnation of the virtuous, which may also have attributed to their popularity, at least in contrast to the Sadducees.

Sadducees

Josephus's description of the Sadducees in *Ant.* 18.1.4 is less than half the length of his section on the Pharisees, a couple of hundred words in English. From that, we learn that they did not believe in any kind of afterlife (a statement that Mark 12:18 corroborates) and that they regarded the Mosaic law to be the sole authority (see also *Ant.* 13.10.6), exclusive of the Pharisees' traditions "according to the fathers." Here Josephus once again manages a reference to the Pharisees' popularity, saying that those Sadducees in administrative power often were forced to adopt Pharisaic positions in order to maintain public favor.

In *Ant.* 13.10.6, Josephus claims that the Sadducees were relatively unpopular with the masses, but well-regarded among the aristocracy, and it is the general assumption among modern interpreters that they were not only aristocratic but specifically of the priesthood. The Gospels associate them more with Jerusalem than with Galilee. Besides Josephus, a number of rabbinic mentions of the Sadducees likewise situate them as the opposite number of the Pharisees, especially concerning control of the High Priesthood.[18]

From these two outlines, we should see that both the Pharisees and the Sadducees were political groupings, and from that we should reflect on the intrinsic inseparability of "religion" and "politics" in the ancient world and, more to the point, the Gospel of Mark. Halakhic issues such as Sabbath observance and food restrictions have implications for everyday living and economics. Control of the high priesthood amounted to control of Jerusalem and Judean politics. It was a crucial factor in Hasmonean and Herodian dynastic disputes and, after Pompey's conquest, became a tool of the Roman senate or emperor to reward loyal and effective client rulers and otherwise maintain a balance of power in the region that benefited Roman agendas.

Herodians

There is little to say about Mark's "Herodians." The nomenclature is (or seems to be) coined by Mark, and the Gospel does not give any description of the group, except that usage differentiates them from other factions such as the Pharisees. There have been various attempts to identify the Herodians with known parties and organizations, including the Sadducees,[19] but none of these have stuck. The major Herodian ruler during the life of Jesus was Antipas, and Agrippa II around the dates of the war, and certainly Mark uses the name "Herod" in ch. 6 strategically, as I have shown in other work.[20] From a historical standpoint, there is no clearly defined "Herodian" group, and the designation in Mark, as much as it can be taken at any face value, may be an umbrella designation for the aristocracy, or it could refer to some collection of individuals, aristocratic or otherwise, in support of or representing Herodian rulership. W. J. Bennett proposed that they were invented by the Gospel of Mark as a means to link the deaths of Jesus and John the Baptist in more than just narrative parallelism.[21]

That may be the case, or it may be that Mark is simply attempting to represent another vector of regional power, and the connection between Herodian involvement in the two executions is coincidental, or at least not primary.

Scribes

Literacy, which is to say the ability to read and/or write, was generally low in the ancient world, and extremely varied in its types and usages. Particularly since the 1980s, most researchers assume an average literacy rate around 10 percent for the Mediterranean world in general, and possibly lower in some peripheral regions. The issue is complicated by the various types of literacy: bills of lading or tax documents require a different level of reading skill than Homer or Isaiah, and reading and writing are two separate skills that are not always taught together.[22]

Therefore, reading and writing were specialized skills in the ancient world, and one who possessed them could market them for various purposes, and in some cases gain certain levels of authority. In Judea and Galilee, the practice of weekly scripture readings in the synagogues[23] put fluent readers in positions of local prominence, in control of text transmission and interpretation to nonliterates. Scribes could be recognized Torah authorities, trusted as readers, copyists, and interpreters of scriptural texts for a variety of contexts. One possible role of a multilingual scribe might be to render a Hebrew text into the local dialect, especially Greek, adding yet another layer of authority and responsibility for transmitting an "accurate" interpretation of the authoritative text.[24]

In Mark, we encounter the scribes in their capacity as legal and halakhic experts, since that is the core substance of their conflicts with Jesus. However, it serves us well to situate that role in the context of literary and scribal culture in general. Literary education, particularly at the level required for fluent reading, Torah interpretation, and, possibly, Hebrew literacy, required both leisure time and resources to employ tutors, and thus was not common among nonaristocrats.[25] We can also at least suspect that at the village level, the person most qualified to read the scriptures in the synagogue might *also* have made a living or amassed influence by interpreting and writing contracts, correspondence, and other everyday writings for local landowners, traders, and peasants. Therefore, while reading Mark's scribes we should be prepared to understand not only "religious" differences with Jesus, but the structural issues of class, status, and leadership.

Priests

Most basically, the role of priests in most ancient Mediterranean contexts was to serve the god of their particular temple, often by means of sacrifice as well as administrative responsibilities, and also in many cases to communicate between the god and the people via various forms of divination. In Jerusalem this role was hereditary, supposedly tracing back to Moses's brother Aaron and, further back, the patriarch Levi. By the Roman period, most priestly lineages were traced to more recent ancestors, as, for example, the Hasmonean lineage through Joarib (1 Macc 2:1).

The administrative power that the Jerusalem priesthood held varied by period and is often not clearly outlined in our sources. Throughout the Persian and Hellenistic periods the priests answered to imperial governors, who may or may not have been fellow Judeans. When the Hasmoneans, a priestly house, gained rulership over the region, they combined traditionally (and scripturally) separate roles into a single family, increasing the power of the priesthood. Under the Herods and the Romans, the priests were, as in pre-Hasmonean times, answerable to a separate administrator, but seem to have maintained administrative control over Jerusalem and its hinterlands, at the very least. 1 and 2 Maccabees, the Gospels, and other sources attest to the existence of a council of priests, variously called the γερουσία, συνέδριον, *senatus*, Sanhedrin, and so on. It is difficult to tell to what extent this body was "official" in the sense of appointed or inherited offices with clear roles and held for a period of time, or whether it was an ad hoc collection of influential priests advising the high priest on case-by-case matters.[26]

Crucially, the priesthood was not necessarily viewed as a venerable and respectable institution by the populace. The Hasmoneans drew some criticism by combining the priesthood and the monarchy into one family,[27] but more damagingly, Herodian and Roman control by the first century ensured a priesthood and a high priest who served at the whim of a non- or barely native authority.

Biblical, intertestamental, and historical sources indicate that the Jerusalem temple received tithes and other revenues whenever it was operational, from monarchic times up to the 60s CE. Although some of these revenues are clearly defined in Torah, in practice there are a number of unclear details. Grabbe highlights some of the inconsistencies and other potential problems in the sources, including the ambiguity of the cattle tax.[28] The so-called Temple Tax, a popular subject of New Testament criticism, is also a tough nut, with conflicting evidence regarding who paid, when, and under what enforcement.[29] Despite these difficulties, however, it is clear that besides administrative power in Jerusalem, by the first century the Jerusalem priesthood commanded no small portion of the economy in Judea proper and possibly in other districts heavily populated by Judeans. Antiochus's and Titus's sacks of the temple were both able to carry away impressive amounts of treasure, according to the accounts we have.

Rome

The Roman empire exercised direct control of the province of Judea through an appointed governor, and indirect control of other nearby districts through client rulers, especially the Herodian dynasty. Control over the province of Judea was in the hands of Herod Agrippa I 41–44 CE, and it went to Agrippa II beginning in 48 until the 90s (although the imperium continued to assign procurators). Thus, although Mark narrates a time when Judea was exclusively under a foreign procurator, at the time of composition rule was Herodian. That does not imply less Roman control, and the lived difference, especially for people who were not members of the aristocracy, was probably minimal.

Outside of Judea proper, Roman control manifested as power over tributes, the Herodian succession, which areas any given ruler was responsible for, and the titles he or she could claim. Even during times when Rome controlled Judea (and therefore Jerusalem) directly, control of the high priesthood was a prize the emperor could grant to a Herodian ruler with no territorial control anywhere near Judea, and administrative matters in Jerusalem itself often rested on the priesthood.

Rome's most direct appearance in Mark is to facilitate the execution of Jesus, as the narrative's Sanhedrin does not seem to have the right to order capital punishment. While Mark's narrative requires the priests to send offenders to the governor for the actual sentence of execution, Josephus is less clear. *Ant.* 20.9.1 suggests that in the early 60s it was not lawful for the priesthood to convene a council without permission from the governor, but does not explicitly say that the council, once legally convened, was not permitted to deliver a death sentence. In *War*, Josephus states that when Rome took direct control of Judea in 6 CE, that the emperor gave the governor "the power of life and death" (2.8.1), but does not mention the priesthood here. On the other hand, the Jerusalem Talmud explicitly states that the priesthood was not permitted to wield the death penalty under Rome (*y. Sanh.* 18a, 24b). Luke gives us an even more difficult picture: the Sanhedrin sends Jesus to Pilate, who determines that, since he is Galilean, Jesus falls under the jurisdiction of Herod Antipas (Luke 23:1–7). However, Acts has the priesthood sentence Stephen to death by stoning (7:58).

Overall, the literary evidence leans away from priestly power of execution, but is less than concrete. Josephus and the Gospel authors, further, are not above manipulating historical fact for narrative and rhetorical purposes. Therefore, it is best to say that *whatever* the real rights of the priesthood regarding capital punishment, the priesthood ultimately required and operated under Roman validation. The emperor and local governors had various means of expressing displeasure if they disagreed with a decision made in Jerusalem.

Finally, the most active representatives of Rome in Mark are soldiers. Although Pilate condemns Jesus to beating and crucifixion, it is the soldiers who carry out the sentence, and specifically a centurion who witnesses Jesus's death. Historically, it is difficult to say who the soldiers might have been. Zeichmann has shown, as discussed in Chapter 1, that no legions entered the region until the war, and that the Herodian armies mostly comprised locals of various ethnicities and cultures. Zeichmann identifies the soldiers in Mark 15 as Judean auxiliaries under Roman command (as opposed to Herodian),[30] which would suggest but not necessarily require local origins.[31] Evidence from first- and second-century Britain suggests that soldiers maintained ethnic identities, rather than or concurrent with a more homogenized "military" identity, even when stationed away from home for long periods,[32] but if the author of Mark knows anything about likely origins of soldiers under Pilate's command, he makes nothing of it, although he shows himself more than capable of highlighting a character's ethnicity or geographic origins in other scenes. The soldiers in Mark are not meant to be distinctive as individuals or representatives of any particular community outside of the Roman military.

The Crowds

Much like "the Pharisees" and other collectives in the narrative, Mark treats "the crowd" (usually ὁ λαός or ὁ ὄχλος, occasionally πολλοί) as a character in its own right, or several of them. They are the common people of Galilee, Judea, and the Decapolis, of the peasant class and generally to be understood as farmers and other laborers. Also like the Pharisees, Sadducees, Herodians, and so on, the crowds in Mark are a narrative invention. We can better understand Mark's use of them if we have a general historical foundation against which to reference them, but we should not mistake them for a true or even necessarily an attempted representation of the local peasantry in the 30s CE.

Most of the population of the Roman empire, and specifically of Judea and the surrounding regions, were of the laboring class. They were overall nonliterate, but skilled in various trades and spheres, such as carpentry, fishing, food or grape farming, and so on. Ethnically, the region was made up of various groups, especially Judeans, Samaritans, and Syrians, but also Nabateans, Idumeans, and others, all heavily Hellenized and variously Romanized. For observers like us, the most obvious markers of ethnic identity are linguistic, such as writings, inscriptions, and names; and "religious," such as food taboos, circumcision (or not), and sacrificial practices. However, these can overlap. Greek names, for example, were common across ethnicities, making personal or place naming patterns unreliable for differentiating between, say, Judeans and Syrians. On the other hand, identity markers can also be easy to overgeneralize. Food laws, one of the most stereotypical features of Jewish practice and identity from a modern standpoint, were the subject of often fierce debate in the centuries straddling the era line. Finally, identities are not always unifying. Although the Judean War is often presented as "Roman versus Jewish," even a cursory reading of Josephus debunks that construction, with Judean actors on both sides, and numerous rivalries and disputes between supposedly aligned factions.

There is another point of consideration for possibly understanding the crowds in Mark. Some evidence suggests an expectation of community authority may have been endemic to Judean culture. In the Tanakh there are frequent references to "all Israel," "Israel," "the elders of Israel," and other such referents, indicating approval of official decrees (Neh 13:5), rejection or approval of candidates for leadership (1 Kgs 12:1-19; 2 Kgs 11:12), judicial functions (Deut 16:18-20; 21:1-9; Num 35:24-25), and demand for constitutional changes (1 Sam 8:1-9). Even Moses, chosen by God, seems to continue his role by the approval of some body of elders (Deut 5:22-27). Deuteronomy in fact heavily limits the privileges and roles of both the kingship (17:14-20) and the priesthood (18:1-8).

Each of these examples needs to be taken in its individual context, so to use them to posit a constitution or formal community structure in Judea, let alone one that persisted from legendary periods to the first century CE, would be methodologically unsound. However, Second Temple and later sources also contain examples of "the people," more or less clearly defined, making, approving, or rejecting administrative decisions before 70. 1 Maccabees has "the great assembly of the priests and the people and the leaders of the nation and the elders of the villages" (14:28) not only honor Simon Maccabeus with an inscription on Mount Zion, but declare him "their leader and high priest forever" (14:41), abrogating their own future authority to depose him (14:44). In a similar vein, Herod the Great declared the succession of his three sons before an assembly gathered in Jerusalem (Jos. *War* 1.24.5). Synagogues seem to have been centers for local community polity, among other functions.[33] Goodman has argued that Rome's misunderstanding of such expectations was instrumental in breeding the disunity that led to the war in 66.[34]

To the extent that such a phenomenon may have existed in Judean society, and to the extent that any form of polity exists at the mercy of the population it governs (certainly, as both Josephus and the Gospels attest, the people are capable of riots), the crowds in Mark can be understood as representative of this crucial popular opinion. However, identity and identification of "the crowds" in first-century Judea and Galilee must take into account economic, ethnic, locational, linguistic, family, political, and other aspects, so that it is not possible, historically, to treat the populace as a collective except in the broadest of terms.

How the War Started

There is rarely a simple, one-track trajectory leading to any armed conflict. Such black-and-white answers are often the product of hindsight and tend to obscure complex and often ambiguous realities. This is no less the case for the Judean War. Simply the usual English nomenclature—"Jewish," "Roman-Jewish," or "Jewish-Roman" War—sets the reader on a path predetermined by ideology. It is no longer the war that took place in Judea, but the one that pitted *Jews* against *Romans* as categorical opposites, two united fronts. Better, it allows Western Christians (confessional or cultural) to take sides in what amounts to a holy war between the comparatively righteous (if, for some authors, fatally nonbelieving) underdog and the heathen, idolatrous oppressor. Such blatantly sectarian language has fallen out of favor over the past century, but the dichotomy survives.

A few episodes from Josephus's narratives of the war are popular proofs of this reading. Pilate's erection in Jerusalem of standards bearing Tiberius's image (*Ant.* 18.3.1; *War* 2.9.2–3); conflicts between Roman soldiers and residents of Judea (especially *War* 2.12.1–2); and Caligula's attempt to erect a statue of himself in Jerusalem (*Ant.* 18.8.1–6) are all moments of extreme tension that include Roman imposition on and disrespect for Judean cultic priorities. The war itself, according to Josephus, began when a group of non-Judean young men sacrificed birds in front of the synagogue at Caesarea (2.17.5), resulting in a snowball effect of violence in Caesarea and Jerusalem, bringing Gallus down from Syria with three legions and thus officially beginning the war.

By framing these incidents as violence against the cultic sensibilities of the Jews, which they met with extreme piety and, at least in the cases of Caligula and Pilate, nonviolent action, Josephus attempted to rehabilitate his *ethnos* before Romans, who prided themselves on their own piety. However, Josephus himself does not attribute the war to cultic insensitivity but to reckless actions by ignoble pretenders to power (*War* 1.1.4).

Scholars looking closely at the war since the 1970s have largely rejected simplistic and dichotomistic explanations. Martin Goodman lays out a number of proposed impetuses, from the "incompetence of the Roman governors" to "quarrels with local gentiles" and debunks each of them with reference to Josephus's unreliability and partisanship, but mostly by claiming that similar conditions (such as relative tax rates and local versus foreign cultic differences) existed throughout the empire without necessarily leading to revolt, and were not exclusive to nor wholly defining of the situation in Judea.[35] He argues that the root cause of the war was internal disputes between Judean elite figures and families. Steve Mason complicates and adds to this reconstruction, in particular bringing in the lens of political realism, which states that nations (for whatever "nation" might mean in historical context, though it generically refers to a region united under a government) will and must see to their own best interests, up to and including war.[36]

What, then, caused the war? Mason's history, pulling together ancient evidence and modern interpretations as well as political theory and even a bit of psychology, probably comes the closest to a helpful answer, if not an easy one. In his conclusion he offers the circular but bleakly plausible suggestion that ultimately *the war itself* caused the war: that incidents mounted in retaliation for each other, and that the arrival of the Syrian legions in a region not used to legionary presence prompted social and psychological responses in both the soldiers and the populace that made war effectively inevitable.[37]

Notes

1. Chris Seeman, *Rome and Judea in Transition: Hasmonean Relations with the Roman Republic and the Evolution of the High Priesthood*, American University Studies. Series VII, Theology and Religion 325 (New York: Peter Lang, 2013), 119–23.
2. Or that later anti-Hasmonean sentiments were loath to credit it to him. *Diod.* 40.2. See Seeman, *Rome and Judea*, 120.
3. On the basis of a bronze tablet recorded in Rome by some medieval sources, Linda Zollschan argues that Judas's alliance with Rome only ever amounted to the less involved *amicitia*, friendship, and was not a military treaty. Linda Zollschan, *Rome and Judaea: International Law Relations, 162–100 BCE* (Abingdon: Routledge, 2016).
4. Seeman, *Rome and Judea*, 203. See also Seeman's analysis of 1 Macc 8 (*Rome and Judea*, 114–19) on possible Roman motives for the treaty with Judas.
5. E.g., ZeevSafrai and Micha Lin, "Geva in the Hasmonean Period / גבע בימי החשמונאים," *Cathedra* 69 (1993): 18–36.
6. Horsley, *Politics*, 44.
7. E.g., Dan 1:8; Tob 1:10–13; *Jub.* 22:16; Mark 7:17–23. David Charles Kraemer, *Jewish Eating and Identity through the Ages*, Routledge Advances in Sociology 29 (London: Routledge, 2009), 26–30.
8. Anthony Keddie, *Class and Power in Roman Palestine: The Socioeconomic Setting of Judaism and Christian Origins* (Cambridge: Cambridge University Press, 2019), https://doi.org/10.1017/9781108656757.

9. Eric C. Stewart, "Social Stratification and Patronage in Ancient Mediterranean Societies," in *Understanding the Social World of the New Testament*, ed. Dietmar Neufeld and Richard E. DeMaris (London: Routledge, 2009), 158–60.
10. Stewart, "Social Stratification," 163–4.
11. Keddie, *Class and Power*, 18–25.
12. Keddie, *Class and Power*, 86.
13. Keddie, *Class and Power*, 90.
14. Keddie, *Class and Power*, 103.
15. Jos. *Ant.* 18.1.1.
16. Stuart Miller provides an illuminating analysis of this dynamic for the cities of Tiberias and Sepphoris. Stuart S. Miller, "Josephus on the Cities of Galilee: Factions, Rivalries, and Alliances in the First Jewish Revolt," *Historia* 50, no. 4 (2001): 453–67.
17. Steve Mason, "Josephus's Pharisees: The Narratives," in *In Quest of the Historical Pharisees*, ed. Jacob Neusner and Bruce D. Chilton (Waco, TX: Baylor University Press, 2007), 20.
18. Hillel Newman and Ruth M. Ludlam, *Proximity to Power and Jewish Sectarian Groups of the Ancient Period: A Review of Lifestyle, Values, and Halakhah in the Pharisees, Sadducees, Essenes, and Qumran*, BRLJ 25 (Leiden: Brill, 2006), 79–81.
19. See especially Harold W. Hoehner, *Herod Antipas*, SNTSMS 17 (Cambridge: Cambridge University Press, 1972), 333–9.
20. Froelich, "Kings of the Jews," 27–36.
21. W. J. Bennett Jr., "The Herodians of Mark's Gospel," *Novum Testamentum* 17, no. 1 (1975): 9–14.
22. For a discussion of the scholarship on literacy in general, as well as a breakdown of various types of literacy (focused on classical Athens but helpful for the general context of the ancient Mediterranean), see Rosalind Thomas, "Writing, Reading, Public and Private 'Literacies': Functional Literacy and Democratic Literacy in Greece," in *Ancient Literacies: The Culture of Reading in Greece and Rome*, ed. William A. Johnson and Holt N. Parker (Oxford: Oxford University Press, 2009), 13–45. For literacy in pre-exilic Israel, see André Lemaire, "Levantine Literacy Ca. 1000–750 BCE," in *Contextualizing Israel's Sacred Writing: Ancient Literacy, Orality, and Literary Production*, ed. Brian B. Schmidt (Atlanta, GA: SBL Press, 2015), 11–46. For a summary with specific relevance for first-century Jewish contexts, see Chris Keith, *Jesus against the Scribal Elite: The Origins of the Conflict* (Grand Rapids, MI: Baker Academic, 2014), 17–37.
23. The evidence for this practice is far from comprehensive, but between Josephus and the Gospels, as well as a few other inscriptions and literary references, it is possible to sketch some broad generalizations. Lee I. Levine, *The Ancient Synagogue: The First Thousand Years*, 2nd ed. (New Haven, CT: Yale University Press, 2008), 45–80; Chris Keith, *Jesus' Literacy: Scribal Culture and the Teacher from Galilee*, LNTS 413 (New York: T&T Clark, 2011), 103–4, https://doi.org/10.5040/9781472550569.
24. Christine Schams, *Jewish Scribes in the Second-Temple Period*, JSOTSup 291 (Sheffield: Sheffield Academic Press, 1998), 127–8.
25. Keith debunks claims that Judeans enjoyed higher literacy rates than other Mediterraneans, and that first-century Jewish piety demanded literate education at all class levels, in Keith, *Jesus' Literacy*, 81–8.
26. Grabbe, *Judaic Religion*, 145–7. Martin Goodman argues that it could have been neither an official body nor a powerful one (Martin Goodman, *The Ruling*

Class of Judaea: The Origins of the Jewish Revolt against Rome, A.D. 66-70 [New York: Cambridge University Press, 1987], 112-16).
27. For a summary of some of the issues see Vasile Babota, "Alexander Janneus as High Priest and King: Struggling between Jewish and Hellenistic Concepts of Rule," *Religions* 11 (2020): 1-17, https://doi.org/10.3390/rel11010040.
28. Grabbe, *Judaic Religion*, 137-8.
29. Sara Mandell, "Who Paid the Temple Tax When the Jews Were under Roman Rule?" *HTR* 77, no. 2 (1984): 223-32.
30. Zeichmann, *Roman Army*, 60.
31. Zeichmann, *Roman Army*, 2.
32. Alexander Meyer, "Approaching 'Ethnic' Communities in the Roman Auxilia," in *New Approaches to Greek and Roman Warfare*, ed. Lee L. Brice (Hoboken, NJ: John Wiley, 2020), 161-72.
33. Levine, *Ancient Synagogue*, 139-45.
34. Goodman, *Ruling Class*, 109-33. Cf. Lawrence H. Schiffman, "Monarchy and Polity: Systems of Government in Jewish Tradition," in *Is Judaism Democratic?: Reflections from Theory and Practice throughout the Ages*, ed. Leonard J. Greenspoon (West Lafayette, IN: Purdue University Press, 2018), 171-84. Schiffman surveys attitudes toward various forms of government in all periods of Jewish history, and focuses especially on monarchy versus priestly aristocracy in the Second Temple period. He makes no mention of popular mandate in any special Judean form for this period.
35. Goodman, *Ruling Class*, 7-19.
36. Steve Mason, *A History of the Jewish War: A.D. 66-74* (Cambridge: Cambridge University Press, 2016), https://doi.org/10.1017/CBO9781139020718. A more complete discussion of realism occurs in Chapter 4.
37. Mason, *Jewish War*, 578-81.

Appendix B

Comparisons with Matthew and Luke

The ἐξουσία, δύναμις, and βασιλ- Texts[1]

	Mark	Matthew	Luke
ἐξουσία			
Temptation narrative		4:9†	4:6
Synagogue exorcism	1:22	7:29	4:32
Commands with a.	1:27		4:36
Authority to forgive sins	2:10	[9:6]	5:24
God gave a. to people		[9:8]	
Delegating to disciples	3:15		6:13†
Centurion's slave		8:9	7:8
Delegating to disciples	6:7	10:1[2]	9:1
Tread on snakes			10:19
Kill the body/cast the soul		10:26–33†	12:5
Baptism of John	11:28 (2)	21:23 (2)	[20:2 (2)]
	11:29	21:24	
	11:33	21:27	[20:8]
On taxes	12:13†	22:15†	[20:20]
Bring you to trial	13:11†	[10:19]†	12:11
Parable of the talents		25:21†	19:17
Watchfulness	13:34		
When I was … in the temple	14:49†	26:56†	22:53
Trial before Pilate			23:7
All a. on heaven and earth		28:18	

	Mark	Matthew	Luke
δύναμις			
Prophecy to Zechariah			1:17
Prophecy to Mary			1:35
Galilean ministry	1:14†	4:12†	4:14
Synagogue exorcism	1:27†		4:36
Healing of the paralytic	2:1–12†	[9:1–8]†	5:17
Healings by the shore	3:10†	4:24–25†	6:19
Bleeding woman	5:30	9:20–22†	8:46
Rejection at Nazareth	6:2	[13:54]	[4:16–30]†
	6:5	[13:58]	
Delegation of the Twelve	6:7†	10:1†	9:1
Tread on snakes			[10:19]
Woes against the cities		11:20	
		11:21	[10:13]
		11:23	[10:15]†
John raised from the dead?	6:14	14:2	9:7†
Coming of the Son of Man	9:1	16:28†	9:27†
Other exorcist/in your name	9:39	[7:22]	13:26†
Triumphal entry	11:9†	21:9†	19:37
Sadducees' question	12:24	22:29	[22:27–40]†
Powers in the heavens	13:25	24:29	21:26
Coming of the Son of Man	13:26	24:30	21:27
Parable of the talents		25:15	[19:13]†
Declaration to High Priest	14:62	26:64	22:69
Clothed with power			24:49
βασιλεύς/βασίλισσα			
Jesse father of King David		1:6	[3:31–32]†
In the days of King Herod		2:1	1:5
King Herod heard		2:3	
Magi hear King Herod		2:9	
Regarding oaths		5:35	
What did you go to see?		11:8	7:25³

	Mark	Matthew	Luke
Queen of the south		12:42	[11:31]
Many kings wanted to see		13:17†	[10:24]
Herod (Antipas)	6:14	14:1†	9:7† 4
	6:22	14:6–7†	
	6:25	14:8†	
	6:26	14:9	
	6:27	14:10†	
Temple tax		17:25	
Unforgiving servant		18:23	
Parable of the Great Supper		22:2	14:16†
		22:7	14:21†
		22:11	
		22:13	
On discipleship			14:31 (2)
Who is the greatest?5	10:42†	20:25†	22:25
Prediction of persecution	13:9	[10:18]	21:12
Jesus as βασιλεύς6			
Born king of the Jews		2:2	
Triumphal entry		21:57	
Hosanna	11:9†	21:9†	19:38
Sheep and goats		25:34	
		25:40	
False charge			23:2
Pilate's charge	15:2	27:11	23:3
Pilate asks the crowd	15:9	27:17†	23:13–17†
Pilate asks again	15:12	27:22†	23:20†
Soldiers' mockery	15:18	27:29	23:37 8
Inscription on the cross	15:26	27:37	23:38
Let him come down	15:32	27:42	[23:35]†
Βασιλεία (general)			
Temptation narrative		4:8	4:5
Beelzebul controversy	3:24	12:25	11:17

	Mark	Matthew	Luke
Kingdom of Satan	3:26†	12:26	11:18
Half of Herod's kingdom	6:23	14:7†	
Kingdom of David	11:10	21:9†	19:38†
Prediction of wars	13:8 (2)	24:7 (2)	21:10 (2)
Parable of the talents	13:34†	25:14†	[19:12]
		25:19†	[19:15]

βασιλεία τοῦ θεοῦ[9]

	Mark	Matthew	Luke
Prophecy to Mary			1:33
John's preaching	1:4†	3:2	3:3†
ἤγγικεν	1:15	4:17	
Calling the disciples	1:16–20†		
Leaving Capernaum	1:38†		4:43
Preaching in synagogues	1:39†	4:23	4:44†
Beelzebul controversy	3:22–27†	[12:28]	[11:20]
Blessed are the poor		5:3	6:20
Blessed are the persecuted		5:10	
Whoever relaxes/observes		5:19 (2)	
Exceed the Pharisees		5:20	
Seek the kingdom		6:33	[12:31]
		6:34†	[12:32]
Lord, Lord		7:21	6:46†
East and west		8:11	[13:29]
Sons of the K thrown out		8:12	[13:28]
Parable saying	4:11	[13:11]	8:10
Sower interpretation	4:15†	[13:19]	8:12†
Parable of the tares		[13:24]	
Parable of the mustard seed	4:30	[13:31]	[13:18]

	Mark	**Matthew**	**Luke**
Parable of the yeast		[13:33]	[13:20]
Tares interpretation		[13:38]	
		[13:41]	
		[13:43]	
Hidden treasure		[13:44]	
Pearl of great value		[13:45]	
Parable of the net		[13:47]	
Every scribe trained		[13:52]	
Preaching in synagogues	6:6†	9:35	[8:1]
Disciples' commission	6:8–10†	10:7	9:2; [10:9]
		10:14†	[10:11]
Feeding 5,000	6:34†	14:14†	9:11
Least is greater than John		11:7	[7:28]
K. suffered violence		11:12	[16:16]
Keys to the kingdom		16:19	
Some will not die	9:1	16:28	9:27
Who is the greatest?	9:34†	18:1	9:46†
Greatest is like a child		18:4	
Assign to you a kingdom[10]			[22:29]
Promise of thrones		[19:28] †	[22:30]
Better to enter with one eye	9:47	18:9	[17:1–2]†
Unforgiving servant		18:23	
Eunuchs for the kingdom		19:12	
Let the dead bury their dead		[8:22]†	9:60
Hand to the plow			9:62
K belongs to such as these	10:14	19:14	18:16
Receive as a child	10:15	[18:3]	18:17
Difficult for wealth to enter	10:23	19:23	18:24
	10:24		
Camel through a needle	10:25	19:24	18:25
Left home and family	10:29†	19:29†	18:29
Parable of the laborers		20:1	

	Mark	Matthew	Luke
Request of the Boanerges	10:37†	20:21	
Tax collectors and harlots		21:31	
Stone that was rejected	12:10–11†	21:43	[20:17]†
Parable of the great supper		22:2	[14:15]
Not far from the kingdom	12:34		[10:28]†
Woes against the Pharisees	12:38–40†	23:13	[11:52]
Testimony to all nations		24:14	
When is the k. coming?			[17:20] (2)
Not coming with signs	13:21†	24:23†	[17:21]
Parable of the fig tree	13:29†	24:33†	21:31
Parable of the virgins		25:1	
Parable of the talents			[19:11]
Sheep and goats		25:34	
Disciples' prayer	[11:25];† 14:35–38†	[6:10]	[11:2]
Passover in the kingdom			22:16
Drink wine new	14:25	26:29	22:18[11]
Penitent thief			23:42
Joseph awaits the kingdom	15:43	27:57†	23:51

† Parallel passages that do not include the relevant vocabulary are marked with the dagger in this chart. These are the only passages in this appendix listed with ranges instead of the individual verse where the vocabulary occurs.

Notes

1. The charts in this Appendix favor Markan order. Matthean and Lukan texts that are out of sequence with the rest of their Gospel because of these efforts are marked with brackets.
2. I have chosen to place this passage here rather than in parallel with Mark 3:15 (cf. Kurt Aland, ed., *Synopsis of the Four Gospels: Greek-English Edition of the Synopsis Quattuor Evangeliorum*, 10th ed. [Stuttgart: German Bible Society, 1993], § 49) especially because of its commands regarding clothing and behavior. Its position relative to the healing of the paralytic (Mark 2:1–12//Matt 9:2–8) relates it to the earlier Markan passage. Perhaps Matthew's author found the repetition unnecessary. Luke's version belongs with Mark 6:7, however, because although Luke redacts both of Mark's missions of the Twelve (Mark 3:13–19//Luke 6:12–16; Mark 6:7–13//Luke

9:1-6), he avoids repetition by removing the mission itself from the first passage, making it simply a selection and list of the Twelve.
3. Here Luke reads ἐν τοῖς βασιλείοις; cf. Matt 11:8, ἐν τοῖς οἴκοις βασιλέων.
4. Here and in v. 3:19 Luke refers to Herod by the correct title, tetrarch.
5. Mark 10:42: ἄρχειν τῶν ἐθνῶν; Matt 20:25: οἱ ἄρχοντες τῶν ἐθνῶν. I have retained the daggers to note the lack of the specific vocabulary, but the sense is not significantly different from Luke's use of βασιλεύς—all three refer to kings or rulers generically. Luke's tendency toward more Septuagintal language perhaps accounts for the difference.
6. For the purposes of this study I treat the titles "king of the Jews" and "king of Israel" as interchangeable with each other, although not in all cases conveying the idea of Jesus as an eschatological king.
7. While Zech 9:9-13 obviously does not refer to Jesus in its original context, its use here in Matthew is clear.
8. Although it does not appear out of order here by chapter and verse, Luke moves the soldiers' mockery of Jesus from the courtyard to the cross, attaching it to the offer of vinegar.
9. Matthew primarily uses βασιλεία τῶν οὐρανῶν. The two phrases are usually treated as functionally identical, and I do not separate them here. This list also includes references to "the kingdom" that are clearly eschatological and/or metaphysical, but do not specify τοῦ θεοῦ or τῶν οὐρανῶν.
10. Although this passage and those of the following entry do not have parallels in Mark, in both of the later Gospels they expand upon Mark 10:41-45.
11. Luke places this verse before the passing of the bread and cup; Mark and Matthew have it after.

Bibliography

Achtemeier, Paul J. *Mark*. 2nd ed. Proclamation Commentaries. Philadelphia, PA: Fortress Press, 1986.
Aland, Kurt, ed. *Synopsis of the Four Gospels: Greek-English Edition of the Synopsis Quattuor Evangeliorum*. 10th ed. Stuttgart: German Bible Society, 1993.
Applebaum, Shimon. "Economic Life in Palestine." In *The Jewish People in the First Century: Historical Geography, Political History, Social, Cultural and Religious Life and Institutions*, edited by Shemuel Safrai and Menahem Stern, 2:631–700. Compendia Rerum Iudaicarum ad Novum Testamentum. Philadelphia, PA: Fortress Press, 1976.
Arnal, William E. "The Parable of the Tenants and the Class Consciousness of the Peasantry." In *Text and Artifact in the Religions of Mediterranean Antiquity: Essays in Honor of Peter Richardson*, edited by Stephen G. Wilson and Michel Desjardins, 135–57. Waterloo, ON: Wilfrid Laurier University Press, 2000.
Babota, Vasile. "Alexander Janneus as High Priest and King: Struggling between Jewish and Hellenistic Concepts of Rule." *Religions* 11 (2020): 1–17. https://doi.org/10.3390/rel11010040.
Balz, Horst, and Gerhard Schneider. *Exegetical Dictionary of the New Testament*. 3 vols. Grand Rapids, MI: Eerdmans, 1990.
Barton, Carlin A., and Daniel Boyarin. *Imagine No Religion: How Modern Abstractions Hide Ancient Realities*. New York: Fordham University Press, 2016.
Beard, Mary. *The Roman Triumph*. Cambridge, MA: Belknap Press of Harvard University Press, 2009.
Beasley-Murray, George Raymond. *Jesus and the Last Days: The Interpretation of the Olivet Discourse*. Peabody, MA: Hendrickson, 1993.
Bennett, W. J., Jr. "The Herodians of Mark's Gospel." *Novum Testamentum* 17, no. 1 (1975): 9–14.
Berger, Klaus. *Formgeschichte des neuen Testaments*. Heidelberg: Quelle & Meyer, 1984.
Bernhardt, Rainer. "Die Immunitas der Freistädte." *Historia: Zeitschrift für alte Geschichte* 29, no. 2 (1980): 190–207.
Berthelot, Katell. "The Biblical Conquest of the Promised Land and the Hasmonean Wars According to 1 and 2 Maccabees." In *The Books of the Maccabees: History, Theology, Ideology. Papers of the Second International Conference on the Deuterocanonical Books, Pápa, Hungary, 9–11 June, 2005*, edited by Géza Xeravits and József Zsengellér, 45–60. Supplements to the Journal for the Study of Judaism 118. Leiden: Brill, 2007.
Bhabha, Homi. *The Location of Culture*. London: Routledge, 1994.
Blidstein, Gerald J. "The Monarchic Imperative in Rabbinic Perspective." *AJS Review* 7/8 (1982): 15–39.
Blomberg, Craig L., and Jennifer Foutz Markley. *A Handbook of New Testament Exegesis*. Grand Rapids, MI: Baker Academic, 2010.
Botha, A. D. "Aspects of Prophecy in Virgil's Aeneid." *Akroterion* 37, no. 1 (1992): 6–14.

Briant, Pierre. "The Greeks and 'Persian Decadence.'" In *Greeks and Barbarians*, edited by Thomas Harrison, 193–210. Edinburgh Readings on the Ancient World. New York: Routledge, 2002.

Broadhead, Edwin K. *Naming Jesus: Titular Christology in the Gospel of Mark*. Journal for the Study of the New Testament Supplement Series 175. Sheffield: Sheffield Academic, 1999.

Broadhead, Edwin K. *Teaching with Authority: Miracles and Christology in the Gospel of Mark*. Journal for the Study of the New Testament Supplement Series 74. Sheffield: JSOT Press, 1992.

Bryan, Christopher. *Render to Caesar: Jesus, the Early Church, and the Roman Superpower*. Oxford: Oxford University Press, 2005.

Bultmann, Rudolf. *The History of the Synoptic Tradition*. Translated by John Marsh. New York: Harper & Row, 1963.

Burger, Christoph. *Jesus als Davidssohn*. Forschungen zur Religion und Literatur des alten und neuen Testaments 98. Göttingen: Vandenhoeck & Ruprecht, 1970.

Burkert, Walter. *Greek Religion*. Translated by John Raffan. Cambridge, MA: Harvard University Press, 1985.

Campbell, Constantine R. *Verbal Aspect and Non-Indicative Verbs: Further Soundings in the Greek of the New Testament*. Studies in Biblical Greek 15. New York: Peter Lang, 2008.

Carter, Warren. "James C. Scott and New Testament Studies: A Response to Allen Callahan, William Herzog, and Richard Horsley." In *Hidden Transcripts and the Arts of Resistance: Applying the Work of James C. Scott to Jesus and Paul*, edited by Richard A. Horsley, 81–94. Semeia 48. Atlanta, GA: Society of Biblical Literature, 2004.

Carter, Warren. *John and Empire: Initial Explorations*. New York: T&T Clark, 2008.

Carter, Warren. *Mark*. Edited by Sarah Tanzer. Wisdom Commentary 42. Collegeville, MN: Liturgical Press, 2019.

Carter, Warren. *Matthew and Empire: Initial Explorations*. Harrisburg, PA: Trinity Press International, 2001.

Carter, Warren. *The Roman Empire and the New Testament: An Essential Guide*. Abingdon Essential Guides. Nashville, TN: Abingdon Press, 2006.

Carter, Warren. "Sanctioned Violence in the New Testament." *Interpretation: A Journal of Bible and Theology* 71, no. 3 (July 2017): 284–97. https://doi.org/10.1177/0020964317698764.

Catchpole, David R. "The Answer of Jesus to Caiaphas (Matt xxvi.64)." *New Testament Studies* 17, no. 2 (1971): 213–26.

Champion, Craige. "The Soteria at Delphi: Aetolian Propaganda in the Epigraphical Record." *American Journal of Philology* 116, no. 2 (1995): 213–20.

Chaniotis, Angelos. "The Divinity of Hellenistic Rulers." In *A Companion to the Hellenistic World*, edited by Andrew Erskine, 431–45. Blackwell Companions to the Ancient World. Malden, MA: Blackwell, 2003.

Cicero, Marcus Tullius. *Cicero: Pro Lege Manilia, Pro Caecina, Pro Cluentio, Pro Rabirio Perduellionis*. Translated by H. Grose Hodge. Reprinted. LCL 198. Cambridge, MA: Havard University Press, 2000.

Collins, Adela Yarbro. *Mark: A Commentary*. Edited by Harold W. Attridge. Hermeneia. Minneapolis, MN: Fortress Press, 2007.

Collins, Adela Yarbro. "Mark and His Readers: The Son of God among Greeks and Romans." *Harvard Theological Review* 93, no. 2 (2000): 85–100.

Collins, John J. *The Apocalyptic Imagination: An Introduction to Jewish Apocalyptic Literature*. 3rd ed. Grand Rapids, MI: Eerdmans, 2016.
Collins, John J. *Daniel: A Commentary on the Book of Daniel*. Edited by Frank Moore Cross. Hermeneia. Minneapolis, MN: Fortress Press, 1993.
Combrink, H. J. Bernard. "Salvation in Mark." In *Salvation in the New Testament: Perspectives on Soteriology*, edited by Jan G. Van der Watt, 33–66. Supplements to Novum Testamentum 121. Leiden: Brill, 2005.
Connolly, Michele A. *Disorderly Women and the Order of God: An Australian Feminist Reading of the Gospel of Mark*. New York: T&T Clark, 2018. https://doi.org/10.5040/9780567674159.
Conway, Colleen. *Behold the Man: Jesus and Greco-Roman Masculinity*. Cary, NC: Oxford University Press, 2008.
Cooley, Alison E. *Res Gestae Divi Augusti: Text, Translation, and Commentary*. Cambridge: Cambridge University Press, 2009.
Crossan, John Dominic. *The Historical Jesus: The Life of a Mediterranean Jewish Peasant*. San Francisco, CA: HarperSanFrancisco, 1991.
Crossley, James G. *The Date of Mark's Gospel: Insight from the Law in Earliest Christianity*. Journal for the Study of the New Testament Supplement Series 266. New York: T&T Clark, 2004.
Danker, Frederick William, ed. *A Greek-English Lexicon of the New Testament and Other Early Christian Literature*. 3rd ed. Chicago: University of Chicago Press, 2000.
Danove, Paul L. *The Rhetoric of Characterization of God, Jesus, and Jesus' Disciples in the Gospel of Mark*. Journal for the Study of the New Testament Supplement Series 290. New York: T&T Clark, 2005.
Dart, Christopher J. "Frontiers, Security, and Military Policy." In *A Companion to the Flavian Age of Imperial Rome*, edited by Andrew Zissos, 207–22. Blackwell Companions to the Ancient World. Chichester: Wiley-Blackwell, 2016.
Davidsen, Ole. *The Narrative Jesus: A Semiotic Reading of Mark's Gospel*. Aarhus, Denmark: Aarhus University Press, 1993.
Dawson, Anne. *Freedom as Liberating Power: A Socio-Political Reading of the Ἐξουσία Texts in the Gospel of Mark*. Novum Testamentum et Orbis Antiquus 44. Freiburg, Schweiz: Universitätsverlag, 2000.
Dibelius, Martin. *Die urchristliche Überlieferung von Johannes Dem Täufer*. Göttingen: Vandenhoeck & Ruprecht, 1911.
DiTommaso, Lorenzo. "Deliverance and Justice: Soteriology in the Book of Daniel." In *This World and the World to Come: Soteriology in Early Judaism*, edited by Daniel M. Gurtner, 71–86. New York: T&T Clark, 2011. https://doi.org/10.5040/9781472551047.
Dittenberger, Wilhelm. *Orientis graeci inscriptiones selectae:Supplementum sylloges inscriptionum graecarum*. 2 vols. Leipzig: S. Hirzel, 1903. http://hdl.handle.net/2027/gri.ark:/13960/t75t7gx7g.
Dodd, C. H. *Parables of the Kingdom*. Rev. ed. New York: Charles Scribner, 1961.
Dreyer, Yolanda. *Institutionalization of Authority and the Naming of Jesus*. Eugene, OR: Pickwick, 2012.
Eck, Werner. *Rom und Judaea: Fünf Vorträge zur römischen Herrschaft in Judäa*. Tubingen: Mohr Siebeck, 2007.

Eckstein, Arthur M. "Macedonia and Rome, 221–146 BC." In *A Companion to Ancient Macedonia*, edited by Joseph Roisman and Ian Worthington, 225–50. Blackwell Companions to the Ancient World. Chichester: Wiley-Blackwell, 2010.

Eckstein, Arthur M. *Mediterranean Anarchy, Interstate War, and the Rise of Rome*. Ebook. Hellenistic Culture and Society 48. Berkeley: University of California Press, 2006. https://doi.org/10.1525/california/9780520246188.001.0001.

Ekroth, Gunnel. *The Sacrificial Rituals of Greek Hero-Cults in the Archaic to the Early Hellenistic Period*. Liége: Presses universitaires de Liège, 2002. http://books.openedition.org/pulg/490.

Elgvin, Torleif. "Hasmonean State Ideology, Wars and Expansionism." In *Encountering Violence in the Bible*, edited by Markus Zehnder and Hallvard Hagelia, 52–67. The Bible in the Modern World 55. Sheffield: Sheffield Phoenix Press, 2013.

Engberg-Pedersen, T. "Review of Hearing the Whole Story. The Politics of Plot in Mark's Gospel." *Journal of Theological Studies* 54, no. 1 (April 1, 2003): 230–45. https://doi.org/10.1093/jts/54.1.230.

Erickson, Kyle. "Another Century of Gods? A Re-Evaluation of Seleucid Ruler Cult." *Classical Quarterly* 68, no. 1 (2018): 97–111. https://doi.org/10.1017/S0009838818000071.

Erskine, Andrew. "Greekness and Uniqueness: The Cult of the Senate in the Greek East." *Phoenix* 51, no. 1 (1997): 25–37.

Evans, Craig A. *Mark 8:27–16:20*. Word Biblical Commentary 34B. Nashville, TN: Thomas Nelson, 2001.

Fanning, Buist M. *Verbal Aspect in New Testament Greek*. Oxford Theological Monographs. Oxford: Oxford University Press, 1990.

Ferron, Benjamin, Claire Oger, and James C. Scott. "'When the Revolution Becomes the State It Becomes My Enemy Again': An Interview with James C. Scott." The Conversation. Accessed December 17, 2019. https://web.archive.org/web/20191217101657/http://theconversation.com/when-the-revolution-becomes-the-state-it-becomes-my-enemy-again-an-interview-with-james-c-scott-98488.

Finney, Mark T. *Honour and Conflict in the Ancient World: 1 Corinthians in Its Greco-Roman Setting*. Library of New Testament Studies 460. London: T&T Clark, 2012.

Flatto, David C. *The Crown and the Courts: Separation of Powers in the Early Jewish Imagination*. Cambridge, MA: Harvard University Press, 2020. https://doi.org/10.4159/9780674249608.

France, R. T. *Divine Government: God's Kingship in the Gospel of Mark*. London: SPCK, 1990.

France, R. T. *The Gospel of Mark: A Commentary on the Greek Text*. The New International Greek Testament Commentary. Grand Rapids, MI: Eerdmans, 2002.

Freedman, David Noel, ed. *The Anchor Bible Dictionary*. 6 vols. New York: Doubleday, 1992.

Frilingos, Christopher A. *Spectacles of Empire: Monsters, Martyrs, and the Book of Revelation*. Divinations. Philadelphia: University of Pennsylvania Press, 2004.

Froelich, Margaret. "Kings of the Jews: Herodian Collaboration with Rome through a Markan Lens." In *Greco-Roman and Jewish Tributaries to the New Testament: Festschrift in Honor of Gregory J. Riley*, edited by Christopher S. Crawford, 27–36. Claremont Studies in New Testament and Christian Origins 4. Claremont, CA: Claremont Press, 2019.

Froelich, Margaret. "Sacrificed Meat in Corinth and Jesus Worship as a Cult Among Cults." *Journal of Early Christian History* (November 3, 2020): 1–13. https://doi.org/10.1080/2222582X.2020.1779101.

Fuks, Gideon. "Some Remarks on Simon Bar Giora." *Scripta Classica Israelica* 8–9 (1988): 106–19.

Galinsky, Karl. *Augustan Culture: An Interpretive Introduction*. Princeton, NJ: Princeton University Press, 1996.

Gandhi, Leela. *Postcolonial Theory: A Critical Introduction*. New York: Columbia University Press, 1998.

Gardner, Gregg. "Jewish Leadership and Hellenistic Civic Benefaction in the Second Century B.C.E." *Journal of Biblical Literature* 126, no. 2 (2007): 327–43. https://doi.org/10.2307/27638437.

Gelardini, Gabriella. *Christus Militans: Studien zur politisch-militärischen Semantik im Markusevangelium vor dem Hintergrund des ersten judisch-romischen Krieges*. Supplements to Novum Testamentum 165. Boston: Brill, 2016.

Gelardini, Gabriella. "The Contest for a Royal Title: Herod versus Jesus in the *Gospel According to Mark* (6,14–29; 15,6–15)." *Annali Di Storia Dell'esegesi* 28, no. 2 (2011): 93–106.

Georgia, Allan T. "Translating the Triumph: Reading Mark's Crucifxion Narrative against a Roman Ritual of Power." *Journal for the Study of the New Testament* 36, no. 1 (September 2013): 17–38. https://doi.org/10.1177/0142064X13495132.

Goldstein, Jonathan A., ed. *I Maccabees: A New Translation, with Introduction and Commentary*. The Anchor Bible 41. Garden City, NY: Doubleday, 1976.

Goodblatt, David M. *The Monarchic Principle: Studies in Jewish Self-Government in Antiquity*. Texte und Studien zum antiken Judentum 38. Tübingen: J.C.B. Mohr (P. Siebeck), 1994.

Goodman, Martin. *The Ruling Class of Judaea: The Origins of the Jewish Revolt against Rome, A.D. 66–70*. New York: Cambridge University Press, 1987.

Gorman, Robert J., and Vanessa B. Gorman. *Corrupting Luxury in Ancient Greek Literature*. Ann Arbor: University of Michigan Press, 2014.

Grabbe, Lester L. *Judaic Religion in the Second Temple Period: Belief and Practice from the Exile to Yavneh*. London: Routledge, 2000.

Gregory, Bradley C. *Like an Everlasting Signet Ring: Generosity in the Book of Sirach*. Berlin: De Gruyter, 2010.

Grindheim, Sigurd. "Sirach and Mark 8:27–9:13: Elijah and the Eschaton." In *Reading Mark in Context: Jesus and Second Temple Judaism*, edited by Ben C. Blackwell, John K. Goodrich, and Jason Maston, 130–6. Grand Rapids, MI: Zondervan, 2018.

Gruen, Erich Stephen. *The Hellenistic World and the Coming of Rome*. 1st paperback printing. Berkeley: University of California Press, 1986.

Gundry, Robert H. *Mark: A Commentary on His Apology for the Cross*. Grand Rapids, MI: Eerdmans, 1993.

Gundry, Robert H. "Richard A. Horsley's *Hearing the Whole Story*: A Critical Review of Its Postcolonial Slant." *Journal for the Study of the New Testament* 26, no. 2 (2003): 131–49.

Hadjittofi, Fotini. "Midas, the Golden Age Trope, and Hellenistic Kingship in Ovid's *Metamorphoses*." *American Journal of Philology* 139, no. 2 (2018): 277–309. https://doi.org/10.1353/ajp.2018.0014.

Hahn, Ferdinand. *Christologische Hoheitstitel: Ihre Geschichte im frühen Christentum.* Forschungen zur Religion und Literatur des alten und neuen Testaments 83. Göttingen: Vandenhoeck & Ruprecht, 1963.

Hammond, Mason. "Res olim dissociabiles: Principatus ac Libertas: Liberty under the Early Roman Empire." *Harvard Studies in Classical Philology* 67 (1963): 93–113.

Hanson, W. S. "Forces of Change and Methods of Control." In *Dialogues in Roman Imperialism: Power, Discourse, and Discrepant Experience in the Roman Empire*, edited by D. J. Mattingly, 67–80. Journal of Roman Archaeology Supplementary Series 23. Portsmouth, RI: JRA, 1997.

Harnack, Adolf. *The Date of the Acts and of the Synoptic Gospels.* Translated by J. R. Wilkinson. Vol. 4. Crown Theological Library 33. London: Williams & Norgate, 1911.

Hellerman, Joseph H. *Reconstructing Honor in Roman Philippi: Carmen Christi as Cursus Pudorum.* New York: Cambridge University Press, 2005. https://doi.org/10.1017/CBO9780511487972.

Henderson, Suzanne Watts. *Christology and Discipleship in the Gospel of Mark.* Society for New Testament Studies Monograph Series 135. Cambridge: Cambridge University Press, 2006.

Hengel, Martin. *The Son of God: The Origin of Christology and the History of Jewish-Hellenistic Religion.* Translated by John Bowden. Philadelphia, PA: Fortress Press, 1976.

Hengel, Martin. *Studies in the Gospel of Mark.* Translated by John Bowden. London: SCM Press, 1985.

Henrichs, Albert. "What Is a Greek God?" In *The Gods of Ancient Greece*, edited by Jan N. Bremmer and Andrew Erskine, 19–40. Identities and Transformations. Edinburgh: Edinburgh University Press, 2010. http://www.jstor.org/stable/10.3366/j.ctt1r236p.8.

Hoehner, Harold W. *Herod Antipas.* Society for New Testament Studies Monograph Series 17. Cambridge: Cambridge University Press, 1972.

Holladay, Carl R. *Theios Aner in Hellenistic Judaism: A Critique of the Use of This Category in New Testament Christology.* Society of Biblical Literature Dissertation Series 40. Missoula, MT: Scholars Press, 1977.

Horsley, Richard A. *Hearing the Whole Story: The Politics of Plot in Mark's Gospel.* Louisville, KY: Westminster John Knox Press, 2001.

Horsley, Richard A., ed. *Hidden Transcripts and the Arts of Resistance: Applying the Work of James C. Scott to Jesus and Paul.* Semeia 48. Atlanta, GA: Society of Biblical Literature, 2004.

Horsley, Richard A. *Jesus and Empire: The Kingdom of God and the New World Disorder.* Minneapolis, MN: Fortress Press, 2003.

Horsley, Richard A. *Jesus and Magic: Freeing the Gospel Stories from Modern Misconceptions.* Eugene, OR: Cascade Books, 2014.

Horsley, Richard A. *Jesus and the Politics of Roman Palestine.* Columbia: University of South Carolina Press, 2014.

Horsley, Richard A. *Jesus and the Spiral of Violence: Popular Jewish Resistance in Roman Palestine.* Minneapolis, MN: Fortress Press, 1993.

Horsley, Richard A. *Mark: A Reader-Response Commentary.* Translated by W. H. Bisscheroux. London: T&T Clark, 2004.

Horsley, Richard A. "'Messianic' Figures and Movements in First-Century Palestine." In *The Messiah: Developments in Earliest Judaism and Christianity*, edited by James H. Charlesworth, 276–95. Minneapolis, MN: Fortress Press, 1992.

Jacoby, Felix. *Die Fragmente der griechischen Historiker.* 3 vols. Berlin: Weidmann, 1923.

Johansson, Daniel. "*Kyrios* in the Gospel of Mark." *Journal for the Study of the New Testament* 33, no. 1 (September 2010): 101–24. https://doi.org/10.1177/0142064X10380130.

Johansson, Daniel. "The Identity of Jesus in the Gospel of Mark: Past and Present Proposals." *Currents in Biblical Research* 9, no. 3 (2010): 364–93.

Johnson, William A., and Holt N. Parker, eds. *Ancient Literacies: The Culture of Reading in Greece and Rome*. Oxford: Oxford University Press, 2009.

Juel, Donald. *Messiah and Temple: The Trial of Jesus in the Gospel of Mark*. Society of Biblical Literature Dissertation Series 31. Missoula, MT: Scholars Press, 1977.

Kaiser, Otto. *Isaiah 13–39: A Commentary*. Translated by R. A. Wilson. The Old Testament Library. Philadelphia, PA: Westminster Press, 1974.

Kallet-Marx, Robert M. *Hegemony to Empire: The Development of the Roman Imperium in the East from 148 to 62 B.C.* Hellenistic Culture and Society 15. Berkeley: University of California Press, 1995.

Keddie, Anthony. *Class and Power in Roman Palestine: The Socioeconomic Setting of Judaism and Christian Origins*. Cambridge: Cambridge University Press, 2019. https://doi.org/10.1017/9781108656757.

Kee, Howard Clark. *Medicine, Miracle and Magic in New Testament Times*. Society for New Testament Studies Monograph Series 55. Cambridge: Cambridge University Press, 1986.

Kee, Howard Clark. *Miracle in the Early Christian World: A Study in Sociohistorical Method*. New Haven, CT: Yale University Press, 1983.

Keith, Chris. *Jesus against the Scribal Elite: The Origins of the Conflict*. Grand Rapids, MI: Baker Academic, 2014.

Keith, Chris. *Jesus' Literacy: Scribal Culture and the Teacher from Galilee*. Library of New Testament Studies 413. New York: T&T Clark, 2011. https://doi.org/10.5040/9781472550569.

Kelber, Werner H. *The Kingdom in Mark: A New Place and a New Time*. Philadelphia, PA: Fortress Press, 1974.

Kelber, Werner H. *Mark's Story of Jesus*. Philadelphia, PA: Fortress Press, 1979.

Kim, Hyun Chul Paul. "Two Mothers and Two Sons: Reading 1 Kings 3:16–28 as a Parody on Solomon's Coup (1 Kings 1–2)." In *Partners with God: Theological and Critical Readings of the Bible in Honor of Marvin A. Sweeney*, edited by Shelley L. Birdsong and Serge Frolov, 83–99. Claremont Studies in Hebrew Bible and Septuagint 2. Claremont, CA: Claremont Press, 2017.

Kim, Tae Hun. "The Anarthrous Υἱός Θεοῦ in Mark 15,39 and the Roman Imperial Cult." *Biblica* 79, no. 2 (1998): 221–41.

Kingsbury, Jack Dean. *The Christology of Mark's Gospel*. Philadelphia, PA: Fortress Press, 1983.

Kittel, Gerhard, ed. *Theological Dictionary of the New Testament*. Translated by Geoffrey W. Bromiley. 10 vols. Grand Rapids, MI: Eerdmans, 1964.

Kloppenborg, John S. "Evocatio Deorum and the Date of Mark." *Journal of Biblical Literature* 124, no. 3 (2005): 419–50.

Kochenash, Michael. "Cornelius's Obeisance to Peter (Acts 10:25–26) and Judaea Capta Coins." *Catholic Biblical Quarterly* 81, no. 4 (2019): 627–40. https://doi.org/10.1353/cbq.2019.0226.

Kochenash, Michael. "Empire without End: Juxtaposing the Kingdom of God with Rome in Luke-Acts." Dissertation, Claremont School of Theology, 2017.

Kotrosits, Maia. *Rethinking Early Christian Identity: Affect, Violence, and Belonging*. Minneapolis, MN: Fortress Press, 2015.

Kraemer, David Charles. *Jewish Eating and Identity through the Ages*. Routledge Advances in Sociology 29. London: Routledge, 2009.

Kraybill, J. Nelson. *Imperial Cult and Commerce in John's Apocalypse*. Journal for the Study of the New Testament Supplement Series 132. Sheffield: Sheffield Academic Press, 1996.

Krentz, Edgar. *The Historical-Critical Method*. Guides to Biblical Scholarship. Philadelphia, PA: Fortress Press, 1975.

Labahn, Michael, and L. J. Lietaert Peerbolte, eds. *A Kind of Magic: Understanding Magic in the New Testament and Its Religious Environment*. T&T Clark Library of Biblical Studies 306. London: T&T Clark, 2007.

Lemaire, André. "Levantine Literacy Ca. 1000–750 BCE." In *Contextualizing Israel's Sacred Writing: Ancient Literacy, Orality, and Literary Production*, edited by Brian B. Schmidt, 11–46. Atlanta, GA: SBL Press, 2015. https://doi.org/10.2307/j.ctt1647cmz.

Levine, Lee I. *The Ancient Synagogue: The First Thousand Years*, 2nd ed. New Haven, CT: Yale University Press, 2008.

Liddell, Henry George, Robert Scott, Henry Stuart Jones, and Roderick McKenzie. *A Greek-English Lexicon*. Rev. and augm. Throughout. Oxford: Clarendon Press; Oxford University Press, 1996.

Liew, Tat-siong Benny. *Politics of Parousia: Reading Mark Inter(Con)Textually*. Biblical Interpretation Series 42. Leiden: Brill, 1999.

Liew, Tat-siong Benny. "Review of *Hearing the Whole Story: The Politics of Plot in Mark's Gospel* by Richard A. Horsley." *Catholic Biblical Quarterly* 64, no. 3 (2002): 576–7.

Lim, Sung U. "A Double-Voiced Reading of Romans 13:1–7 in Light of the Imperial Cult." *HTS Teologiese Studies/Theological Studies* 71, no. 1 (March 23, 2015). https://doi.org/10.4102/hts.v71i1.2475.

Litwa, M. David. *Posthuman Transformation in Ancient Mediterranean Thought: Becoming Angels and Demons*. Cambridge: Cambridge University Press, 2021. https://doi.org/10.1017/9781108921572.

Litwa, M. David. *We Are Being Transformed: Deification in Paul's Soteriology*. Beihefte zur Zeitschrift für die neutestamentliche Wissenschaft und die Kunde der älteren Kirche 187. Berlin: De Gruyter, 2012.

Livy. *History of Rome*. Translated by B. O. Foster, J. C. Yardley, Frank Gardner Moore, Evan T. Sage, and Alfred Cary Schlesinger. 14 vols. LCL. Cambridge, MA: Harvard University Press, 1919.

Lorberbaum, Yair. *Disempowered King: Monarchy in Classical Jewish Literature*. Kogod Library of Judaic Studies 9. New York: Continuum, 2010. https://doi.org/10.5040/9781472548481.

Lucan. *The Civil War*. Translated by J. D. Duff. Loeb Classical Library. London: W. Heinemann, 1928.

Lührmann, Dieter. *Das Markusevangelium*. Handbuch zum neuen Testament 3. Tübingen: Mohr [Siebeck], 1987.

MacDonald, Dennis R. *The Gospels and Homer: Imitations of Greek Epic in Mark and Luke-Acts*. Lanham, MD: Rowman & Littlefield, 2015.

Mack, Burton L. *A Myth of Innocence: Mark and Christian Origins*. 1st paperback ed. Philadelphia, PA: Fortress Press, 1991.

MacMullen, Ramsay. "Social Ethic Models: Roman, Greek, 'Oriental.'" *Historia: Zeitschrift für alte Geschichte* 64, no. 4 (2015): 487–510.
Maier, Gerhard. *Biblische Hermeneutik*. Monographien Und Studienbücher. Wuppertal: R. Brockhaus, 1990.
Malbon, Elizabeth Struthers. *Mark's Jesus: Characterization as Narrative Christology*. Waco, TX: Baylor University Press, 2009.
Mandell, Sara. "Who Paid the Temple Tax When the Jews Were under Roman Rule?" *Harvard Theological Review* 77, no. 2 (1984): 223–32.
Marcus, Joel. "Crucifixion as Parodic Exaltation." *Journal of Biblical Literature* 125 (2006): 73–87.
Marcus, Joel. "The Jewish War and the *Sitz im Leben* of Mark." *Journal of Biblical Literature* 111 (1992): 441–62.
Marcus, Joel. *Mark 1–8: A New Translation with Introduction and Commentary*. Anchor Bible 27. New York: Doubleday, 1999.
Marcus, Joel. *Mark 8–16: A New Translation with Introduction and Commentary*. Anchor Bible 27a. New Haven, CT: Yale University Press, 2009.
Mason, Steve. *A History of the Jewish War: A.D. 66–74*. Cambridge: Cambridge University Press, 2016. https://doi.org/10.1017/CBO9781139020718.
Mason, Steve. "Josephus's Pharisees: The Narratives." In *In Quest of the Historical Pharisees*, edited by Jacob Neusner and Bruce D. Chilton, 3–40. Waco, TX: Baylor University Press, 2007.
McKnight, Scot, and Joseph B. Modica. *Jesus Is Lord, Caesar Is Not: Evaluating Empire in New Testament Studies*. Downers Grove, IL: InterVarsity Press, 2013.
McVann, Mark. "The 'Passion' of John the Baptist and Jesus before Pilate: Mark's Warnings about Kings and Governors." *Biblical Theology Bulletin* 38, no. 4 (2008): 152–7.
Mellor, Ronald. ΘΕΑ ΡΩΜΗ: *The Worship of the Goddess Roma in the Greek World*. Hypomnemata 42. Göttingen: Vandenhoeck & Ruprecht, 1975.
Meyer, Alexander. "Approaching 'Ethnic' Communities in the Roman Auxilia." In *New Approaches to Greek and Roman Warfare*, edited by Lee L. Brice, 161–72. Hoboken, NJ: John Wiley, 2020.
Michalak, Aleksander R. *Angels as Warriors in Late Second Temple Jewish Literature*. Wissenschaftliche Untersuchungen zum neuen Testament. 2. Reihe 330. Tübingen, Germany: Mohr Siebeck, 2012.
Miller, Amanda C. *Rumors of Resistance: Status Reversals and Hidden Transcripts in the Gospel of Luke*. Emerging Scholars. Minneapolis, MN: Fortress Press, 2014.
Miller, Stuart S. "Josephus on the Cities of Galilee: Factions, Rivalries, and Alliances in the First Jewish Revolt." *Historia: Zeitschrift für alte Geschichte* 50, no. 4 (2001): 453–67.
Miller, Susan. *Women in Mark's Gospel*. Journal for the Study of the New Testament Supplement Series. London: Bloomsbury, 2004.
Müller, Mogens. *The Expression "Son of Man" and the Development of Christology: A History of Interpretation*. Copenhagen International Seminar. London: Routledge, 2012.
Myers, Ched. *Binding the Strong Man: A Political Reading of Mark's Story of Jesus*. Maryknoll, NY: Orbis Books, 1988.
Nestle, Eberhard, Erwin Nestle, Barbara Aland, Kurt Aland, and Institut für Neutestamentliche Textforschung, eds. *Novum Testamentum Graece*. 28., rev. Aufl., 2. korr. Druck. Stuttgart: Deutsche Bibelges, 2013.
Neusner, Jacob, and Bruce D. Chilton, eds. *In Quest of the Historical Pharisees*. Waco, TX: Baylor University Press, 2007.

Newman, Hillel, and Ruth M. Ludlam. *Proximity to Power and Jewish Sectarian Groups of the Ancient Period: A Review of Lifestyle, Values, and Halakhah in the Pharisees, Sadducees, Essenes, and Qumran*. Brill Reference Library of Judaism 25. Leiden: Brill, 2006.

Nortje, S. "John the Baptist and the Resurrection Traditions in the Gospels." *Neotestamentica* 23 (1989): 349–58.

O'Hara, James J. *Death and the Optimistic Prophecy in Vergil's Aeneid*. Princeton, NJ: Princeton University Press, 1990.

Olson, Kelly. "Masculinity, Appearance, and Sexuality: Dandies in Roman Antiquity." *Journal of the History of Sexuality* 23, no. 2 (2014): 182–205.

Oprisko, Robert L. *Honor: A Phenomenology*. London: Taylor & Francis, 2012.

Packard Humanities Institute. "PHI Greek Inscriptions." Accessed March 24, 2021. https://inscriptions.packhum.org/.

Peppard, Michael. "Torah for the Man Who Has Everything: 'Do Not Defraud' in Mark 10:19." *Journal of Biblical Literature* 134, no. 3 (2015): 595–604. https://doi.org/10.15699/jbl.1343.2015.3006.

Pero, Cheryl. *Liberation from Empire: Demonic Possession and Exorcism in the Gospel of Mark*. Studies in Biblical Literature 150. New York: Peter Lang, 2013.

Phillips, Thomas E. *Reading Issues of Wealth and Poverty in Luke-Acts*. Studies in the Bible and Early Christianity 48. Lewiston, NY: Edwin Mellen Press, 2001.

Price, S. R. F. *Rituals and Power: The Roman Imperial Cult in Asia Minor*. Cambridge: Cambridge University Press, 1984.

Räisänen, Heikki. *The "Messianic Secret" in Mark*. Translated by Christopher Tuckett. Studies of the New Testament and Its World. Edinburgh: T&T Clark, 2003.

Reed, J. D. "Vergil's Roman." In *A Companion to Vergil's Aeneid and Its Tradition*, edited by Joseph Farrell and Michael C. J. Putnam, 69–79. Blackwell Companions to the Ancient World. Chichester: Wiley-Blackwell, 2010.

Reeves, John, and Annette Yoshiko Reed. *Enoch from Antiquity to the Middle Ages, Volume I: Sources From Judaism, Christianity, and Islam*. Enoch from Antiquity to the Middle Ages, Volume I. Oxford: Oxford University Press, 2018.

Rich, John, and Graham Shipley, eds. *War and Society in the Roman World*. Leicester-Nottingham Studies in Ancient Society 5. London: Routledge, 1993.

Rohrbaugh, Richard L. "Honor: Core Value in the Biblical World." In *Understanding the Social World of the New Testament*, edited by Dietmar Neufeld and Richard E. DeMaris, 109–25. London: Routledge, 2009. https://doi.org/10.4324/9780203865149-17.

Rosenfeld, B. Z., and H. Permutter. "The Attitude to Poverty and the Poor in Early Rabbinic Sources (70–250 CE)." *Journal for the Study of Judaism* 47 (2016): 411–38.

Safrai, Zeev, and Micha Lin. "Geva in the Hasmonean Period / גבע בימי החשמונאים." *Cathedra: For the History of Eretz Israel and Its Yeshuv* 69 (1993): 18–36.

Samuel, Simon. *A Postcolonial Reading of Mark's Story of Jesus*. Library of New Testament Studies 340. London: T&T Clark, 2007.

Sanders, E. P., and Margaret Davies. *Studying the Synoptic Gospels*. London: SCM Press, 1989.

Schäfer, Peter. *The History of the Jews in the Greco-Roman World: The Jews of Palestine from Alexander the Great to the Arab Conquest*. Rev. ed. London: Routledge, 2003.

Schams, Christine. *Jewish Scribes in the Second-Temple Period*. Journal for the Study of the Old Testament Supplement Series 291. Sheffield: Sheffield Academic Press, 1998.

Scheffler, Eben. "Luke's View on Poverty in Its Ancient (Roman) Economic Context: A Challenge for Today." *Scriptura* 106 (2011): 115–35.

Schiffman, Lawrence H. "Monarchy and Polity: Systems of Government in Jewish Tradition." In *Is Judaism Democratic?: Reflections from Theory and Practice throughout the Ages*, edited by Leonard J. Greenspoon, 171–84. West Lafayette, IN: Perdue University Press, 2018.

Schmidt, Thomas E. *Hostility to Wealth in the Synoptic Gospels*. London: Bloomsbury, 1987.

Schmithals, Walter. *Das Evangelium nach Markus*. 2 vols. Ökumenischer Taschenbuchkommentar zum neuen Testament. Gütersloh: Gütersloher Verlagshaus Mohn, 1979.

Schreiber, Johannes. *Theologie des Vertrauens*. Hamburg: Furche, 1967.

Scott, James C. *Domination and the Arts of Resistance: Hidden Transcripts*. New Haven, CT: Yale University Press, 1990.

Scott, James C. *Weapons of the Weak: Everyday Forms of Peasant Resistance*. New Haven, CT: Yale University Press, 1985.

Scullion, Scott. "Olympian and Chthonian." *Classical Antiquity* 13 (1994): 75–119.

Seeman, Chris. *Rome and Judea in Transition: Hasmonean Relations with the Roman Republic and the Evolution of the High Priesthood*. American University Studies. Series VII, Theology and Religion 325. New York: Peter Lang, 2013.

Serrati, John. "A Syracusan Private Altar and the Development of Ruler-Cult in Hellenistic Sicily." *Historia: Zeitschrift für alte Geschichte* 57, no. 1 (2008): 80–91.

Shively, Elizabeth. "Characterizing the Non-Human: Satan in the Gospel of Mark." In *Character Studies and the Gospel of Mark*, edited by Christopher W. Skinner and Matthew Ryan Hauge, 127–51. Library of New Testament Studies. London: T&T Clark, 2014. https://doi.org/10.5040/9780567669766.

Silva, Moisés, ed. *New International Dictionary of New Testament Theology and Exegesis*. 2nd ed. 5 vols. Grand Rapids, MI: Zondervan, 2014.

Smith, Abraham. "Tyranny Exposed: Mark's Typological Characterization of Herod Antipas (Mark 6:14–29)." *Biblical Interpretation* 14, no. 3 (July 1, 2006): 259–93. https://doi.org/10.1163/156851506776722994.

Smyth, Herbert Weir, and Gordon M. Messing. *Greek Grammar*. 13th ed. Cambridge, MA: Harvard University Press, 1984.

Snodgrass, Klyne. "Streams of Tradition Emerging from Isaiah 40:1–5 and Their Adaptation in the New Testament." *Journal for the Study of the New Testament* 8 (1980): 24–45.

Spivak, Gayatri Chakravorty. *In Other Worlds: Essays in Cultural Politics*. New York: Routledge, 1988.

Stegemann, Ekkehard, and Wolfgang Stegemann. *The Jesus Movement: A Social History of Its First Century*. Translated by O. C. Dean, Jr. Minneapolis, MN: Fortress Press, 1999.

Stewart, Eric C. "Social Stratification and Patronage in Ancient Mediterranean Societies." In *Understanding the Social World of the New Testament*, edited by Dietmar Neufeld and Richard E. DeMaris, 156–66. London: Routledge, 2009.

Stratton, Kimberly, and Andrea Lieber, eds. *Crossing Boundaries in Early Judaism and Christianity: Ambiguities, Complexities, and Half-Forgotten Adversaries. Essays in Honor of Alan F. Segal*. Supplements to the Journal for the Study of Judaism 177. Leiden: Brill, 2016.

Suetonius. *Lives of the Caesars*. Translated by J. C. Rolfe. 2 vols. LCL. Cambridge, MA: Harvard University Press, 1914.
Sweeney, Marvin A. *Isaiah 1–39: With an Introduction to Prophetic Literature*. The Forms of the Old Testament Literature 16. Grand Rapids, MI: Eerdmans, 1996.
Swete, Henry Barclay. *The Gospel According to St. Mark: The Greek Text with Introduction, Notes, and Indices*. 3rd ed. London: Macmillan, 1913.
Talmon, Shemaryahu. "The Concepts of Māšîaḥ and Messianism in Early Judaism." In *The Messiah: Developments in Earliest Judaism and Christianity*, edited by James H. Charlesworth, 79–115. Minneapolis, MN: Fortress Press, 1992.
Tannehill, Robert C. "The Disciples in Mark: The Function of a Narrative Role." *Journal of Religion* 57 (1977): 386–405.
Tannehill, Robert C. "The Gospel of Mark as Narrative Christology." *Semeia* 16 (1979): 57–95.
Taylor, N. H. "Palestinian Christianity and the Caligula Crisis. Part II. the Markan Eschatological Discourse." *Journal for the Study of the New Testament* 18, no. 62 (October 1996): 13–40. https://doi.org/10.1177/0142064X9601806202.
Telford, William. *The Theology of the Gospel of Mark*. New Testament Theology. Cambridge: Cambridge University Press, 1999.
Theissen, Gerd. *The Gospels in Context: Social and Political History in the Synoptic Tradition*. Minneapolis, MN: Fortress Press, 1991.
Thomas, Rosalind. "Writing, Reading, Public and Private 'Literacies': Functional LIteracy and Democratic Literacy in Greece." In *Ancient Literacies: The Culture of Reading in Greece and Rome*, edited by William A. Johnson and Holt N. Parker, 13–45. Oxford: Oxford University Press, 2009.
Twelftree, Graham H. "Jesus the Exorcist and Ancient Magic." In *A Kind of Magic: Understanding Magic in the New Testament and Its Religious Environment*, edited by Michael Labahn and Bert Jan Lietaert Peerbolte, 57–86. Library of New Testament Studies 306. London: T&T Clark, 2007.
Tyson, Joseph B. "The Blindness of the Disciples in Mark." *Journal of Biblical Literature* 80, no. 3 (1961): 261–8.
van Iersel, Bas M. F. *"Der Sohn" in den synoptischen Jesusworten: Christusbezeichnung der Gemeinde oder Selbstbezeichnung Jesu?* Supplements to Novum Testamentum 3. Leiden: Brill, 1964.
Van Leeuwen, Raymond C. "Wealth and Poverty: System and Contradiction in Proverbs." *Hebrew Studies* 33 (1992): 25–36.
Virgil. *Virgil*. Translated by H. Rushton Fairclough. Revised ed. 2 vols. LCL. Cambridge, MA: Harvard University Press, 1967.
Watson, David F. *Honor among Christians: The Cultural Key to the Messianic Secret*. Minneapolis, MN: Fortress Press, 2010.
Watson, David F. "The 'Life of Aesop' and the Gospel of Mark: Two Ancient Approaches to Elite Values." *Journal of Biblical Literature* 129, no. 4 (2010): 699–716.
Weeden, Theodore J. *Mark: Traditions in Conflict*. Philadelphia, PA: Fortress Press, 1971.
Williams, Craig A. *Roman Homosexuality: Ideologies of Masculinity in Classical Antiquity*. Ideologies of Desire. Oxford: Oxford University Press, 1999.
Winn, Adam. "Resisting Honor: The Markan Secrecy Motif and Roman Political Ideology." *Journal of Biblical Literature* 133, no. 3 (2014): 583–601.
Winter, Bruce W. *Divine Honours for the Caesars: The First Christians' Responses*. Grand Rapids, MI: Eerdmans, 2015.

Witulski, Thomas. "Der römische Kaiser Hadrian und die neutestamentliche Johannesapokalypse." In *Die Johannesapokalypse: Kontexte - Konzepte - Wirkungen*, edited by Jörg Frey, James A. Kelhoffer, and Franz Tóth, 79–116. Wissenschaftliche Untersuchungen zum neuen Testament 287. Tübingen: Mohr Siebeck, 2012.
Wood, Shane J. *The Alter-Imperial Paradigm: Empire Studies and the Book of Revelation*. Biblical Interpretation Series 140. Leiden: Brill, 2016.
Woolf, Greg. "Literacy or Literacies in Rome?" In *Ancient Literacies: The Culture of Reading in Greece and Rome*, edited by William A. Johnson and Holt N. Parker, 46–68. Oxford: Oxford University Press, 2009.
Woolf, Greg. "Roman Peace." In *War and Society in the Roman World*, edited by John Rich and Graham Shipley, 171–94. Leicester-Nottingham Studies in Ancient Society 5. London: Routledge, 1993.
Wrede, William. *Das Messiasgeheimnis in den Evangelien*. Göttingen: Vandenhoeck & Ruprecht, 1901.
Wrede, William. *The Messianic Secret*. Translated by J. C. G. Greig. Library of Theological Translations. Cambridge: James Clark, 1971.
Wright, J. Edward. "Whither Elijah? The Ascension of Elijah in Biblical and Extrabiblical Traditions." In *Things Revealed: Studies in Early Jewish and Christian Literature in Honor of Michael E. Stone*, edited by Esther G. Chazon, David Satran, and Ruth A. Clements, 123–38. Supplements to the Journal for the Study of Judaism 89. Leiden: Brill, 2004.
Young, Robert. *Postcolonialism*. A Very Short Introduction. Oxford: Oxford University Press, 2003.
Zeichman, Christopher. "Military-Civilian Interactions in Early Roman Palestine and the Gospel of Mark." University of St. Michael's College, 2017.
Zeichmann, Christopher. "Capernaum: A 'Hub' for the Historical Jesus or the Markan Evangelist?" *Journal for the Study of the Historical Jesus* 15, no. 1 (August 20, 2017): 147–65. https://doi.org/10.1163/17455197-01501003.
Zeichmann, Christopher. "Military Forces in Judaea 6–130 CE: The *Status Quaestionis* and Relevance for New Testament Studies." *Currents in Biblical Research* 17, no. 1 (2018): 86–120.
Zeichmann, Christopher. *The Roman Army and the New Testament*. Lanham, MD: Fortress Academic, 2018.
Zollschan, Linda. "Macedonian Libertas." *Classical Bulletin* 78, no. 2 (2002): 169–94.
Zollschan, Linda. *Rome and Judaea: International Law Relations, 162–100 BCE*. Abingdon: Routledge, 2016. https://doi.org/10.4324/9781315678900.
Zuiderhoek, Arjan. "Benefactors, Markets, and Trust in the Roman East." In *The Extramercantile Economies of Greek and Roman Cities: New Perspectives on the Economic History of Classical Antiquity*, edited by David B. Hollander, Thomas R. Blanton, and John T. Fitzgerald, 51–62. London: Routledge, 2019. https://doi.org/10.4324/9781351004824.

Subject Index

Alexander the Great 54, 78, 127
angels 69–70
apocalypse/apocalyptic 11, 13, 15, 17–18, 33, 36, 48–50, 72–5
auctoritas 50, 66
Audience of Mark 8–9, 10–11, 23 n.2, 27 n.76, 50, 53–4, 74
Augustus Caesar 29–31, 40 n.18, 42–3, 66, 83, 86, 95, 96, 98–9, 102, 104 n.34, 114, 124

baptism
    of Jesus by John 49, 52, 99
βασιλεύς 45–7
Beelzebul (see *Satan*)

Caligula 55, 73, 139
Christology 9–11, 50, 52, 96–7, 115
colonization/colonialism (definition) 26 n.51

date of Mark 2, 5 nn.4–6, 25 n.38
demons/demonic 36–8, 78, 85, 114, 123
    exorcism 36–7, 49–50, 70–1, 72, 75, 86, 98, 102
    Legion 37, 114
disciples 8–10, 17, 20, 37, 48, 51, 55, 113, 117–18
discipleship 114–16
δύναμις 48, 75, 99–102

elect 19, 33, 54, 56, 74
evocatio 69
ἐξουσία 48–52, 100, 101

freedom 48–9, 78, 83, 84, 123–4

Galilee
    historical/political 20, 37, 45, 56, 61, 64, 102, 128, 130–9

in Mark 72, 78, 86, 117
Markan provenance 2, 5 n.7, 77

healing 50, 52, 60 n.64, 71, 86, 100, 101
halakhah 49, 130, 134–5, 138
Hasmonean/s 72, 127, 131, 135
    dynastic struggles 65, 128, 134
    expansion 64, 129
    Mattathias 44, 129
    propaganda 64, 85, 140 n.2
    and Rome 127, 128
Herod/Herodian 20, 37, 129, 131, 134, 136
    Agrippa I 136
    Agrippa II 46, 128, 134, 136
    Antipas 22, 45–6, 51, 55, 58 n.21, 113, 134, 137
    dynastic struggles 128, 137
    the Great 111, 131, 139
    "Herodians" in Mark 134–5
    military 65, 67, 129, 137
    and Rome 128–9, 131
hidden transcript 12–14, 24 n.21, 48, 106
honor 106–8, 112–16

identity (community/ethnic) 31, 67, 76, 77, 137–8
imperium 50, 63, 64, 65
infrapolitics 12–14, 106

Jerusalem
    administration 49
    aristocracy 19–20, 37
    church 21, 115
    ideological value 49
    in Mark 22, 72, 76–8
    sack of 3, 15, 67, 72
    strategic value 65, 128
Judean War
    Masada 25 n.38
    military 22–3, 67, 140

Simon bar Giora 44–5, 56
Julius Caesar 42, 43, 94, 96, 98, 99

κύριος 52–4

legio X Fretensis (see *Rome: military*)
legions (see *Rome: military*)
Life of Aesop 119
literacy 135

Messiah/messianism 14, 44–5, 48, 74, 85
   Davidic 44, 47, 115
   first-century claimants 44–5, 73
miracle 50, 54, 68, 86, 97, 100, 113, 115
Mithridatic Wars 62–3

Nero 27 n.94, 72–3, 107–8, 110

Octavian (see *Augustus Caesar*)

parousia (of Christ) 17, 75, 87, 99
παρουσία (ritual) (see *triumph*)
Pharisees 133–4
political realism 35, 49, 62, 140
Pompey Magnus 30, 50, 63–4, 65–6, 67, 78, 128
Pontius Pilate 22, 45, 46, 47, 51, 137, 139
potestas 48
private transcript (see *hidden transcript*)
prophecy
   biblical 33, 69
   in Mark 33, 53, 72–5
   Roman 29–30
   vaticinium ex eventu 2, 5 n.4, 72
public transcript (see *hidden transcript*)

ransom 88
Realpolitik (see *political realism*)
Rome
   civil wars 65, 66, 128

expansion 61–3
military 25 n.38, 37–8
propaganda 31, 62, 65
ruler cult 30
   Hellenistic 93–5
   Roman imperial 94, 98, 139

Sadducees 134
salvation 19, 29, 68–9, 73–4, 83–9, 98
Satan 33, 36–8, 49–51, 54, 56, 71, 72, 75, 76, 100, 101, 112, 116, 123
Seleucid 54, 63, 83, 93, 95, 127–8, 129
   Antiochus IV 18, 44, 64, 73, 78
Septuagint 32, 53, 75, 87, 88, 111, 129
slavery (see *freedom*)
Son of God
   for Jesus 10, 99, 102, 114, 124
   imperial title 98–9
Son of David 47–8
Son of Man 10, 15, 19, 73–4, 75, 87, 98, 99, 124
   necessity of suffering 17, 34
stratification 54, 56, 106
   of the Kingdom of God 34, 54–6
suffering 4, 8, 17, 33, 46, 73–4, 87–8, 116

temple (Jerusalem)
   destruction of 15, 67, 72
   in Mark 2, 69, 78, 113, 117–18
   priesthood and cult 85, 102, 105, 131, 135–6
   taxes and payments to 88, 131, 136
   violations of 22, 73
θεῖος ἄνηρ 97
Titus (Roman emperor) 78
triumph 76–8

Vespasian 2, 67, 75, 77

wealth 111, 109–14

Index of Ancient Authors

Hebrew Bible
Genesis
1:8   93
5:24   96
31:3 (LXX)   53

Exodus
18:25   70
19:20   93
23:25–27   111
24:9–11   93

Leviticus
19:9–10   111
23:22   111
25:35   111

Numbers
8:1 (LXX)   53
35:24–25   138

Deuteronomy
1:15   70
5:8   92
5:22–27   138
15:7–11   111
16:18–20   138
17:14–20   138
18:1–8   138
21:1–9   138
33:2–3   69

1 Samuel
2:7 (LXX)   53
8:1–9   138
24:7   44

2 Samuel
6:2   75

1 Kings
12:1–19   138

2 Kings
2:1–12   96
4:9   50
11:12   138
19:31   69, 75

2 Chronicles
15:6   39 n.13

Nehemiah
13:5   138

Job
1–2   40 n.29
42:7–17   40 n.29

Psalms
84:10   44
130:4   59 n.47

Proverbs
10:4   111
10:4 (LXX)   120 n.19
11:1–2   111
11:4   111
11:7   111
11:18–19   111
11:21   111
11:24–26   111
11:28   111
11:31   111
12:3   111
13:25   111
14:19   111

Isaiah
10:21–23   69

11:1	44	27:10	111
11:3–5	44	40:25	112
11:6–9	44	40:28–30	112
11:12–16	44		
19:2	33	1 Maccabees	
25:4	111	1:1	64
		1:11	64
Jeremiah		1:20–23	64, 78
5:28	111	1:54	73
22:16	111	2.1	135
23:5–6	44	2:42	64
		2:46	129
Ezekiel		7:5	127
16:49	111	8:23–32	127
		14:4–15	85
Daniel		14:25–49	109
1:8	140 n.7	14:28	138
7 (LXX)	48	14:41	139
7:13–14 (LXX)	74	14:44	139
8:15–25	69		
9:20–27	69	2 Maccabees	
10:21	69	2:7–17	64
12:1–3	69, 85	4:35–38	64
12:11 (LXX)	73	5:11	64
Hosea		2 Esdras	
8:6	92	5:9	73
		6:24	73
Amos			
8:4–6	111	*Pseudepigrapha*	
		1 Enoch	
Habakkuk		1:1–9	69
3:13	44	6:7–8	70
		9:1	70
Zechariah		10	69–70
9:9	47	10:8–13	70
		10:17–22	70
Deuterocanonical Books		22	85
Tobit		99:4	39 n.13
1:10–13	140 n.7		
		Jubilees	
Wisdom of Solomon		22:16	140 n.7
6	32	23:22–31	85
Ben Sira		*Dead Sea Scrolls*	
3:30	111	Damascus Document	
10:13	111	12.22–23	44
20:21	112	13.20–22	44

Ancient Jewish Writers
Josephus (Jos.)
Life

1.2	133
122–25	108

Antiquities of the Judeans (Ant.)

8.2.5	70
11.8.4	81 n.56
12.6.2	129
13.6.2	133
13.9.1	129
13.10.5–6	133, 134
14.4.4	128
14.11.2	131
14.13.2	131
15.5	65
17.2.4	133
17.10.5–6	44
17.10.7	14, 44
17.10.8	58 n.16
18.1.1	55, 141 n.15
18.1.2	133
18.1.4	134
18.3.1	139
18.4–10	133
18.7.1–2	58 n.19
18.8.1–6	139
20.5.1	44
20.8.6	44
20.9.1	137

Wars of the Judeans (War)

1.1.4	139
1.2.1	64
1.3.7	75
1.5.2	133
1.19.4	65
1.24.5	139
2.4.1–2	44
2.4.3	58 n.16
2.8.1	44, 137
2.9.2–3	139
2.12.1–2	139
2.13.4–5	44
2.13.5	14
2.17.5	139
2.17.6	56
2.17.8–9	44
2.20.3	40 n.33
2.21.1–5	37
3.8.1–7	85
4.3.2	73
4.3.6–14	40 n.33
6.3.3	72
6.4	72
6.4.1	81 n.40
6.5.2	72
6.6.1–2	73
6.8–10	78
7.1	72
7.3.1	73
7.5.1–2	67
7.5.3–7	77
7.5.4–6	67
7.5.8	67

Philo of Alexandria
Legum allegoriae (Leg alleg.)

3.161	85

New Testament[1]
Matthew

4:1–11	36, 112
4:8	32
7:29	51
8:9	51
9:8	51
10	51
10:19	52
12:26	33
13:24–30	35
13:36–43	35
13:47–50	35
13:58	101
14:1–10	46
18:1	40 n.23
19:28	35
21:5	47
21:9	47
24:9	39 n.16
25:14–30	51

---

[1] Not including citations of Matthew, Mark, and Luke available in Appendix B.

25:31–46	47	4:1–9	116
26:55	51	4:1–34	29, 35, 115
		4:10–20	86
Mark		4:11	8
1:1	14	4:24–25	55
1:2–3	33, 53	4:26–29	86
1:4	34	4:30–32	86
1:9–11	99	4:35–41	34, 68, 86
1:11	50, 98	5:1–20	37, 86, 114
1:12	36	5:7	36
1:13	36–7, 49	5:19	53, 98
1:14	37	5:19–20	113, 114, 119
1:15	34, 72, 86, 114	5:21–43	86
1:16–20	116, 117	5:23	83
1:17	114	5:25–34	55
1:21–22	51	5:28	83
1:21–28	37, 49–50, 85–6	5:30	100, 101
1:24–25	114	5:34	83, 101
1:29–34	86	5:35–43	54
1:22	48, 52	6:1–6	97, 101–2
1:27	48, 52, 71	6:2	100, 101
1:29	117	6:3	98, 104 n.41
1:32–34	50, 72	6:4	113
1:34	114	6:5	100, 101
1:38	98	6:7	48, 49, 51
1:39	37	6:7–13	115, 119
1:40–45	53, 86, 113, 114	6:11	113
2:1–12	50–1, 86, 112	6:12	34
2:5–12	34	6:14	75, 100
2:10	48, 52, 71, 98	6:14–27	46, 113
2:13–14	116, 117	6:16–17	22
2:15	117	6:21	22
2:17	86, 98	6:22–23	46
2:18–20	118	6:30–44	34, 86, 115
2:21–22	33	6:45–52	34, 68, 115
3:3–12	72	6:56	83, 89 n.8
3:4	83	7:1–23	86
3:11	98	7:17–23	140 n.7
3:11–12	114	7:21–22	86
3:13–19	116	7:24–30	54, 113
3:20–30	116	7:37	98
3:14	51	8:1–10	34, 86
3:15	48, 49	8:27–38	115
3:19–35	100	8:29–30	47
3:20–30	36–8, 51, 71, 101	8:31	36, 74
	101	8:32	14
3:22	33, 38	8:32–33	116
3:23–24	98	8:33–34	114
3:31–35		8:34–37	55

8:35	83	13:3–8	72
9:1	34, 35, 75, 100	13:8	33, 46, 74
9:2–8	33, 96, 99	13:9	33
9:14–29	37	13:9–13	73
9:31	74	13:11	52
9:34	40 n.23	13:12	73
9:38–41	37	13:13	83, 98
9:39	100	13:14	8, 73
9:42–48	35, 72	13:14–16	73
9:47	34	13:20	73, 83, 99
10:15	34, 35	13:24	73
10:17–22	114	13:24–27	35
10:17–27	34	13:25	100
10:17–31	54, 117	13:26	100
10:21	118	13:25–27	75
10:23–25	34	13:27	98, 99
10:26	83	13:34	48, 51
10:28	117, 118	14:3–9	34, 55, 117–
10:30–40	73		18, 119
10:33–34	74	14:9	55
10:35	117	14:28	2
10:35–40	8, 33	14:32–42	116
10:35–45	115	14:49	51
10:28	118	14:61–62	45, 47, 74–5
10:39	116	14:62	100
10:42	53, 56	15	15, 76
10:42–45	55, 116, 118	15:2	45
10:46–52	47–8, 55	15:16–20	22
10:48	33, 47	15:21	8
10:52	83	15:30–31	83
11:1–11	76–8	15:32	45
11:9	47	15:33	34, 99
11:11	47	15:34	36
11:15–19	34, 37, 78	15:38	2, 34, 78, 99
11:25	34	15:39	98
11:27–33	51, 52, 101	15:43	34
11:28–29	48	15:57–58	2
11:33	48	16	54
12:1–12	54	16:7	2
12:13	133		
12:18	134	Luke	
12:24	100	4:1–12	36, 112
12:34	34	4:5	32
12:35–37	34, 47–8	4:6	51
12:38–44	34	4:16–30	101
12:41–44	34, 117–18	4:31–32	51
13	2, 8, 36,	6:12–16	51
	68, 72–5	6:20–49	116
13:1–2	15	7:1–10	131

7:8	51	2 John	
9:7	46	8	39 n.16
11:18	33		
12:11	52	Revelation	
16:19–31	117	2:14	105
19:12–27	32, 36, 51		
20:20	51, 52	*Rabbinic Works*	
21:12	39 n.16	*y. Sanhedrin (y. Sanh.)*	
22:3	36	18a	137
22:53	51	24b	137
23:1–3	58 n.17		
23:1–7	137	*Early Christian Writings*	
23:7	51–2	Origen (Orig.)	
		Contra Celsum (Cels.)	
John		1	26 n.48
14:1–30	21	9	26 n.48
Acts		*Greco-Roman Literature*	
1:6	14	Aeschylus (Aesch.)	
1:7	36	*Agamemnon (Ag.)*	
5:12–16	100	104–7	59 n.49
5:36–38	44	*Persae*	
7:58	137	589	32
10:1–31	117		
19:12	100	Aesop (Aes.)	
21:38	44	*Fabulae (Fab.)*	
24	58 n.17	103.1	58 n.31
Romans		Appian (App.)	
8:38	75, 100	*Mithridatic Wars (Mith.)*	
		10–11	80 n.16
1 Corinthians		13	80 n.16
8–10	105	58	80 n.16
8:4	92	105	80 n.20
15:12–28	85	115	80 n.20
		Syrian Wars (Syr.)	
Ephesians		63	103 n.8
6:12	75		
		Augustus	
Philippians		*Res gestae divi Augusti (RGDA)*	
3:5	133	1	42
		1.1	31
Colossians		3.1–2	86
1:16	48	5	42
		8	43
1 Thessalonians		11	43
4:13–17	74	13	31
		15	40 n.18

17	40 n.18	Dionysius of Halicarnassus (Dion. Hal.)	
25.1	31	*Antiquitates romanae* (*Ant. Rom.*)	
26	31	2.34	76
appx.	40 n.18		
		Greek Magical Papyri (*PGM*)	
Cassius Dio (Dio)		4.1248–52	71
Historiae romanae			
36.50.3	80 n.20	Herodotus (Hdt.)	
49.41.1	104 n.34	*Historiae*	
51.21.5–7	77	9.108–13	58 n.22
Cicero (Cic.)		Homer (Hom.)	
De inventione rhetorica (*Inv.*)		*Iliad* (*Il.*)	
2.53	43	2.335–43	92
		22.166–336	68
Pro Lege manilia (*Leg. man.*)	50, 80 n.18		
2.6	30	Horace (Hor.)	
10.28	66	*Carmen Saeculare* (*Carm. Saec.*)	
11.29	66	53–56	67
13.36–39	66	*Odes*	
		2.25–28	69
De natura deorum (*Nat. d.*)			
1.10.26	92	Hyperides (Hyp.)	
1.11.28	92	5.3	81 n.46
2.2.6	92		
		Livy	
Orationes philippicae (*Phil.*)		*Ab urbe condita*	
2.43	104 n.34	1.pr.10–12	40 n.18, 43
		1.18	57 n.1
De republica (*Rep.*)		29.11.7–8	92
1.35–37	41	45.18	79 n.9
1.36	31	45.18.1–2	84
1.42	41	45.29.4–14	84
2.3–22	42		
2.12	57 n.2	Lucan (Luc.)	
2.23	41	*Pharsalia*	
		1.121–43	66
Demosthenes (Dem.)		1.299–351	66
Exordia (*Ex.*)			
21.3		Macrobius	
Speeches		*Saturnalia* (*Sat.*)	
4.28	75	3.9.7–8	69
19.264	75		
		Pausanias	
Diodorus Siculus (Diod.)		*Graciae descriptio*	
Bibliotheca historica		1.2.1	116
37.26	81 n.56	10.22.12	68
40.2	128	10.23.1–10	68

Plato (Pl.)
Republic (*Rep.*)
427c   43

Pliny the Elder (Plin.)
Naturalis historia (*Nat.*)
28.18–19   69
37.6   76, 110

Pliny the Younger
Letters
10.96   26 n.48

Plutarch (Plut.)
Antonius (*Ant.*)
60.3   95
Demosthenes (*Dem.*)
10.4   103 n.21
12.1   103 n.21
Pompeius (*Pomp.*)
8.4   65
10.3–5   65
10.6–7   66
13.1–2   65
13.5   65
14   65
18.2   65
45.1   77
70.1–2   66
76.2–3   66

Polybius (Polyb.)
Historiae (*Hist.*)
4.28   79 n.8
36.10   79 n.12

Quintus Curtius Rufus (Curt.)
Historia Alexandri Magni
5.1.17–23   78

Strabo (Strab.)
Geographica
1.1.16   30

Suetonius (Suet.)
Divus Augustus (*Aug.*)
33–34   43
40.5   43
94   102

97   34
Gaius Caligula (*Cal.*)
52   34
Nero
1.2   107
2–5   107
7   107
7.2   110
8.1   107
8.2   107
10   107
10.1   43
10.1–2   110
11–13   107, 110
11.2   110
12.4   107
16–17   107
16.1   110
19.3   108
20–25   108
23.2   108
25   43
29   108
30–34   43
30–31   110
41   110
41.1   107
45.1   110
47–49   43
51   108
Tiberius (*Tib.*)
33–35   43
42–43   43
48   43
50–53   43
69   43
72   34

Sybilline Oracles
3.268–55   18

Thucydides (Thuc.)
Historiae
1.38   58 n.32
7.86.4   1.2.1

Virgil
Aeneid (*Aen.*)
1.76–80   31

1.234–37	30	8.626–728	30
1.278–79	30		
1.286–87	30	Xenophon (Xen.)	
3.97	30	*Anabasis* (*Ana.*)	
6.703–885	30	1.1.6	75, 81 n.6

www.ingramcontent.com/pod-product-compliance
Lightning Source LLC
Chambersburg PA
CBHW061836300426
44115CB00013B/2414